Edwin Arlington Robinson
Centenary Essays

Edwin Arlington Robinson
Centenary Essays

Edited by Ellsworth Barnard

University of Georgia Press
Athens

The editor, contributors, and publisher acknowledge permission to quote passages from the following material:

Collected Poems by Edwin Arlington Robinson. Copyright 1916, 1917, 1920, 1921, 1924, 1925, 1930, 1931, 1933, 1934 by Edwin Arlington Robinson. Copyright 1935 by The Macmillan Company. Copyright renewed 1944, 1945, 1949, 1951 by Ruth Nivison. Copyright renewed 1953, 1955, 1958 by Ruth Nivison and Barbara R. Holt. Copyright renewed 1963 by The Macmillan Company. By permission of the publisher.

Unpublished manuscripts by Edwin Arlington Robinson from the Houghton Library collections. By permission of the Harvard College Library.

The editor and the University of Georgia Press wish to thank the author and the publisher for permission to reprint "Robinson's Modernity" by J. C. Levenson, an essay which originally appeared in the *Virginia Quarterly Review* for Autumn 1968. Copyright 1968 by the *Virginia Quarterly Review*.

The text of this book was set in Electra. The book was printed from the type on Warren's Olde Style Wove by Heritage Printers, Inc., Charlotte, N.C., and bound in Columbia's Riverside by Carolina Ruling and Binding Co., Charlotte, N.C. Manufactured in an edition of 2,000.

Contents

Preface

This is not a "memorial" volume, offering solemn tributes by elder statesmen of the literary world to a poet who was once America's most famous, but who may since have seemed to be largely forgotten. Its aim is rather to illuminate for present and potential readers of Robinson's poetry certain aspects of his achievement which, one hundred years after his birth, attract the critical attention of persons of varying ages, backgrounds, and tastes who all, in one sense or another, practice the profession of literature.

It was this aim that led the editor to solicit original essays rather than articles previously published. The one exception is J. C. Levenson's essay "Robinson's Modernity," which appeared in the Autumn 1968 issue of the *Virginia Quarterly Review* and may therefore be fairly regarded as current. It is perhaps proper to mention also that Nathan Starr's essay "The Transformation of Merlin," although written for this volume, was presented in abridged form at the International Arthurian Congress at Cardiff, Wales, in August 1969.

All quotations from Robinson's poetry, unless otherwise noted, follow the text of the *Collected Poems* (1937) and are used with the permission of the publisher, The Macmillan Company.

In conclusion, I wish to express on behalf of the contributors our thanks to the University of Georgia Press for undertaking publication of the volume and especially to George Core for his unstinted aid in making it, as we hope it is, worthy of the occasion.

E. B.

Shelburne Falls, Massachusetts
September 1969

Edwin Arlington Robinson: A Chronology

December 22, 1869.	Born at Head Tide, Maine.
September 1870.	Removal of family to Gardiner, Maine.
June 1888.	Graduation from Gardiner High School.
September 1888–June 1889.	Postgraduate study at Gardiner High School.
1889–1891.	Residence in Gardiner, doing odd jobs and writing verse.
September 1891.	Matriculation at Harvard as special student.
July 1892.	Death of his father.
June 1893.	Conclusion of study at Harvard.
1893–1897.	Residence in Gardiner, doing odd jobs and writing: poetry, short stories (later destroyed), and a translation, with Harry de Forest Smith, of Sophocles' *Antigone* (fragments published in *Untriangulated Stars*).
November 1896.	Death of his mother.
December 1897.	First visit to New York.
1898.	Residence in New York, Cambridge, Gardiner, and Winthrop, Maine.
January–June 1899.	Employment in President Eliot's office at Harvard.
September 1899.	Death of his brother Dean.

October 1899.	Return to New York.
Autumn 1903–August 1904.	Employment on New York subway project.
January–May 1905.	Employment in drygoods store of his friend William E. Butler in Boston.
June 1905.	Appointment by Theodore Roosevelt to sinecure in the office of the Collector of Customs, New York.
August 12, 1905.	Review of *The Children of the Night* by Theodore Roosevelt in the *Outlook*.
1906–1913.	Attempts at commercial play writing and later at writing novels (which he destroyed).
January 1909.	Death of his brother Herman.
June 1909.	Resignation from Customs Service.
Autumn 1909.	Visit to Herman's widow and her family in Farmingdale, Maine. Last extended visit to his native state.
July–October 1910.	Residence at Chocorua, New Hampshire.
July–September 1911.	Residence at the MacDowell Colony at Peterborough, New Hampshire (where he spent each succeeding summer until his death).
December 21, 1919.	Fiftieth anniversary tributes by contemporary poets in *New York Times Book Review*.
1922.	Award of Pulitzer Prize for *Collected Poems*.
April–July 1923.	Visit to England.
1924.	Award of Pulitzer Prize for *The Man Who Died Twice*.
1927.	Sensational success of *Tristram*. Award of Pulitzer Prize.
April 5, 1935.	Death from cancer at New York Hospital.

Robinson's Major Publications

The date given is usually that of the first trade edition, and the publisher, unless otherwise stated, is The Macmillan Company.

The Torrent and The Night Before. Privately printed, November 1896.
The Children of the Night. Richard J. Badger, December 1897. Second Edition: Scribner's, 1905.
Captain Craig. Houghton Mifflin, October 1902. Revised Edition: Macmillan, 1915.
The Town Down the River. Scribner's, October 1910.
Van Zorn (prose play). September 1914.
The Porcupine (prose play). September 1915.
The Man Against the Sky. February 1916.
Merlin. March 1917.
Lancelot. Thomas Seltzer, April 1920.
The Three Taverns. September 1920.
Avon's Harvest. March 1921.
Collected Poems. October 1921. Expanded editions in 1927, 1929, 1937.
Roman Bartholow. March 1923.
The Man Who Died Twice. March 1924.
Dionysus in Doubt. April 1925.
Tristram. May 1927.
Cavender's House. April 1929.
The Glory of the Nightingales. September 1930.
Matthias at the Door. September 1931.
Nicodemus. September 1932.
Talifer. October 1933.
Amaranth. September 1934.
King Jasper. November 1935.

Bibliography

The following listings are selective, especially in the "Essays and Articles" section under the heading "Biography and Criticism."

I. BIBLIOGRAPHY.

Anderson, Wallace L. *Edwin Arlington Robinson: A Critical Introduction.* Boston: Houghton Mifflin, 1967, pp. 155–165.

Barnard, Ellsworth. "Edwin Arlington Robinson," in *Fifteen Modern American Authors,* ed. Jackson Bryer. Durham: Duke University Press, 1969.

Hogan, Charles Beecher. *A Bibliography of Edwin Arlington Robinson.* New Haven: Yale University Press, 1936.

———. "Edwin Arlington Robinson: New Bibliographical Notes," *Papers of the Bibliographical Society of America,* XXXV (Second Quarter 1941), 115–144.

Lippincott, Lillian. *A Bibliography of the Writings and Criticisms of Edwin Arlington Robinson.* Boston: F. W. Faxon, 1937.

White, William. "A Bibliography of Edwin Arlington Robinson, 1941–1963," *Colby Library Quarterly,* Series VII, No. 1 (March 1965), pp. 1–26.

II. WORKS.

1. *Collections of Poems (in print).*

Collected Poems. New York: Macmillan, 1937.

Selected Early Poems and Letters, ed. Charles T. Davis. New York: Holt, Rinehart, and Winston, 1960. (Contains the original texts of all the poems in *The Torrent and The Night Before, The Children of the Night,* and *Captain Craig,* including some omitted from the *Collected Poems.*)

Selected Poems of Edwin Arlington Robinson, ed. Morton Dauwen Zabel. Introduction by James Dickey. New York: Macmillan, 1965. (Also New York: Collier Books, 1966.)

2. Letters.

Selected Letters of Edwin Arlington Robinson, ed. Ridgely Torrence. New York: Macmillan, 1940.

Untriangulated Stars: Letters of Edwin Arlington Robinson to Harry de Forest Smith, 1890–1905, ed. Denham Sutcliffe. Cambridge: Harvard University Press, 1947.

Edwin Arlington Robinson's Letters to Edith Brower, ed. Richard Cary. Cambridge: Harvard University Press, 1968.

III. BIOGRAPHY AND CRITICISM.

1. Books and Pamphlets.

Anderson, Wallace L. *Edwin Arlington Robinson: A Critical Introduction.* Boston: Houghton Mifflin, 1967. (Also Cambridge: Harvard University Press, 1968.)

Barnard, Ellsworth. *Edwin Arlington Robinson: A Critical Study.* New York: Macmillan, 1952. (Reprinted, New York: Octagon Books, 1969.)

Bates, Esther Willard. *Edwin Arlington Robinson and His Manuscripts.* Waterville, Maine: Colby College Library, 1944.

Brown, Rollo Walter. *Next Door to a Poet.* New York: Appleton-Century, 1937.

Cestre, Charles. *An Introduction to Edwin Arlington Robinson.* New York: Macmillan, 1930.

Coffin, Robert P. Tristram. *New Poetry of New England: Robinson and Frost.* Baltimore: Johns Hopkins Press, 1938.

Coxe, Louis O. *Robinson.* University of Minnesota Pamphlets on American Writers. Minneapolis: University of Minnesota Press, 1962.

————. *Edwin Arlington Robinson: The Life of Poetry.* New York: Pegasus, 1969.

Franchere, Hoyt. *Edwin Arlington Robinson.* New York: Twayne Publishers, 1968.

Fussell, Edwin S. *Edwin Arlington Robinson: The Literary Background of a Traditional Poet.* Berkeley: University of California Press, 1954.

Hagedorn, Hermann. *Edwin Arlington Robinson.* New York: Macmillan, 1938. (The standard biography to date.)

Humphry, James, III. *The Library of Edwin Arlington Robinson.* Waterville, Maine: Colby College Press, 1950.

Kaplan, Estelle. *Philosophy in the Poetry of Edwin Arlington Robinson.* New York: Columbia University Press, 1940.

Morris, Lloyd. *The Poetry of Edwin Arlington Robinson: An Essay in Interpretation.* New York: George H. Doran, 1923.

Neff, Emery. *Edwin Arlington Robinson.* New York: William Sloane Associates, 1948. (Reprinted, New York: Russell & Russell, 1968.)

Redman, Ben Ray. *Edwin Arlington Robinson.* New York: Robert M. McBride, 1926.

Richards, Laura E. *E. A. R.* Cambridge: Harvard University Press, 1936.

Robinson, W[illiam] R. *Edwin Arlington Robinson: A Poetry of the Act.* Cleveland: The University Press of Case Western Reserve, 1967.

Smith, Chard Powers. *Where the Light Falls: A Portrait of Edwin Arlington Robinson.* New York: Macmillan, 1965.

Untermeyer, Louis. *Edwin Arlington Robinson: A Reappraisal.* Washington: Library of Congress, 1963.

Van Doren, Mark. *Edwin Arlington Robinson.* New York: The Literary Guild, 1927.

Winters, Yvor. *Edwin Arlington Robinson.* Norfolk: New Directions, 1946.

2. *Essays and Articles.*

Adams, Richard P. "The Failure of Edwin Arlington Robinson," *Tulane Studies in English,* XI (1961), 97–151.

Aiken, Conrad. *Collected Criticism.* New York: Oxford University Press, 1968. (Except for a brief preface by I. A. Richards, the text is identical with that of *A Reviewer's ABC.*)

Anderson, Wallace L. "E. A. Robinson's 'Scattered Lives,'" *American Literature,* XXXVIII (January 1967), 498–507.

Brooks, Van Wyck. *New England: Indian Summer.* New York: Dutton, 1940.

Beatty, Frederika. "Edwin Arlington Robinson As I Knew Him," *South Atlantic Quarterly,* XLIII (October 1944), 375–381.

Cambon, Glauco. *The Inclusive Flame.* Bloomington: Indiana University Press, 1963.

Carpenter, Frederic Ives. "Tristram the Transcendent," *New England Quarterly,* XI (September 1938), 501–523.

Coxe, Louis O. "E. A. Robinson: The Lost Tradition," *Sewanee Review,* LXII (Spring 1954), 247–266.

Crowder, Richard. "E. A. Robinson and the Meaning of Life," *Chicago Review,* XV (Spring 1961), 5–17.

———. " 'Here Are the Men . . .': E. A. Robinson's Male Character Types," *New England Quarterly,* XVIII (September 1945), 346–367.

Daniels, Mabel. "Edwin Arlington Robinson: A Musical Memoir," *Colby Library Quarterly,* Series VII, No. 6 (June 1963), pp. 219–233.

Dauner, Louise. "The Pernicious Rib: E. A. Robinson's Concept of Feminine Character," *American Literature,* XV (May 1943), 139–158.

———. "Vox Clamantis: Edwin Arlington Robinson As a Critic of American Democracy," *New England Quarterly,* XV (March 1942), 401–426.

Davis, Charles T. "Image Patterns in the Poetry of Edwin Arlington Robinson," *College English,* XXII (March 1961), 380–386.

Donaldson, Scott. "The Alien Pity: A Study of the Characters in E. A. Robinson's Poetry," *American Literature,* XXXVIII (May 1966), 219–229.

Donoghue, Denis. *Connoisseurs of Chaos: Ideas of Order in Modern American Poetry.* New York: Macmillan, 1965.

Evans, Nancy. "Edwin Arlington Robinson," *Bookman,* LXXV (November 1932), 675–681.

Fisher, John Hurt. "Edwin Arlington Robinson and the Arthurian Legend," in *Studies in Language and Literature in Honor of Margaret Schlauch.* Warsaw, Poland, 1966.

Free, William J. "E. A. Robinson's Use of Emerson," *American Literature,* XXXVIII (March 1966), 69–84.

Frost, Robert. Introduction to *King Jasper.* New York: Macmillan, 1935. (Reprinted in *Selected Prose of Robert Frost,* ed. Hyde Cox and Edward C. Latham. New York: Holt, Rinehart, and Winston, 1966.)

Gregory, Horace, and Zaturenska, Marya. *A History of American Poetry, 1900–1940.* New York: Harcourt Brace, 1946.

———. "The Vein of Comedy in E. A. Robinson's Poetry," *American Bookman,* I (Fall 1944), 43–64.

Hepburn, James G. "E. A. Robinson's System of Opposites," *PMLA,* LXXX (June 1965), 266–274.

Hertz, Robert N. "Two Voices of the American Village: Robinson and Masters," *Minnesota Review,* II (1962), 345–358.

Isaacs, Lewis M. "E. A. Robinson Speaks of Music," *New England Quarterly,* XXII (December 1949), 499–510.

Kilmer, Joyce. *Literature in the Making.* New York: Harper, 1917.

Levenson, J. C. "Robinson's Modernity," *Virginia Quarterly Review,* XLIV (Autumn 1968), 590–610.

Lowell, Amy. *Tendencies in Modern American Poetry.* Boston: Houghton Mifflin, 1917.

Mark Twain Quarterly, II (Spring 1938), 1–26. (Contains a critical essay by Charles Cestre and brief reminiscences by a number of Robinson's friends and acquaintances.)

Monroe, Harriet. *Poets and Their Art.* Freeport, N. Y.: Books for Libraries Press, 1967. (A reprint of the 1932 edition.)

———. "Robinson As Man and Poet," *Poetry,* LXVI (June 1953), 150–157.

Pearce, Roy Harvey. *The Continuity of American Poetry.* Princeton, N. J.: Princeton University Press, 1961.

Perrine, Laurence. "Contemporary Reference of Robinson's Arthurian Poems," *Twentieth Century Literature,* VIII (July 1962), 74–82.

Schriftgiesser, Karl. "An American Poet Speaks His Mind," Boston *Evening Transcript,* November 4, 1933, Book Section, pp. 1–2.

Scott, Winfield Townley. "To See Robinson," *New Mexico Quarterly,* XXVI (Summer 1956), 161–178.

Skard, Sigmund. "E. A. Robinson: 'Eros Turannos,' A Critical Survey," *Americana Norvegica,* Vol. I (ed. Sigmund Skard and Henry H. Wasser, Philadelphia, 1966).

Starr, Nathan C. *King Arthur Today.* Gainesville: University of Florida Press, 1954.

Stevick, Robert D. "Robinson and William James," *University [of Kansas City] Review,* XXV (June 1959), 293–301.

Stovall, Floyd. "The Optimism Behind Robinson's Tragedies," *American Literature,* X (March 1938), 1–23.

———. "Edwin Arlington Robinson in Perspective," in *Essays on American Literature in Honor of Jay B. Hubbell,* ed. Clarence Gohdes. Durham, N. C.: Duke University Press, 1967.

Sutcliffe, Denham. "The Original of Robinson's Captain Craig," *New England Quarterly,* XVI (September 1943), 407–431.

Tate, Allen. *On the Limits of Poetry.* New York: Swallow Press, 1948. (The essay on Robinson is reprinted from *Reactionary Essays.*)

Torrence, Olivia Dunbar. "The Poet at the Breakfast Table," *Colophon,* n. s., III (Winter 1938), 92–99.

Waggoner, Hyatt H. *The Heel of Elohim.* Norman, Okla.: University of Oklahoma Press, 1950. (Contains a revised version of "E. A. Robinson and the Cosmic Chill," *New England Quarterly,* XIII (March 1940), 65–84.)

———. *American Poets from the Puritans to the Present.* Boston: Houghton Mifflin, 1968.

Walsh, William T. "Some Recollections of E. A. Robinson," *Catholic World*, CLV (August, September 1942), 522–531, 703–712.

Wells, Henry W. *New Poets from Old*. New York: Columbia University Press, 1940.

Williams, Stanley T. "Edwin Arlington Robinson," Chapter 69, *Literary History of the United States*. New York: Macmillan, 1948.

Zietlow, Paul. "The Meaning of Tilbury Town," *New England Quarterly*, XL (June 1967), 188–211.

Ziff, Larzer, *The American 1890's: The Life and Times of a Lost Generation*. New York: Viking, 1966.

Edwin Arlington Robinson
Centenary Essays

"Of This or That Estate": Robinson's Literary Reputation

Ellsworth Barnard

Edwin Arlington Robinson was born in 1869. His first volume of poetry—actually a thin paper-bound pamphlet—called *The Torrent and The Night Before* from the titles of the first and last poems, was printed at his own expense in 1896. Most of the poems in it were reprinted the following year, with some others added, in *The Children of the Night*, put out by a vanity publisher named Badger and paid for by a friend. Five years later, in 1902, after many rejections and disappointments, a substantial volume entitled *Captain Craig* was issued by Houghton Mifflin after two other friends had guaranteed the publisher against loss. His next book was a thin volume called *The Town Down the River* published in 1910 by Scribner.

After errant ventures into playwriting and fiction, he returned permanently to poetry and began his richest creative period with *The Man Against the Sky*, published in 1916 by Macmillan. This period ended with *Tristram*, his one great popular success, in 1927; although the years from 1929 until his death in 1935 saw the appearance of annual volumes, all but one devoted to a single long poem, and all dutifully reviewed in the leading magazines.

Robinson's ascendancy during the twenties is in sharp contrast to the harrowing and at times almost hopeless struggle for recognition during the first two decades of his poetic career. His first volume, indeed, was commended by a number of the eminent men of letters to whom he sent it (despite the dedication "To any man, woman, or critic who will cut the edges of it—I have done the top"); but *The Children of the Night* received scant notice and less praise, and so did *Captain Craig*. Magazine editors were even more hostile or indif-

ferent than the critics. When, in 1905, under the prodding of Theodore Roosevelt, the *Century Magazine* accepted a humorous trifle
called "Uncle Ananias," it was, says his biographer Hermann Hagedorn, "the first acceptance by any other magazine than the *Globe* or
the *Harvard Monthly* in eight years; the first paid acceptance since
Lippincott's had taken his sonnet on Poe eleven years before"—and
left it unpublished. Robinson had sufficient reason to remark in a
letter, "My poetry is rat poison to editors."

The main cause of this rejection seems clear enough. Frost had a
similar struggle for a similar reason. What both poets were trying to
do—like Wordsworth a century before—was to bring poetry back into
touch with life; to take it out of the drawing room, out of the realm
of hearts and flowers, and onto drab small town streets and dusty
country roads; to tell the stories of humdrum and even sordid lives
and show that these were after all the lives of human beings; and to
tell these stories in "the real language of men." "There is poetry in
all types of humanity—even in lawyers and horse-jockeys," Robinson
had written to his friend Harry de Forest Smith in 1893, with the
evangelical fervor of young men who have seen visions; and he put his
faith to the test in the abrasive snarl of "Aaron Stark," the inarticulate
grief of "Reuben Bright," and the shopworn courtesy of "The Clerks."

But America was not interested. Poetry was one thing and reality
was another. Poetry was for ladies and lady-like professors; the mode
for men was action. Or, if the national temper of expansive materialism was not wholly unleavened by intangibles, what caught men's
imaginations was not the meager graspings of Main Street misers but
the aspirations to illimitable wealth of Wall Street operators. Not
Aaron Stark but John D. Rockefeller was the symbolic man against
the sky whom Americans saw moving toward an uncertain but surely
grandiose fate. Not Captain Craig but Andrew Carnegie was the true
benefactor of American culture. Not the defeated knights or jesters
at Calverly's saloon but the ruthless political bosses in the halls of
Congress were the makers or the destroyers of the American dream.

The national mood was as little receptive to another feature of
Robinson's early volumes—what the critics called "pessimism." "The
world is not beautiful to him," wrote Harry Thurston Peck in the
Outlook, "but a prison house"; to which the poet retorted: "The
world is not a prison house but a kind of spiritual kindergarten where
millions of bewildered infants are trying to spell God with the wrong

blocks." Even if the critics had accepted the substitute metaphor, however, their feeling would not have changed. Though in "The Children of the Night" the poet at the end invites his readers to be "Children of the Light" instead, it is at best a chill and twilit world that he pictures, where the dominant mood is one of bewildered suffering. He may affirm in the *Octaves* and certain sonnets that he who endures to the end shall be saved, but the salvation is abstract and uncomforting, while the endurance is painfully concrete. A belated strain of Puritanism and the grimness of his personal experience were stronger in effect than his conscious formulation of faith. And the society around him had little interest in either.

It is true that in *Captain Craig* Robinson fought his way out of the shadows. The Captain himself, in fact, may have seemed to some of the book's few readers more cheerful than a pauper has a right to be. But still, the joy was sober and not unmeasured; the triumph lay in acceptance and not in conquest. And at any rate, as already noted, the nation did not share the poet's desire to consecrate the commonplace, whether the atmosphere was somber or sunlit.

By 1916, however, the scene had changed. A one-time college professor was now President, and his proclaimed "new freedom" was not the freedom of the strong to exploit the weak. Moreover, the lurid light of Europe's holocaust, visible even across the Atlantic, brought into darker relief the doubts that had never been quite erased concerning America's manifest destiny.

And an even greater change had made itself felt in America's literary climate. Frost's success in England had followed him back to America. Amy Lowell's crusade to make verse freer in theme as well as form was fluttering the dovecotes of the genteel tradition. Vachel Lindsay was chanting new rhythms that transmuted verbal pop art into poetry that haunted the memory of his readers or hearers. Carl Sandburg was persuading people that Chicago's hog-butchery and harlotry were not beyond the pale of poetry. Edgar Lee Masters was uncoffining the hitherto voiceless tragedies of that Midwestern Tilbury Town, Spoon River. And Harriet Monroe in her magazine *Poetry* provided a focus for this coruscation of fresh personalities, themes, and techniques.

Robinson, too, had changed, although more subtly, and in ways not clearly contributory to the public acceptance of his work. Nearing the half-century mark, still empty-handed and unknown, after harsh years of unproductive effort or unacknowledged achievement, he had nevertheless found a new and surer footing in the march where many were now moving with less certitude. The sometimes too insistent sermonizing in *The Children of the Night*; the sometimes too easy optimism in "Captain Craig"; the sharply drawn but essentially simple and static characters of the early volumes; these had given way to a more detached, ironic, and subdued observance of life's absurdities and other mysteries (if some readers feel that parts of "The Man Against the Sky" are still too declamatory, there is "Hillcrest's" more quiet admonishment against man's pride of intellect), and to the portrayal of situations where characters are not merely described by the poet but are viewed by other characters whose traits in turn the reader must assess, with a resultant deeper involvement. Who exactly, for instance, is the "we" of "Flammonde" and "Eros Turannos"?

These qualities and others, in a more hospitable atmosphere, not only gained for Robinson the hearing that he had been so long denied, but brought him during the twenties an unchallenged preeminence among American poets. On December 21, 1919, the day before his fiftieth birthday, the *New York Times Book Review* featured a collection of critical estimates by a number of famous and less famous American poets which were almost wholly laudatory—as perhaps the occasion demanded. The significant fact, however, is that the occasion and the demand did occur. In the next nine years came the first *Collected Poems* and seven new volumes; and, along with them, three Pulitzer prizes, *Tristram's* sale of 57,000 copies in its first year (which, as the author remarked in a letter, "isn't so bad for blank verse"), and three book-length critical studies by Lloyd Morris, Ben Ray Redman, and Mark Van Doren; to which was added in 1930 a still more substantial one by the French scholar Charles Cestre.

This was the climax of Robinson's renown. The decline in poetic power during the early thirties was accompanied by a decline in status. No major critical works were published, and no great excitement was aroused by Hagedorn's biography in 1938 (an admirable work in view of the difficulties faced by the author) or the *Selected Letters* in 1940, edited (rather poorly) by Ridgely Torrence.

During the forties, however, while Robinson's popularity continued to diminish, academic interest increased. Several doctoral dissertations received full or partial publication. In 1944 Yvor Winters published a book designed to rescue Robinson from those who admired his work for what Winters decreed to be the wrong reasons; and in 1948 Robinson was given a volume written by Emery Neff in the new American Men of Letters series. Meanwhile, in 1947, the Harvard University Press had lent its prestige to a solid volume of Robinson's letters to his friend Harry de Forest Smith, *Untriangulated Stars,* ably edited by Denham Sutcliffe.

None of these volumes, however, caused any noticeable revival of popular interest in Robinson; and the same was true of the present writer's critical study of his poetry in 1952, which Macmillan accepted with the prophetic statement that it would "not be an easy book to sell." The optimistic first printing—and the last—was 3,500 copies, of which about half were sold at the list price and the rest remaindered. (When, in 1953, I noted a copy in a Chicago bookstore near the University and asked the proprietor if he had sold many copies, he replied that somebody had asked him to order one and that he had taken a chance and ordered two. He said, when I confessed my identity, "Would you mind autographing it? It might help move it.")

For more than a dozen years after this date it seemed that the appeal of Robinson's poetry, even to scholars, was declining toward the vanishing point. The 1965 *PMLA* bibliography listed exactly two Robinson items—one an unpublished letter, the other a two-page article in an Italian periodical. The average number of items during the preceding ten years was a little over four. As for less scholarly writings, the *Reader's Guide,* after listing a review of my book in the *Saturday Review of Literature* early in 1952, contained no Robinson entry for the next thirteen years. In the anthologies, also, successive editions of old standbys found less and less space for Robinson, while some newer collections ignored him altogether.

The reputation of no other American poet has followed so strange a pattern—nearly total neglect for the first twenty years of a late-starting career; a dozen years of acknowledged national supremacy; and thirty years of slow return to obscurity. One naturally wonders about the causes of such a loss of status. Was the general judgment during the middle period so wildly wide of the mark that the poet's work deserves to be forgotten? Or is the later judgment the product, at least in part, of ultimately irrelevant historical events and social changes, and of temporary trends in poetic taste?

One cause of Robinson's decline in fame after the mid-thirties was of course simply that he died. If there is any law ("the statement of a process in nature not known to vary") governing changes in literary reputations, it is that the death of a famous author signals the demotion of his work. Without the continuing appearance of new works, without fresh stories in the press concerning his actions or opinions, the public begins to forget him; and even in the groves of academe (where the television screen that mirrors the outside world is not altogether obscured by the dust of scholarship), his name is heard less often and with a muted resonance. Already Eliot and Frost are moving into the shadows; and the violence in the work of Faulkner and Hemingway, transmuted though it is at times by poetry, has become for many persons less relevant than the violence in the streets or on the campus.

That there was a lessening regard for Robinson's work even before his death—that there was a widespread lack of enthusiasm for the long poems that followed *Tristram*—is of course no mystery. Critics as a rule found the plots thin-spun and unoriginal, usually involving a more or less conventional triangle (*Amaranth* is a notable exception); the characters increasingly garrulous (though even in the earlier long narratives Robinson's people had not been notably taciturn); the style less appealing because of the involved syntax, the relaxed metrical pattern, the sparseness of vivid epithets and images. And most readers today would doubtless arrive at the same judgment. Clearly, the poet's energy was failing. The "choral golden overflow / Of sound and fire" that he had once been able to invoke, at least on occasion, came no more.

And once more the times had turned against him. Ironically, the Great Depression, descending as if it were the doom that he, like Merlin, had prophesied for a society built on a rotten foundation, made his habitual theme of conflict within or between individuals seem scarcely pertinent. Even his departure from habit in *Amaranth*, in which he explored with humor as well as tolerance the nightmarish "wrong worlds" into which human beings were led by ill-conceived ambitions, brought little response. The victims of the Depression did not feel that they had been "betrayed by what [was] false within"; they felt trapped by forces from without. The reform of society and not the regeneration of the individual was what they saw as the road to salvation. And even when Robinson himself in *King Jasper* dealt with the theme of revolution, he did so in moral terms that to many seemed outdated.

To be sure, the relation between social and literary trends is often cloudy, and prudent critics will not push it too far. But whatever the degree to which contemporary history, as well as Robinson's death, contributed to his decline in fame, it is painfully clear that his publishers cooperated. One reason why interest in his work languished for so long is as simple as it is incomprehensible—the failure of the Macmillan Company to make a selection of his best work available in an inexpensive edition. Between 1935 (the year of his death) and 1953, anyone who wished to go beyond the anthologies was limited to a dwindling number of separate long works—not his best—and the *Collected Poems*, with its 1,500 pages of bare text, priced in proportion to its bulk. (Sales of this formidable volume have remained at a fairly steady 600 a year.) When a volume of selections finally appeared, eighteen years after the poet's death, it turned out to be a thin cloth-bound volume containing no sample of the long poems and costing the then not-inconsiderable sum of $3.50. Twelve years later the first printing of 6,000 copies was not yet sold out. And when at last, in 1960, Robinson appeared in paperback in a Rinehart edition, the editor was compelled to limit his selection of poetry to what was then in the public domain and hence could not go beyond the *Captain Craig* volume of 1902. (In spite of this severe limitation, sales during the first years were about 2,500 copies annually.) Not until 1966 did Macmillan issue a paperback of its own—still without any of the long poems.

Another obvious cause of the general neglect has been the almost total absence of a dramatic public image. One thinks, for instance, of Hemingway's embodiment of his own legend, appealing not only to bored suburbanites but also to college professors. To plant a bullet in the brain of a buffalo is obviously a more manly achievement than to plant an idea in the mind of a freshman, and the aesthetic and spiritual exaltation of an MLA meeting is obviously meager compared to that offered by a bullfight. One thinks also of Faulkner's association with the decadence and violence of the South, and of the public appearances and recorded readings of Frost and Eliot. Frost, especially (be it said without disparagement), was a superb salesman of Frost; Eliot, despite his donnishness, had a flair for public relations; and Faulkner quietly but effectively cultivated romantic legends about his personal and family history. Among other writers approximately of Robinson's generation whose vogue is still current, and whose private lives caught the public eye, one may note the political aberrancy of Ezra Pound, whose treatment by the U. S. government provided a cause eagerly accepted by the many critics who insist that the world of art is absolute and self-contained, with no relation to politics or morals; the blighted life of Hart Crane, appealing to a generation preoccupied with the hero as victim; and the unexpected linking of poetry and medicine in the career of William Carlos Williams. Only Wallace Stevens, satisfied with the unspectacular role of insurance executive, rose to eminence without the aid of personal drama.

Like Stevens, Robinson was an exception. Few lives of men famous in any way can have been outwardly less dramatic, partly because few such persons have been so self-effacing in a competitive society, so self-distrustful in a world of action. The fact was that Robinson was hopelessly sedentary; he read his own poetry badly and knew it; he could not have been dragged upon a public stage; he shunned newspaper publicity; and he had no inclination to exploit whatever regional uniqueness New England or New York City might possess. As for his personal habits, only a few friends worried when he seemed in danger of drinking himself to death; and rumors that he was homosexual were never supported by enough evidence, or even widely enough talked about, to earn him a really respectable status with certain recent critics. His one notable triumph in the realm of sex was negative: Isadora Duncan tried, and failed, to seduce him. So when interest in the work itself subsided, there was no interest in the man to lend it support.

So much for the public. But what of the academic marketplace— the true source, in our time, of literary fame, or at least prestige? Here the explanation is that Robinson was never taken up by the New Critics (though Allen Tate in reviewing *Talifer* in 1933 credited him with "a score of great lyrics"), who dominated the literary-academic establishment during the thirty years after his death. This neglect is a little hard to understand, for his work contains several of the qualities most often taken as touchstones by these critics. No poet is more pervasively ironic; not many poets can create greater tension in fewer lines than Robinson in the dramatic lyrics and sonnets that are perhaps his favorite genre; and his verse contains enough types of ambiguity, if not the magic seven, to have been a boon to the *Explicator*.

Perhaps what the New Critics found lacking in Robinson's poetry was, first of all, strangeness. His metaphors do not dazzle readers with their explosive brilliance; he does not (as a rule) garnish his verses with erudite allusions; his meters, as distinct from his language, do not flirt with prose, nor do they aim at the nuclear reconstitution of traditional rhythms through either fission or fusion; he does not invent exotic symbols to entice and then baffle the reader. In sum, as he himself often said, he is not an "intellectual" poet.

Or perhaps in another sense he is too intellectual. There may be some truth in the suggestion that he had, up to a point, a Puritan distrust of the senses, and of the world that existed in them. His images do not, as a rule, have the visual, aural, or tactual force which regularly animates those of Eliot or Yeats. None of his characters who, like Prufrock, are appalled at the vacuity of their lives describe their revulsion in such a savage metaphor as "I should have been a pair of ragged claws / Scuttling across the floors of silent seas." Instead, they suffer unprotestingly, like "The Poor Relation"; or they quietly and undemonstratively shoot themselves, like Richard Cory; or they analyze their predicaments in low-key comments to a confidant, like Tasker Norcross. Even in the concluding stanza of what is possibly Robinson's most admired poem, "Eros Turannos"—

> Meanwhile we do no harm; for they
> That with a god have striven,
> Not hearing much of what we say,
> Take what the god has given;
> Though like waves breaking it may be,
> Or like a changed familiar tree,
> Or like a stairway to the sea,
> Where down the blind are driven—

even here the imagery is so undemanding that it can hardly excite those to whom it has never occurred that what is clear need not be banal and what is familiar need not be trite.

A second source of alienation from the New Criticism was that Robinson is primarily interested in *people*—simply for their own sake, as unique individuals. The anthologists' liking for "Richard Cory" and "Miniver Cheevy" has been based at least on a sound perception of where Robinson's own concern chiefly lies. In contrast, contemporary poetry and poetry criticism have generally not been concerned with people as such, but have preferred fleshless mythic figures in symbolic garb. The very concept of Eliot's "objective correlative" implies that the primary subject matter of poetry is an idea or emotion, for which the poet is to seek out a suitable metaphorical incarnation. And from this point of view, "Eros Turannos" is not a poem about two people, from whose story we may, if we wish, infer a general comment on human nature; it is a poem in which two people illustrate a certain kind of relationship, and the merit lies in the poet's technical skill in fitting the illustration to the idea.

Finally, in this age where many persons seek refuge in various dogmas, even dogmas of despair, from life's terrifying intractability, Robinson may fail to appeal because of his anti-absolutist temper. He rarely (in his mature work, at least) raises his voice; he never rages or despairs; he never shouts his faith or his defiance. Although he was, as he once said, "born with his skin inside out," his hypersensitiveness does not lead to hyperbole. Not pity and terror, still less outrage and revulsion, but compassionate or ironic acceptance is his characteristic response to the human drama. And stoicism has had little part in the modern temper.

This seeming alienation from the age leads to a further comment. Surveying the long erosion of Robinson's fame, one notes a curious fact—that even in the years of eminence he was never the center of a cult, never the master of admiring disciples, never a major influence on younger poets. Whereas echoes of the manner of Eliot and Frost are almost omnipresent in the work of such poets during the thirties and forties, and one of the most stringent tests of talent has been the avoidance of such echoes, no reminiscences of Robinson occur. Why?

Since few poets come to mind whose work has been inimitable, the answer is perhaps, again, that Robinson was out of tune with his time; that although his work contained something that appealed to the public taste of the twenties, it was alien to the deeper currents of the national mood. Like Thoreau before him, he was marching to a different drummer from that which most of his countrymen were hearing.

But the drummer that he marched to—or at least the rhythm—is not necessarily dead. In fact, there are signs of a Robinson revival, reserved and unobtrusive, as befits the man and his work. Macmillan would not have issued a paperback selection of his poems if it had not thought there would be buyers. And after an interval of a dozen years, books about the poet are again appearing: Chard Powers Smith's long biographical and interpretative study, *Where the Light Falls*, in early 1965; William R. Robinson's critical study subtitled *A Poetry of the*

Act in 1967; Wallace L. Anderson's *Edwin Arlington Robinson: A Critical Introduction* in the Riverside Studies in Literature in the same year (issued in 1968 in a trade edition by the Harvard University Press); Hoyt C. Franchere's study in Twayne's United States Authors Series; and Louis O. Coxe's substantial work subtitled *The Life of Poetry,* issued in both hard cover and paperback in 1968 (though dated 1969). Work is also under way on a multi-volume collected edition of Robinson's thousands of letters, to be published by Harvard. (With what ironic amusement—perhaps after an initial shock of resentment at the invasion of his private life—would he have contemplated such a prospect.) And from the nadir of 1965 the number of items in the *PMLA* bibliography has been steadily rising.

Literary predictions are hazardous, but it may not be irresponsible to conclude that a readjustment of Robinson's reputation is under way, and to speculate once more about the causes.

It has been suggested more than once that Robinson was at heart a Victorian, or even a late Romantic—troubled about the state of the world, concerned about his relation to it, unreservedly dedicated to what he conceived to be his "calling," not ashamed to produce on occasion a poetry of statement, incorrigibly fascinated (like Dickens, whom he never ceased to admire) by the infinite variety of human nature. And today, as every college or university teacher of English knows, the Romantic and the Victorian authors, after decades of neglect or contempt on the part of both teachers and students, are recapturing the status accorded them a hundred years ago—in the year of Robinson's birth. It is now recognized that these authors were not escapists and sophists respectively, victims alike of self-delusive certitudes, but passionate rebels against their own Establishment, speaking in a tongue intuitively understood by many of the new generation. This revival of respect for nineteenth-century literature augurs well for Robinson's future.

If, however, his future reputation depends merely on fluctuations of taste; if, that is, the appeal of his work as a whole is not anchored in unchanging human needs and desires and beliefs, then this essay, and indeed this volume, has no point. The only question finally worth asking about Robinson's work is, "To what extent is such an appeal present, and whence does it spring?"

Of course, many of Robinson's poems are relative failures. Like other poets, he did not always write as well as he did sometimes, and

no one will wish to defend all his poems—though defenders can doubtless be found for any one of them. On the other hand, the number of
pieces that in quality are quite or nearly equal to his best is sufficient,
if his best is good enough, to establish him as a major poet.

First, then, in assessing his achievement, there is his way with
words—the high frequency of success in "gambling" for "the possible
conjunction of a few inevitable words." And these may or may not be
the plain words of ordinary people that in his headstrong youth he
had seemed to say were best. In later life he vehemently denied that
he had any poetic system or theory, and in practice he never cuts himself off from the full traditional resources of the English language. In
"Mr. Flood's Party," recalling the warm reality and shining hopes that
Eben Flood had once enjoyed and then been dispossessed of, Robinson uses a long-voweled assonance to awaken distant echoes of sub-
limity, and an allusion to a dying hero of medieval myth to accent the
infinite remoteness of Eben's remembered triumphs.

> Alone, as if enduring to the end
> A valiant armor of scarred hopes outworn,
> He stood there in the middle of the road
> Like Roland's ghost winding a silent horn.

But at the end, no words could be more simple, or more moving, than
those in which the poet suggests Eben's unspoken acknowledgement
of final defeat.

> There was not much that was ahead of him,
> And there was nothing in the town below—
> Where strangers would have shut the many doors
> That many friends had opened long ago.

Or if love is the theme, there is the great scene in *Merlin*, where
the sage forsakes the chill wisdom of eternity for the wisdom of the
hot heart that beats in the world of time. Here, for once at least, the
poet like the magician surrenders gladly to the sway of sense, and amid
seductive lights and music yields himself to the total embrace of earthly love incarnate in Vivian.

> With a long-kindling gaze that caught from hers
> A laughing flame, and with a hand that shook

> *Like Arthur's kingdom, Merlin slowly raised*
> *A golden cup that for a golden moment*
> *Was twinned in air with hers; and Vivian,*
> *Who smiled at him across their gleaming rims*
> *From eyes that made a fuel of the night*
> *Surrounding her, shot glory over gold*
> *At Merlin, while their cups touched and his trembled.*

In contrast to this sensuous splendor is the picture of another kind of love, no less intense, in another kind of language, no less inevitably right, in "Vain Gratuities"; where an unseeing outward world wastes its pity on a woman apparently mismated:

> *But she, demure as ever, and as fair,*
> *Almost, as they remembered her before*
> *She found him, would have laughed had she been there;*
> *And all they said would have been heard no more*
> *Than foam that washes on an island shore*
> *Where there are none to listen or to care.*

And second, there is the poet's sense of form, together with his gift for achieving its "inevitable conjunction" with theme. No modern poet, for instance, has held more assured though unostentatious mastery of the sonnet, or made it serve so faultlessly so many ends: meditation ("Many Are Called"), parable ("Alma Mater"), portraiture ("Cliff Klingenhagen"), drama ("Ben Trovato"), satire ("Karma"). This very distinction, indeed, may be why Robinson's achievement in this form has been so often overlooked; the traditional mood of the sonnet is confessional, and no poet since Milton has so widened its range. Likewise, no poet in English has dealt more successfully with similar themes in a variety of lyric forms: "Hillcrest," "The Wandering Jew," "For a Dead Lady," "The Mill." In such poems the adaptation of rhythm and rhyme to the increasing or diminishing intensity of passion or pathos is managed with a sureness of touch belonging only to an adept. And finally, there is the blank verse (when it was still an adventure and not a habit), which makes Robinson clearly the greatest American master (though Frost might have his supporters) of the meter in which much of the greatest poetry in the language has been written. And again one finds the movement suited to many moods: tender in "Aunt Imogen," Eden-innocent in "Isaac and Archibald," familiar and reflective in "Ben Jonson" and "Rembrandt to Rembrandt," passionate or stoical in *Merlin,* ironic or exalted in *The Man Who Died Twice.*

To be sure, these are all traditional forms, and in the middle third of the twentieth century traditional forms have been out of fashion. Many critics and poets evidently feel that in this age, sonnets, rhymed stanzas, and blank verse are as outdated as blank verse tragedy on the Elizabethan model. But perhaps the analogy is invalid, and it is not the form itself that is at issue but the effect. We do not reject blank verse tragedy because it is in blank verse; we reject it because it does not come alive—because, as an experienced fact, no contemporary dramatist can speak to his audience through that medium. But experience does not justify the rejection of nondramatic verse because it follows conventional forms. The question is, "Can a contemporary poet speak to us through these forms and make us listen, if we give him the chance?"

My answer is that Robinson can, and will increasingly. For, finally —granting that, in art, form and substance cannot be separated and that how a poet writes is part of what he says—it is still what he says that counts. The medium is not the message. The message is never new though the medium may change. The message is always man, and the *Odyssey* is still read (one may guess, without prejudice to Joyce) more widely than *Ulysses,* and Sophocles more widely than Beckett. And in Robinson's poetry, also, there is a vision of life that assuredly the world will not let die; a vision rendered, not rarely, through the medium of inevitable words and flawless form; a vision whose intensity is sometimes scarcely bearable, though presented with irony as well as sympathy and with humor as well as pathos; a vision that reveals, without the luxury of rage or the patronage of pity or the vanity of piety, the human character in all its grime and glory, its abasement and exaltation, its endurance of fate and its dream of freedom, and all the other attributes that poets incarnate—and that critics anatomize. But critics, also, as Robinson in his mellower moods would certainly have agreed, despite the dedication of his first book, may be seekers for the Light.

The Strategy of "Flammonde"

William J. Free

When Edwin Arlington Robinson arranged the contents of his *Collected Poems* for the Macmillan Company in 1935, he chose to place the poems from his 1916 volume *The Man Against the Sky* at the beginning. Robinson's intention is lost in time, but the effect of the violation of chronology is to emphasize these poems above his early work. Indeed, *The Man Against the Sky* does contain many of Robinson's better known and most frequently anthologized poems: "Ben Jonson Entertains a Man from Stratford," "The Man Against the Sky," "Eros Turannos," "Cassandra," "Bewick Finzer," and one of his most controversial, "Flammonde," which, as the initial poem in *The Man Against the Sky*, also begins the *Collected Poems*.

Some critics have argued that such a placement indicates that Robinson valued the poem highly; however, few agree on why "Flammonde" should occupy such an honored place. Most commentators simply paraphrase the obvious: Flammonde belongs to that category of Robinson's characters who, although failures themselves, miraculously dispose the destinies of those with whom they come in contact. Few seem willing to pursue the meaning and artistry of the poem beyond that point. Indeed, scrutiny of Robinson criticism scarcely justifies Emery Neff's contention that "Flammonde" is secure as an American classic.

Particularly interesting is the failure of Robinson's defenders to confront the criticism of Yvor Winters, who was one of the first to analyze the poem in depth. Winters dismisses "Flammonde" as "repulsively sentimental." Specifically he attacks it on two counts. First, he expresses his personal distaste for the character Flammonde, whom he describes as "the sensitive parasite or . . . the literary or academic sponge. . . ." He links Robinson's interest in such a character to the poet's obsession with his own personal problems, particularly his poverty and the romanticism of his youth. Secondly, and perhaps more significantly, Winters quarrels with the poem's language, "which is reminiscent of the worst sentimentalism of the nineties, or even of lachrymose popular balladry."

Winters objects particularly to two of the examples of Flammonde's munificence: his saving the reputation of the woman whose past was marked by "a long-faded scarlet fringe" and his revealing the germ of talent in a boy overlooked by less sensitive townspeople. Winters' criticism of these lines is telling and accurate. Undoubtedly, much of the language and imagery of "Flammonde" is sentimental and derived from the second- and third-rate popular literature of the time. Robinson scholars have observed a discreet silence on this point.

The poem is not sentimental in its total effect and cannot be so easily dismissed. Not only is it interesting in its own right, but, perhaps more significantly, Robinson's strategy of language, character, and viewpoint in "Flammonde" illuminates one aspect of the problem which he faced in finding a suitable language in which to express his vision of life.

As "The Man Against the Sky" clearly indicates, Robinson rejected the materialism which dominated the philosophy of his time. Throughout his career, Robinson tried to express a sense of mystery to counteract what he believed to be the dead end of materialism. The solution to life, Robinson believed, lay in faith in a numinous existence. His faith developed in the direction of a traditional dualism of temporal and eternal being. He wrote to Harry de Forest Smith in 1897 that man can live in hell because hell, material progress, and Herbert Spencer are "temporal necessities, . . . damned uninteresting to one who can get a glimpse of the real light through the clouds of time." But that light, an image which haunted Robinson for the rest of his career, proved elusive. Robinson believed in the human spirit, but he could not find in earthly experience proof of its existence. He wrote in "Two Sonnets" in *The Torrent and The Night Before*:

> *No, I have not your backward faith to shrink*
> *Lone-faring from the doorway of God's home*
> *To find Him in the names of buried men;*

> Nor your ingenious recreance to think
> We cherish, in the life that is to come,
> The scattered features of dead friends again.

God's home was in mystery, not matter. To Robinson the light was seen far away and through a glass dimly, known only by the faint glimmers emitted from the inexplicable mysteries of life. Faith in physical immortality or in material proofs was cowardice because it turned the believer from confronting the uncertainty of mystery, the only true basis of faith.

As a poet Robinson found himself in a situation comparable to Matthew Arnold at Grande Chartreuse—caught between two worlds, one dead, the other powerless to be born. Robinson inherited a language in which metaphor had ceased to serve its poetic function. The tradition of metaphor which dominated the late nineteenth century was romantic. But the romantic sensibility, which saw nature as a mediating language between God and man and metaphor as the nexus of the communion, collapsed after Darwin and, by the end of the century, had disintegrated into sentimental cliché. The Romantic poets had found in nature images which satisfied their emotional and philosophical needs. But, as Wordsworth came to realize in *The Prelude*, the meaning of nature was not inherent in the image but was a coloring of the poet's imagination which he expressed by associating the concrete image with the abstract emotion or idea. In *English Poetry and the English Language* F. W. Bateson stated: "In the metaphysical period the connotation of a word *grew* out of its denotation—the two are so entangled that it is impossible to know where one begins and the other ends. But the connotation of a nineteenth-century word was *superimposed* upon its denotation—the denotation it had possessed in the eighteenth century—and the two meanings exist separately and, as it were, side by side" (italics Bateson's). Nature was useful to the Romantic mind precisely because it was neutral. The neutrality of the image allowed the poet to superimpose his own connotation on it by associating it with his emotion or idea.

By Robinson's time nature had abandoned its neutrality to enlist in the cause of materialism. A nature red in tooth and claw was useless as a source of metaphor to Robinson because he rejected the materialistic philosophy which it connoted. Being unwilling to accept the pessimism which nature communicated to Arnold in "Dover Beach,"

Robinson found himself cut off from the richest source of metaphor in his time. To find metaphors he was forced to fall back on images so commonplace and over-used that they had lost all meaning, denotative or connotative.

Concurrent with the collapse of the Romantic sensibility, poetic language fell under attack from logical positivism, a movement with which Robinson, oddly, felt affinity. William James in *Principles of Psychology* asserted that the cognitive use of language was superior to the metaphorical. Savages, he said, speak in parables and similes, civilized men in abstractions. James left no doubt as to which is the higher order of mind.

Robinson was a man of his time. His imagination was basically cognitive rather than sensuous, and he leaned toward abstraction. Robinson belonged to the late-Victorian world of ontological questions in which apes and angels were not realities but theoretical positions and the "law of the jungle" connoted less of human and animal actions than of sociological and psychological theorems. Although Robinson could not accept the materialists' vision, he sought his own largely in their idiom.

Thus the nature of his faith and the language of his time posed Robinson a formidable problem. The poet must work through the material. His medium forces him to seek meaning through concretely realized experience or metaphor. As a translator of the Greek dramatists, Robinson the apprentice poet must have been acutely aware of this fact. But, given the tradition of language in which he worked, he had difficulty finding an appropriate strategy in which to express his faith in mystery.

An interesting example of this problem occurs in the last sestet of his "Two Sonnets":

> Nor ever shall we know the cursed waste
> Of life in the beneficence divine
> Of starlight and of sunlight and soul-shine
> That we have squandered in sin's frail distress,
> Till we have drunk, and trembled at the taste,
> The mead of Thought's prophetic endlessness.

It is an amazingly abstract passage. Although the purpose of the lines is to express Robinson's passionate dedication to belief in a numinous world, most of the effect must come from emotionally loaded general adjectives such as "cursed," "divine," "frail," and "prophetic." These words have no denotative function in the lines but exist merely for their connotative value.

One of the passage's metaphors—the "mead of Thought's prophetic endlessness"—parodies the breakdown of Romantic metaphor. The connection of the concrete image "mead" with the abstract phrase "Thought's prophetic endlessness" is forced. The metaphor contains neither a "literal base of operations" in denotation nor the connotative shock of recognition which makes an effective metaphor. When Keats says that melancholy is "seen of none save him whose strenuous tongue / Can burst Joy's grape against his palate fine . . . ," we sense an appropriateness in his metaphor turned paradox that is lacking in Robinson's lines. The sweetness of the grape is a concrete, sensuous joy and experiencing that sweetness in the context of mutability makes the grape a powerful image of melancholy. But mead is not a kind of endlessness or thought except through a very arbitrary connection. The context gives Keats's grape connotations which are expressive of his emotion and the grape in turn gives the emotion concrete expression; Robinson's mead remains dissociated from his thought and feeling. The metaphor misfires and the abstract nouns and verbs are left to carry the meaning.

The other concrete image, the metaphor of light to represent the Holy Spirit, is one of the oldest and most common in western literature. But Robinson's attempt to mix the concrete and abstract in starlight, sunlight, and the comically weak coinage "soul-shine" falls flat. The worn-out image cannot carry so heavy a burden of meaning without stronger support from the context. Robinson expects the traditional connotation of light to stand alone, as does Tennyson in many similarly weak uses of the same image, as for example in "The Two Voices." Unless included in a fresh context, such a conventional image fails. In "Two Sonnets" the abstract nouns and adjectives are asked to carry the entire load of Robinson's philosophy, and they cannot.

This inability to find fresh metaphors to express his thought is the greatest failing in Robinson's work. Only when he is able to assimilate his ideas into the poem through the objectivity of character is he able to escape abstraction's debilitating effect. Benedetto Croce has pointed out that ideas become poetry only when included in the larger context of a poetic intuition: "philosophical maxims placed in the mouth of a personage of tragedy or comedy, perform there the function, not of concepts, but of characteristics of such persons. . . ." Critics have long sensed that Robinson's character poems are his best work. The reason is that the presence of character enabled Robinson to objectify his ideas in a way not possible in the more lyrical forms (that is, octaves, quatrains, sonnets and other short poems in which the poet speaks in his own voice).

But Robinson's character poems do not have the structural qualities of tragedy or comedy. They are perceptions. And highly abstract perceptions. The Tilbury Town characters are psychological studies in the strictest sense of that word. We seldom perceive them as flesh and blood; they are textures of ideas. Except in one last concrete act, Richard Cory exists in the subjective reflections and judgments of "we people on the pavement" who watch him from a distance. Robinson never allows the perception to reach personal intimacy. His characters don't sweat when they love, they don't bleed when they die; they finally exist only as embodiments of Robinson's philosophy. The superiority of these poems to his lyrics lies not in what they say but in their form and technique.

Perhaps we can clarify Robinson's technique by borrowing the language of T. S. Eliot's "The Three Voices of Poetry." In the early lyrics Robinson speaks in the voice of the poet talking to himself. In this voice he is unable to transform his ideas about life's meaning into poetry because he cannot place between himself and his ideas a sufficient distance. Russian critic Victor Shklovsky contends that "The technique of art is to make objects 'unfamiliar,' to make forms difficult, to increase the difficulty and length of perception because the process of perception is an aesthetic end in itself and must be prolonged. *Art is a way of experiencing the artfulness of an object . . .*" (italics Shklovsky's). Metaphor is one of the chief means by which poetry "defamiliarizes" objects and ideas and emphasizes their artfulness. It produces the distance necessary to intensify perception. Robinson's early lyrics contain no artfulness; metaphor, as a means of distancing, fails him, leaving only flat verse, not poetry. In the character poems he attempts to use other voices as a means to aesthetic distance. Here Robinson speaks through a persona, or in some cases two personae. Two patterns emerge: in one the personified "I" who narrates the poem describes the subject character without having the subject speak. In the second both the "I" and the subject speak. These two modes correspond to Eliot's second and third voices—the persona mask assumed by the poet in addressing his audience and the dramatic character. The first is the strategy of "Flammonde," the second of "Captain Craig."

"Captain Craig" illuminates the strategy of "Flammonde." The two poems have a common source: an itinerant Englishman named Alfred Louis whom Robinson met in 1897. Robinson apparently saw in the paradoxical nature of Louis's character evidence for the mystery of life he sought. To the materialist everything was explicable through science; to Robinson, Louis was inexplicable. On the one hand, the aristocrat—Cambridge educated, intimate of Browning, Longfellow, Ruskin, and George Eliot (he claimed to be the original of Mordecai in *Daniel Deronda*), correspondent of Mill, member of the bar, author, glib philosopher on the vicissitudes of life; on the other, a smelly bum, an habitual drunk, a sponger off his friends, and a former patient in a mental hospital. Evolution and sociology could no more explain Louis than they could the drunk little man in William Vaughan Moody's poem "The Menagerie."

Louis, transformed into Captain Craig, is the dramatic voice of that poem. Robinson's mask is the persona "I" who, with his friends Morgan, Killigrew, and Plunket, befriends the Captain and plays Plato to his Socrates. The analogy is doubly meaningful. The relationship between the Captain and his young friends is that of teacher and pupils: Craig, through his monologues and letters teaches them his interpretation of the meaning of life. At the same time both Craig and "I" speak for Robinson just as Socrates and his pupils actually speak for Plato.

Robinson states his meaning in "Captain Craig" through two devices. First, the Captain, through direct statement, teaches the paradox of compensation, an answer to the question of life's meaning with which Robinson flirted briefly and unsuccessfully early in his career. Craig describes a man who dreamed he was Aeschylus and was driven mad by remembering only one line from his new Eumenides:

> *That measure would have chased him all his days,*
> *Defeated him, deposed him, wasted him,*
> *And shrewdly ruined him—though in that ruin*
> *There would have lived, as always it has lived,*
> *In ruin as in failure, the supreme*
> *Fulfilment unexpressed, the rhythm of God*
> *That beats unheard through songs of shattered men*
> *Who dream but cannot sound it. . . .*

The situation of the dreamer and the words of Craig describing him repeat the ideas which Robinson in his own voice had stated in Octave VIII, resorting there to his commonplace metaphor of light:

> *And though forlornly joyless be the ways*
> *We travel, the compensate spirit-gleams*
> *Of Wisdom shaft the darkness here and there*
> *Like scattered lamps in unfrequented streets....*

In "Captain Craig" Robinson gives the abstract idea of compensation the appearance of concreteness by placing it in the mouth of a character; in Octave VIII it remains an abstract thought expressed through a commonplace metaphor. The language of "Captain Craig" is as prosaic as the language of the octave—general nouns and verbs, emotionally charged adjectives, and the simple metaphor of sound replacing that of light as the embodiment of mystery. But the sense of distance and artfulness gained by placing the words in Craig's mouth produces the illusion of a more complex context which makes the idea seem more poetic to us.

In his second device Robinson has the persona "I" overtly state the sense of mystery which he has learned from the example of Captain Craig. At the end of the poem "I" identifies the road to Craig's grave with life in another commonplace metaphor, but one which the context makes effective:

> *A windy, dreary day with cold white shine,*
> *Which only gummed the tumbled frozen ruts*
> *That made us ache. The road was hard and long,*
> *But we had what we knew to comfort us,*
> *And we had the large humor of the thing*
> *To make it advantageous....*

The "what we knew" which gives comfort for Craig's death and advantage for the future is the knowledge of compensation contained in the torrent of words from his lips. Thus, in a sense, "I" merely repeats what Craig had been saying all along. But he repeats it, not conceptually, but indirectly through a metaphor which works because it suggests the whole context of the poem which lies behind it and gains its connotation from that context. Furthermore, it is an image in which the actual road along which Craig's coffin moves and the metaphorical road that is life are united, making it one of the most effective images in Robinson's early work.

The weakness of "Captain Craig" is that Robinson, as in the personal lyrics, continues to communicate his ideas directly rather than to assimilate them into a poetic intuition. Except for the last metaphor the dramatic context of the poem is weak. Nothing happens, except the didactic message, which has been transferred from the poet's voice to his personae Captain Craig and "I." The presence of character gives the illusion that the poem is more concrete than the lyrics, but, really, on the level of language, it uses the same abstractions and conventional metaphors as the sonnets and octaves. "Captain Craig" occupies a middle ground between the artistically ineffective lyrics and the more successful character poems like "Flammonde."

Robinson worked much more effectively in the restricted form of "Flammonde" because the brevity of the poem caused him to adopt a new strategy. He distances "Flammonde" a step beyond "Captain Craig" by centering the entire knowledge of the character in the mind of the persona, thus giving the poem a stronger unity. Unlike Captain Craig, Flammonde is silent; unlike the persona voice in "Captain Craig" who learns a specific idea—that spiritual growth is a compensation for temporal misfortune—the persona voice of "Flammonde" gains only a vague sense that there exists some mysterious force which cannot be rationally understood, yet which makes enduring one's darkening hills worthwhile.

Robinson further complicates the poem by universalizing the persona voice. J. C. Levenson has pointed out that frequently Robinson's "I" is not merely an eccentric individual but a chorus representing Tilbury Town and us all. Moreover, he is to a degree unreliable and says more than he knows. Thus an element of irony must enter our understanding of the poem, for we must judge the extent and meaning of the unreliability.

Such is the case in "Flammonde." Uses of the collective pronoun far outnumber the singular which occurs only in parenthetical statements, "Nor can I say" and "And these I mention." In those places in the poem in which the viewpoint is important, "we" dominates: "He never told *us* what he was . . . ," "And what he saw *we* wondered at . . . ," "*We* could understand, / But none of *us* could lift a hand . . . ," "What was he, when *we* came to sift / His meaning . . ." (italics mine). All are cases in which the point at issue is understanding Flammonde's nature. More importantly, the final meaning of his life is communicated not to an individual or four individuals as in "Captain Craig," but collectively:

> We've each a darkening hill to climb;
> And this is why, from time to time
> In Tilbury Town, we look beyond
> Horizons for the man Flammonde.

The problem which we face is one of perception. We must intuit Flammonde within some framework which makes possible our perceiving the mystery which is at the heart of the poem. Flammonde stands before us unyielding, like a block of stone upon which recognizable features must be carved.

The nature of this framework, I believe, led Yvor Winters into misunderstanding the poem. Winters' error lies in mistaking the language of the persona for the voice of the poet. He does not see the poem ironically. The cognitive understanding which the persona has of Flammonde is, as Winters says, sentimental and trite. But Winters does not see that the triteness itself functions in context to communicate Robinson's deeper meaning. The strategy of "Flammonde" is to make sentimental metaphor the viewpoint from which we understand Flammonde and then to demonstrate the inadequacy of the vision, leaving us in the presence of mystery.

The portrait of Flammonde is almost absurdly oversimplified. The controlling metaphor is built of a few cliché actions and images commonplace in the popular literature of the time where they were used as a shorthand iconography to communicate values quickly and simply. Structurally the poem divides into three sections of four stanzas each. The division parallels the perceptual pattern of the persona. The first section introduces the image of aristocracy, the second illustrates it, and the third destroys it.

The first stanza describes the strange man "from God knows where" as royalty. The key images are "foreign air," "news of nations in his talk," "something royal in his walk," and "held his head / As one by kings accredited." They represent a progression from objective detail into metaphor. Flammonde talks about foreign countries. This fact easily becomes transferred into "foreign air." The characterization of a man's "air" is a personal, subjective, and metaphorical judgment, and to characterize the air as "foreign" doubles the metaphor.

The same kind of linguistic process appears in "something royal in his walk." The phrase tells us nothing descriptive about the manner of Flammonde's motion. "Something" is as vague a noun as can be applied to an action, and "royal" is a metaphorical characterization of that vagueness. However, the concept of royalty suggests a third idea, Flammonde's being accredited by kings. This judgment is put in the form of the simile, "as if," which recognizes the fictional nature of the connection while at the same time forcing it on our minds. The stanza thus provides us with a simplified framework of royalty within which to judge Flammonde.

This framework gives rise, in the third stanza, to a tag epitaph, "The Prince of Castaways." The epitaph reinforces the aristocratic framework and becomes the mask through which we view Flammonde's actions. Flammonde's princely nature is strengthened by the details of the second stanza—the "cleansing heritage of taste," and the dependence upon tradition. Both are aristocratic characteristics which we notice as such because the metaphor of royalty has predisposed us to see them that way.

The aristocratic metaphor colors our perception of the actions described in the second section. Although these acts of Flammonde's munificence are not specifically related to aristocracy, they suggest the principle of *noblesse oblige,* the bounty of the village squire. The nature of the actions, combined with the linguistic echoes of the term Prince, further suggest an identity of Flammonde as the Prince of Peace.

The events described produce associations on two different levels. On the one hand they suggest the actions of Christ—the teaching of humility and forbearance, the rescue of the woman taken in adultery, and the physical healings which can be seen to parallel Flammonde's social and psychological healings. In this frame of reference the image of Flammonde furthers the aristocratic metaphor by connecting him with a moral and spiritual royalty. On the other hand the actions are drawn from the sentimental fiction and poetry to which Yvor Winters so strenuously objects. The rescue of a talented lad from oblivion is an action not unknown in the pages of Horatio Alger. Sentimentalizing the fallen woman was a popular theme in melodrama and fiction and appears specifically in the novels of Edgar Saltus, which Robinson had read and condemned as "slimy."

Not only these actions, but the image of aristocracy through which we view them, were commonplace in popular literature in Robinson's time. Americans of the 1880s and '90s were obsessed with aristocracy. Magazines were filled with articles on the lives and style of European aristocrats and with fiction which drew heavily on aristocracy, ranging in quality from Henry James to William Black, a novelist featured in *Harper's* and the *Atlantic* and read by Robinson, who used images of aristocracy to extol the virtues of his heroes and heroines. The image extended into stage melodrama, a form of entertainment with which Robinson was quite familiar. An honest shop girl in *The White Slave* defends her honor with the words "rags are royal raiment when worn for virtue's sake."

Robinson's use of these cliché images and situations has two effects. First it reduces the perception of Flammonde to a commonplace level appropriate for the average resident of Tilbury Town whom "we" represents. Secondly it forces on the reader a recognition of the unreliability of this perception.

Robinson stimulates our ironic understanding of the persona's perception by undercutting it throughout the poem. In the first section Robinson contradicts Flammonde's royal appearance by recognizing the deceitfulness of the metaphor of aristocracy. The persona raises the question, is Flammonde merely playing the Prince of Castaways?

> *Meanwhile he played surpassing well*
> *A part, for most, unplayable;*
> *In fine, one pauses, half afraid*
> *To say for certain that he played.*

The metaphor of stage performance, of make-believe, contradicts the metaphor of Flammonde's royalty, and the persona cannot, given the evidence of Flammonde's appearance, decide which is the more accurate. In the fourth stanza he says that to those who watch Flammonde's social success the question is irrelevant; but it is not irrelevant to the sense of mystery which lies at the heart of the poem. The persona does not have the courage of his metaphors and can neither accept nor deny either of them. The paradox leaves the reader puzzled.

The last section of the poem further undermines the image of Flammonde as aristocrat, this time skilfully using an aspect of the controlling metaphor itself. The persona, curious about Flammonde's

"small Satanic sort of kink" which "Withheld him from the destinies / That came so near to being his . . . ," raises another question:

> *Why was it that his charm revealed*
> *Somehow the surface of a shield?*
> *What was it that we never caught?*
> *What was he, and what was he not?*

The shield can have two functions. As bearer of an heraldic device it
can proclaim the aristocracy of its owner. In that sense it unites with
the other aristocratic images to indicate Flammonde's special nature.
But it can also function as protection. In the context of the poem the
protection is ambiguous. Flammonde's charm is a shield which protects
him from the reality of his failing and at the same time a cover which
hides his true nature from the prying eyes of the townspeople. Flammonde escapes the moral and spiritual degradation which his destitute
state implies by shielding himself with his charm. His charm is both
an aristocratic badge, a coat-of-arms which identifies him as royalty
in spite of himself, and a distraction from his failure. To the persona
the shield prevents complete understanding. He cannot answer the
questions about who and what Flammonde is because the shield of
charm hides the real man. The shield is a special kind of distance
which serves the cause of Flammonde's mystery and, at the same time,
is a point of reference which enables the reader to see the image of
aristocracy in an ironic light.

The mystery is furthered by the recognition that Flammonde's
royal nature cannot compensate for his failure.

> *How much it was of him we met*
> *We cannot ever know; nor yet*
> *Shall all he gave us quite atone*
> *For what was his, and his alone;*
> *Nor need we now, since he knew best,*
> *Nourish an ethical unrest:*
> *Rarely at once will nature give*
> *The power to be Flammonde and live.*

The stanza has several implications. First it repeats the mystery which
the image of the shield had stated in the previous stanza. Secondly it
denies the possibility of a rational explanation of Flammonde such as
the one offered in "Captain Craig." Captain Craig's life was a triumph

because his pupils perceived the spiritual growth which compensated for his material failure. Such an idea is as much an oversimplified and rationalistic explanation of life as is the materialist's heredity and environment. By denying the possibility of such an explanation, Robinson again moves the poem into the realm of mystery.

The last four lines of the stanza further justify the refusal to explain. The enigmatical "ethical unrest" I interpret to mean questioning the ethics of Flammonde's playing the Prince. If his aristocratic appearance is merely a role or shield, is it ethical for him to practice such deceit in exchange for his living? Robinson's answer is to place Flammonde in a category of special existence which makes the question meaningless. Nature, in violation of its usual workings, has allowed Flammonde to encompass the paradox. Robinson suggests that to most men such an ambiguous existence is impossible. Flammonde is too complex a being for ethical questions just as he is too complex to be encompassed by metaphors of aristocracy or pretense. We cannot understand or explain Flammonde through any normal human faculties of perception. We must simply accept him as mystery.

It is this sense of mystery which causes us to look to Flammonde when climbing darkening hills. Flammonde exists beyond the horizons of our understanding. He is the substitute for light, the embodiment of the numinous world for which the image of light is a poor symbol. Flammonde succeeds as symbol because he is both present and mysterious. "We," the persona, through the screen of metaphor, see him moving before us, yet do not really see at all. Behind the screen is the shield. In a sense, the harder we look, the less we see.

"Flammonde" succeeds where "Captain Craig" and the lyrics fail because Robinson's strategy forces our intense perception of the poem's artfulness and meaning. Robinson embodies mystery in the process of the poem by showing that the consciousness of "we people on the pavement" cannot understand or explain what it sees and thus is forced to fall back upon faith in a mystery which passes understanding.

Robinson's use of the commonplace and cliché image strengthens our sense of the inadequacy of our usual modes of perception to deal with the essential. The persona is conditioned by the common metaphors of his time and forced into an unreliable perception, just as the age, Robinson believed, was limited by material explanations of life. In this sense the poem is epistemological; its subject, the limitation and ultimate failure of human perception. By using cliché images to reveal, through irony, the unreliability of perception, Robinson calls our attention to the failure of consciousness to form "true" explanations for the suffering, defeat, and triumph of human life.

The poem also demonstrates that materialism, as an ontological position, is unsatisfactory because it is based on a flawed epistemology. The materialist depends upon human observation and reason for his answers. "Flammonde" demonstrates the unreliability of these merely human tools. The tantalizing hint that there must be some higher meaning behind the shield and behind the screen enables Robinson to use the very uncertainty as a powerful comment on his faith in the numinous world.

Robinson's poetic problem, I have tried to show, was to transform the abstract ideas and sentimental, cliché-ridden metaphors of his day into poetry. In a sense he was trying to restore life to a worn-out language without abandoning that language. He succeeded to the degree to which he could place sufficient distance between his ideas and his own voice through the use of character. When, as in "Captain Craig," the persona voice articulates Robinson's ideas, the success is qualified. When, as in "Flammonde," the idea is embodied in the whole perceptual process of the poem, Robinson achieves a degree of artfulness superior to that of anyone writing at the turn of the century.

The strategy of "Flammonde" forms the basis of Robinson's most successful character poems. "Richard Cory," "Old King Cole," "Ben Jonson Entertains a Man from Stratford," "Bewick Finzer," "Cliff Klingenhagen," "Aaron Stark"—all are ultimately as mysterious as is "Flammonde." In each case the simple perception of the persona voice falls into an unresolved paradox which leaves the final impression of a spiritual order above man's comprehension, yet controlling his destiny with an unswerving necessity. Although such poems use the language of a materialistic century, Robinson's strategy of character allowed him to make it express his faith in the power of spirit.

Part of Robinson's triumph as a poet is that he could formulate such a strategy given the language with which he had to work. Part of his limitation is that he could never go beyond it. The new poetic language born with Pound and Eliot achieved an integration of image and feeling and an artful distance produced by density of context which remained beyond Robinson's talent. Robinson's characters are incapable of such statements as:

> Here I am, an old man in a dry month,
> Being read to by a boy, waiting for rain.
> I was neither at the hot gates
> Nor fought in the warm rain
> Nor knee deep in the salt marsh, heaving a cutlass,
> Bitten by flies, fought.

The images here generate their own feeling and meaning, unlike Robinson's lights and kings, which must be almost tricked into freshness by manipulating the perceptual fields in which they appear.

Robinson was a transitional poet, bringing fruit from stony ground. The wonder was that he was able to succeed at all, given the hardness of the stones and the coldness of the season. Whatever else its meaning, "Flammonde" testifies to the difficulty and triumph of his achievement.

"The Man Against the Sky" and the Problem of Faith

David H. Hirsch

"The Man Against the Sky" is one of those poems about which controversy—both philosophical and aesthetic—persists without any apparent hope of resolution. Some critics find the poem a failure, though they continue to find it interesting as E. A. Robinson's fullest statement of his beliefs on ultimate questions. Others cannot agree on just what the ultimate beliefs stated in the poem are. It is not clear, or at least it has not been unanimously agreed upon, whether Robinson intends the poem as an affirmation or as a statement of despair.[1]

I suspect that much of this controversy is owing to the tendency of critics to read the poem exclusively in discursive terms. My purpose is to resolve some of the questions that have clustered about the poem, by reading it more "poetically," that is, with more attention given to poetic conventions. More specifically, I believe that an examination of the fire imagery and the allusions in the poem will dispel some of the reservations critics have had with regard to the "loose structure" of the poem. I hope it will become apparent as this paper develops that the so-called split in the poem, which occurs when the "man" disappears and the poet embarks on a series of questions that he asks seemingly in his own person, is actually a transition from the attempt to re-create an emotional experience of high intensity on the one hand to the attempt to give that experience meaning on the other.

It may be relevant to start by saying that one of the elements of oddness in the poem is that it starts with a situation more suitable to an ending than a beginning. The opening scene envisages a speaker who faces the setting sun. The speaker describes another man, in front of him, who also faces the setting sun. This man, as Hyatt Waggoner

aptly puts it, is ". . . seen in the ultimate perspective of death."[2]
This beginning of the final and title poem in the volume which was
published in 1916 takes up where the first poem in the volume, "Flammonde," had ended. "Flammonde" closes on what can best be described as a hopeful, albeit somber, note:

> We've each a darkening hill to climb;
> And this is why, from time to time
> In Tilbury Town, we look beyond
> Horizons for the man Flammonde.

The people of Tilbury Town look "beyond horizons" seeking this man
with the odd name which may be translated "world on fire."

In "The Man Against the Sky" the naturalistic surface has been
stripped away, and instead of Flammonde placed in relation to the
populace of a fictional town which resembles the actual town of Gardiner, Maine, we have a nameless narrator placed in relation to naked
nature, and even nature appears not in its ordinary form but as a
flaming world:

> Between me and the sunset, like a dome
> Against the glory of a world on fire,
> Now burned a sudden hill,
> Bleak, round, and high, by flame-lit height made higher,
> With nothing on it for the flame to kill
> Save one who moved and was alone up there
> To loom before the chaos and the glare
> As if he were the last god going home
> Unto his last desire.

Robinson has not been considered a poet who works with a deep sense
of tradition, but these opening lines suggest at least two possible parallels. The less obvious of the two I want to discuss later. The more
obvious parallel is Coleridge's "Kubla Khan," in which there are mea-
sureless caverns, a "pleasure-dome," the "river Alph," "a sunless sea,"
"twice five miles of fertile ground," "gardens bright," and "many an
incense-bearing tree." Coleridge shows a daemonic Garden of Eden in
which are mingled exotic pleasures and horrors. The sun in Coleridge's
poem is ambivalent, while in Robinson's poem it is clearly destructive.
Similarly the dome in Robinson's poem is in no way associated with
pleasure, but is shown being assaulted by the fiery sun. Six years later

T. S. Eliot was to announce to the intellectual world the secret of these
patterns of fire imagery. He used them to perfection to create the poetic idea that for more than a quarter of a century remained the metaphor for the age, the waste land. But it is no exaggeration to say that
Robinson had discovered the twentieth-century waste land without
quite being able to name it.

The opening image of "The Man Against the Sky" is of someone
straining to see beyond horizons, but instead of that Flammonde
whom the inhabitants of Tilbury Town seek, the speaker in this poem
sees a stranger in isolation who is surrounded by a lifeless burned-out
countryside, "Bleak, round, and high, by flame-lit height made
higher, / With nothing on it for the flame to kill. . . ." One commen-
tator has pointed out that the opening image of the world on fire is
"one of the few figures in the poem that have several levels of meaning.
The 'world on fire' against which [the man] is outlined," writes Hyatt
Waggoner, "is at once the sunset, the conflagration of World War I,
and the universe described by science, with its live stars and dead stars,
the electrical nature of matter, and so on."[3]

The fire imagery, it should be added, is important not only for its
several levels of meaning, but as a unifying motif that runs through
the poem, and that functions principally by linking both the speaker
of the poem and the "man" to the biblical age, when "fire" was a
meaningful force that could be either creative or destructive. The three
biblical texts that are especially relevant as a gloss on Robinson's
poem are Exodus 3:1–8, the episode of Moses and the burning bush;
Daniel 3, the casting of Shadrach, Meshach, and Abed-nego into the
fiery furnace; and Revelation, 16:8–9 and 20:9–10, the episodes of the
fourth angel and of the lake of fire.

Two of these texts are explicitly alluded to in the poem, and these
I should like to consider initially. The one that seems to me of primary
importance, both thematically and in the organization of the poem, is
the allusion to Exodus 3. Speculating on the identity of the "man,"
the narrator of the poem projects the following possibility:

> Or, mounting with infirm unsearching tread,
> His hopes to chaos led,
> He may have stumbled up there from the past,
> And with an aching strangeness viewed the last
> Abysmal conflagration of his dreams, —
> A flame where nothing seems

To burn but flame itself, by nothing fed;
And while it all went out,
Not even the faint anodyne of doubt
May then have eased a painful going down
From pictured heights of power and lost renown,
Revealed at length to his outlived endeavor
Remote and unapproachable forever. . . .

The skillfulness of Robinson's counterpoint can be appreciated when placed next to the account of Moses' confrontation with the burning bush:

Now Moses kept the flock of Jethro his father-in-law, the priest of Midian: and he led the flock to the back side of the desert, and came to the mountain of God *even* to Horeb. And the Angel of the Lord appeared unto him in a flame of fire out of the midst of a bush: and he looked, and, behold, the bush burned with fire, and the bush *was* not consumed. And Moses said, I will now turn aside, and see this great sight, why the bush is not burnt. And when the Lord saw that he turned aside to see, God called unto him out of the midst of the bush, and said, Moses, Moses. And he said, Here *am* I. And he said, Draw not nigh hither: put off thy shoes from off thy feet; for the place whereon thou standest *is* holy ground.

Thus begins one of the fateful dialogues in the history of human religious consciousness. What is striking in the biblical text is that miraculously God appears and speaks, and man answers. But if we consider Robinson's antiphon, what is striking in it is the silence that encompasses the image, and indeed, the entire poem. In Robinson's poem God does not speak, and the primary impression that is conveyed throughout is of either silence or noise. Audial images are sparse in this poem, and when they occur they occur as images of non-rational discourse or meaningless noise: "Under these . . . shafts and agonies . . . [man] may cry out and stay on horribly." Or, again,

Is this the music of the toys we shake
So loud,—as if there might be no mistake
Somewhere in our indomitable will?
Are we no greater than the noise we make
Along one blind atomic pilgrimage
Whereon by crass chance billeted we go
Because our brains and bones and cartilage
Will have it so?

In so far as the visual imagery is concerned, this man who stands silhouetted against the sky or who sets himself in opposition to it has ascended accidentally ("he may have stumbled up there from the past") just as Moses seems to have stumbled on to Mount Horeb. But whereas Moses is granted a vision of God, Robinson's man is envisaged by the speaker as seeing only "the last / Abysmal conflagration of his dreams." What once was "vision" has, in the twentieth century, become dream or illusion. And while the biblical flame is a manifestation of the Divine Presence, Robinson's flame embodies nothing and is nothing. Finally, while Moses, who stands on holy ground, may not approach too close to the Divine Presence, Robinson's man finds, anti-climactically, that the speechless flame is also "remote and unapproachable forever." There is one more element worth noting, and that is that the parallel situations suggest a parallel, albeit a disjunctive one, between the man of the poem and the biblical Moses, a parallel which is further supported by the lines,

> Again, he may have gone down easily,
> By comfortable altitudes, and found,
> As always, underneath him solid ground
> Whereon to be sufficient and to stand
> Possessed already of the promised land,
> Far stretched and fair to see. . . .

The second biblical allusion, which is more direct, is no less suggestive than the one I have just discussed:

> . . . Even he who climbed and vanished may have taken
> Down to the perils of a depth not known,
> From death defended though by men forsaken,
> The bread that every man must eat alone;
> He may have walked while others hardly dared
> Look on to see him stand where many fell;
> And upward out of that, as out of hell,
> He may have sung and striven
> To mount where more of him shall yet be given,
> Bereft of all retreat,
> To sevenfold heat,—
> As on a day when three in Dura shared
> The furnace, and were spared
> For glory by that king of Babylon
> Who made himself so great that God, who heard,
> Covered him with long feathers, like a bird.

It has become too pat, perhaps, to talk about Christ figures in the works of American writers; nevertheless, this long, nervous sentence, which I have quoted only in part, is insistently dotted with Christ imagery: the descent into Hell ("perils of a depth not known"), the bread of affliction ("that every man must eat alone"), the possible allusion to Christ's walking on the water ("He may have walked while others hardly dared / Look on to see him stand where many fell"), the ascent from hell, the reference to self-sacrifice ("To mount where more of him shall yet be given"), and the allusion to the Book of Daniel itself. After Shadrach, Meshach, and Abed-nego have been cast into the furnace raging at sevenfold heat, Nebuchadnezzar looks in and sees, to his dismay, the three Jews unharmed, and with them yet another figure, "and the form of the fourth is like the Son of God." But again, the allusion is disjunctive, and seems to lead to a blank wall rather than to any affirmation.

The third possible source for the fire imagery is the Book of Revelation. One of the pervasive underlying motifs of the Apocalypse is the threat of the destruction of the world by fire. In verses 8 and 9 of Chapter 16 we are told that "the fourth angel poured out his vial upon the sun; and power was given unto him to scorch men with fire. And men were scorched with great heat, and blasphemed the name of God. . . ." In Chapter 20 it is asserted that Satan and his cohorts ". . . went up on the breadth of the earth, and compassed the camp of the saints about, and the beloved city: and fire came down from out of heaven and devoured them. And the devil that deceived them was cast into the lake of fire and brimstone, where the beast and the false prophet *are*, and shall be tormented day and night for ever and ever" (9, 10). The pattern of imagery that appears in Revelation is echoed in the opening lines of Robinson's poem. But whereas the fire of Revelation is a purifying flame that consumes evil and prepares the way for the New Jerusalem, the fire in Robinson's poem simply creates a waste land, or at best it is ambiguous. If it does not purify, it may illuminate, but to what end is not clear. Does the flame help to cast light "over ways that save," or does it simply discover "life a lighted highway to the tomb?"

If consideration of the fire imagery, with its evocation of Moses and Jesus, is useful in highlighting some of the problems that cluster about the identity of the man against the sky as a projection out of the religious consciousness of the narrator of the poem, a consideration of affinities between Robinson's poem and the tradition may help to call attention to the presence of the narrator himself, which has not elicited much comment.[4] In Book XI of *Paradise Lost* there is a scene that closely resembles the image with which Robinson opens his poem.[5] Adam, having fallen, asks the angel Michael for guidance:

> "Ascend, I follow thee, safe guide, the path
> Thou lead'st me, and to the hand of heaven submit,
> However chastening, to the evil turn
> My obvious breast, arming to overcome
> By suffering, and earn rest from labor won,
> If so I may attain." So both ascend
> In the visions of God: It was a hill
> Of Paradise the highest, from whose top
> The hemisphere of earth in clearest ken
> Stretched out to the amplest reach of prospect lay.
> Not higher that hill nor wider looking round,
> Whereon for different cause the tempter set
> Our second Adam in the wilderness,
> To show him all earth's kingdoms and their glory.

Robinson's scene and Milton's are similar. In both we have the image of two beings made in God's image ascending a hill, one preceding the other. But the opening of Robinson's poem comes through as a disharmonious rendition of the scene described by Milton. The two figures remain, one in the vanguard, the other behind. "Earth's kingdoms and their glory" is transmuted into "the glory of a world on fire," and the "hill of paradise" becomes a "sudden hill" that is aflame. Moreover, the angelic mission of guidance has been sidetracked. Whereas Milton may stand outside the events and portray them in a rational and orderly progression, Robinson's narrator is directly involved. The hill, which in Milton is a hill in Paradise, in Robinson seems to be rather a hill in Hades. And instead of ascending "in the visions of God" (with all the ambiguities implicit in that phrase), Robinson's pair "loom before the chaos and the glare."

Milton, that is, can provide a narrative that expresses certainty about human experience. He sets out to "justify the ways of God to man," and he is as good as his word. His periodic sentences justify their length by encompassing infinite riches of simile, myth, and allusion; and the myths to which he so often alludes, both pagan and

biblical, still have meaning for him. As Basil Willey puts it, "Milton
. . ., although himself a considerable rationaliser, could still employ
the concrete symbols of the faith without feeling that he was deliberately utilizing what was fictitious."[6] After Milton, Willey continues,
such confidence is no longer possible. Robinson's periodic sentences
reflect the post-Renaissance, post-Enlightenment diminished universe.
His similes do not clarify or decorate, but rather push faith into a small
corner of the imagination. Immediately following the opening fire
image, the narrator goes on to explain:

> *Dark, marvelous, and inscrutable he moved on*
> *Till down the fiery distance he was gone, —*
> *Like one of those eternal, remote things*
> *That range across a man's imaginings*
> *When a sure music fills him and he knows*
> *What he may say thereafter to few men, —*
> *The touch of ages having wrought*
> *An echo and a glimpse of what he thought*
> *A phantom or a legend until then . . . .*

It is as if Robinson's narrator is stuttering, hesitating to reach the
end of a sentence because he cannot be quite sure where the sentence
will lead. The man appears, in these lines, to be a revelation, "Dark,
marvelous, and inscrutable," but a revelation, like all modern revela-
tions, that must be concealed. The simile that begins "Like one of
those . . ." turns the poem away from the "man" and back upon the
narrator himself. The astonishing thing about the revelation is its extraordinary tentativeness. It is, to begin with, eternal and yet remote. It
is a sure music which once heard is next to unutterable, and the knowledge it brings is a knowledge of the futility of trying to communicate it
to others. And the revelation ends by being eroded away like a house of
cards: "an echo and a glimpse," the vision is the quintessence of in-
tangibility. Moreover, it is not even an echo and a glimpse, but an
echo and a glimpse of what was thought, and not only an echo and a
glimpse of what was thought, but an echo and a glimpse of what was
thought a phantom or a legend. The revelation recedes into a void; it
is like a block of ice that is transformed from a solid to a liquid to an
ever-elusive vapor before one's very eyes. And all of these kaleidoscopic
phantom shapes "range across a man's imaginings."

This internalizing of the motions of faith is a typically twentieth-century posture, one that is brought to perfection by Wallace Stevens, and it is only by such internalization, by making faith a quality of imagination, that faith becomes susceptible of coherent discussion in the twentieth century. By internalizing the "man" of the opening sections of the poem, by making him a figure in the imagination of the narrator, Robinson can present him as a kind of composite of the western religious consciousness. The man, then, within the narrator's imagination becomes metamorphosed into something "eternal," albeit "remote." And the perception of the "man" by the inner eye of the narrator is conveyed in terms of a refraction of a shattered mirror image.

It is this internalizing of the intimations of the transcendent, I believe, that bursts out in the questions and answers of the final lines of the poem, and makes them not simply a discursive appendage but a fulfillment of the narrator's dilemma as it is projected throughout the poem. By the time he has reached these closing lines, the narrator's situation has changed. He is no longer attempting to communicate the experience of a "revelation," as he is with the image of the man facing the sunset, but is now trying to extract meaning from the "revelation."[7] These questions come only after the narrator has balanced the description of man as a decayed religious consciousness by describing man in his many secular guises, as scientist, communist, automaton, artist, actor, philosopher, pleasure seeker, stoic, doubter, and as the accidental descendant of equally accidental non-human ancestors. The questions that the narrator asks at this point resolve into two general categories: If man can no longer believe as he once did, does that mean that he cannot believe at all? And if man has no hope beyond the grave, if he is nothing better than this quintessence of dust, then what is there to keep him from suicide?

Robinson's answer to the first question is that faith itself not only persists but is ineradicable, even though the specific beliefs that men can retain are subject to change:

> But this we know, if we know anything:
> That we may laugh and fight and sing
> And of our transience here make offering
> To an orient Word that will not be erased,
> Or, save in incommunicable gleams
> Too permanent for dreams,
> Be found or known.

The Word, or Revelation, may come fleetingly in dreams and visions and through a glass darkly, but it comes undeniably. What the new beliefs will be or can be or must be, this Robinson does not say.

The second question, the question of suicide, is answered implicitly in the poem, but perhaps unsatisfactorily. Robinson's intent is clear. Without the knowledge of something beyond this material globe man would inevitably choose death, actively seek it instead of passively waiting for it:

> *If after all that we have lived and thought,*
> *All comes to Nought,—*
> *If there be nothing after Now,*
> *And we be nothing anyhow,*
> *And we know that,—why live?*
> *'Twere sure but weaklings' vain distress*
> *To suffer dungeons where so many doors*
> *Will open on the cold eternal shores*
> *That look sheer down*
> *To the dark tideless floods of Nothingness*
> *Where all who know may drown.*

It is interesting that in the closing lines, which represent the narrator trying to give meaning to the events of history that have culminated in the loss of faith, the dominant imagery is of water, whereas in the opening lines, which convey the emotional impact of the experience of the erosion of faith, the dominant imagery is of fire. It may be worth noting, too, that *The Waste Land* follows a similar pattern and that "The Love Song of J. Alfred Prufrock" actually ends, probably coincidentally, with exactly the same word as Robinson's poem, "drown."

Hyatt Waggoner has argued cogently and persuasively that "The Man Against the Sky" is a negative poem. He has pointed out, rightly, that the three capitalized words of the last section, which are also rhyme words, are "Nought," "Now," and "Nothingness." And he concludes that

> . . . lacking precision, the 'dungeons,' 'cold eternal shores,' and 'dark tideless floods' can have only a vague emotional import. They are evidences not only that Robinson too often availed himself of worn nineteenth-century language, but also that he did not really quite know, so far as he expressed himself in this poem, what it was he feared and what it was he hoped.[8]

Yet I think that we may surmise what Robinson hoped and feared. He feared a world devoid of values. What he hoped is more difficult to get at but may be inferred from these lines:

> Shall we, because Eternity records
> Too vast an answer for the time-born words
> We spell, whereof so many are dead that once
> In our capricious lexicons
> Were so alive and final, hear no more
> The Word itself, the living word
> That none alive has ever heard
> Or ever spelt,
> And few have ever felt
> Without the fears and old surrenderings
> And terrors that began
> When Death let fall a feather from his wings
> And humbled the first man?

Waggoner takes these lines as further evidence of the poem's negativity: "Since no one today has 'ever heard or ever spelt' the Word without experiencing the 'fears and old surrenderings and terrors' that beset us, the conclusion [reached in the poem] can only be considered negative in fact, despite its apparent intention of affirming some kind of faith."[9] The immediate meaning and initial emotional impact of these lines is assuredly negative. I think, however, that it is possible to take these lines as presenting an alternative to the vacuous world produced by science and the twentieth-century sensibility. The alternatives envisaged by Robinson are the death-in-life of a world without values as opposed to the threatening but meaningful world of faith. Faith, I take Robinson to be saying, is not a source of instant joy but of intensified anxiety. In an age of spiritual lethargy, faith is, as T. S. Eliot so aptly puts it, the stirring of dull roots with spring rain.

NOTES

1. Essentially, the argument is one of intention and achievement. Robinson said that he meant the poem to be a statement of faith, but some critics have seen only negation in the poem itself. Two recent critics, however, agree that the poem is an affirmation. See Ellsworth Barnard, *Edwin Arlington Robinson, A Critical Study* (New York, 1952), pp. 22, 113–115, and Wallace L. Anderson, *Edwin Arlington Robinson, A Critical Introduction* (Boston, 1967), pp. 146–149. Louis

O. Coxe, *Edwin Arlington Robinson, The Life of Poetry* (New York, 1969), pp. 104–106, treats the poem as a more problematic work of art.

2. *The Heel of Elohim* (Norman: University of Oklahoma Press, 1950), p. 31.

3. *Ibid.*, p. 31.

4. W. R. Robinson asserts that "the observer is able to identify himself with the figure he observes and thereby meditate on his own spiritual being as an externalized phenomenon" (*Edwin Arlington Robinson, A Poetry of the Act,* Cleveland, 1967, p. 67).

5. Although it is not customary to analyze Robinson's poems as if he were a poet in "the tradition," the fact is that Robinson read and absorbed the classic English poets. To Milton he devoted part of a year of post-graduate study at Gardiner High School. And Esther Willard Bates writes: "During the years in which he was engaged on the longer poems, especially *Cavender's House* and *Matthias at the Door,* I saw a volume of Ibsen's plays lying on his studio table. A volume of Milton was there more regularly: he said he liked to read Milton's blank verse when he was writing it himself" (*Edwin Arlington Robinson and His Manuscripts,* Waterville, Maine, 1944, p. 30).

6. *The Seventeenth Century Background* (Garden City: Doubleday, 1953), p. 293.

7. In a letter, Robinson wrote, "The world has been made what it is by upheavals, whether we like them or not. I've always told you it's a hell of a place. That's why I insist that it must mean something. My July work was a poem on this theme and I call it 'The Man Against the Sky.'"

8. *The Heel of Elohim,* p. 36.

9. *Ibid.*, p. 35.

The Book of Scattered Lives

Scott Donaldson

In the sonnet "New England" Edwin Arlington Robinson takes ironic issue with the stereotype of the cold, reticent New Englander driven by his Puritan conscience. Elsewhere, he writes, poets boil

> . . . with such a lyric yeast
> Of love that you will hear them at a feast
> Where demons would appeal for some repose,
> Still clamoring where the chalice overflows
> And crying wildest who have drunk the least.

But in New England, children stumble on frozen toes, Passion is suspect, "Love a cross . . . to bear," and Joy shivers, knitting, in the corner. The sheer delight in Robinson's overstatement undercuts his surface message; he is having some fun with the stereotype, the kind of fun, for example, that is hard to imagine Robert Frost having.

For if Frost, despite his boyhood in San Francisco, is pre-eminently the twentieth-century American poet most versed in country things, Robinson, despite his Maine origins, learns lessons deriving as much from the city as the country, and taught him by people, not places. Every critic from Yvor Winters to Louis Coxe[1] has noted the preoccupation with character of this poet with a prose in view, telling his elliptical tales of people—of Tilbury Town, to be sure, but the people of that town down the river, New York, as well.

Before he was thirty years old Robinson had moved to New York City, and for the rest of his life he returned there with regularity, living much of every winter on the seacoasts of Bohemia following sojourns the rest of the year to write at Peterborough and visit friends in Boston and elsewhere. After his brief employment at Harvard, for example, Robinson found a place on Washington Square in 1899, and wrote a friend that he was settled there, "maybe for six months, maybe for the rest of my natural life."[2] The rest of his natural life it turned out to be, as he was no more able to resist New York than the Watcher by the Way who finally yields, in "The Town Down the River," to the lure of the city. He was not insensitive, as his poetry testifies, to the *anomie* and the loneliness of urban existence. He nearly lost his wits working on the subway construction project, where his already sensitively painful ears were subjected to the torture of riotous noise. Even a demon would appeal for some repose from that clamor. Yet Robinson came back, and came back, even after the idyllic, productive summers at the MacDowell Colony. Late in life he found the city's unreasonable, ill-planned growth oppressive, but still he returned—and for the best of reasons: "New York is getting beyond the bounds of material decency, with fifty or sixty story buildings standing up everywhere, like some unholy growth of mushrooms after a warm rain. It is no longer a place for me to live in, and if it weren't for a lack of ordinary consideration on the part of most of my friends, who persist in living here, I'd go somewhere. The trouble is, I don't know where."[3]

There was no place else to go, and his friends were there.

Many of his poems, especially those in *The Town Down the River* (1910) and *A Man Against the Sky* (1916), deal with the particular persons and situations he encountered as a poet no longer young but seeking recognition in the city. Among failed men of near-genius, among brilliant dropouts from the world of competition, Robinson found, not without the aid of substantial quantities of liquor, the kind of camaraderie unavailable in Gardiner, Maine, where the townspeople persisted in wondering when Win Robinson would finally give up this poetry business and come to his senses. At night he went the rounds of the taverns in lower Manhattan and Greenwich Village, "establishing warm relationships" the only way he knew how, "by way of booze," drinking whiskey straight until he could smile, or talk with unwonted fluency, or listen to the nickelodeon in a pleasant alcoholic haze.[4]

There is little of the urban mystique of Walt Whitman or Hart Crane in Robinson's poetry: he was no more enchanted by the soaring buildings and magnificent bridges of New York than by the flora and fauna of New England. But the people and their situations he recorded, in unanthologized verse, with a sensitivity that justifies Louis Coxe's claim that Robinson was indeed "a city poet, perhaps our first and finest."[5]

Holed up in his room-study at Gardiner in the mid-nineties, E. A. Robinson wrote some fifteen prose sketches for a projected book to be called *Scattered Lives*. "Some day," he announced to Harry de Forest Smith, "you will see a printed edition of *Scattered Lives* though it be printed on toilet paper with a one-hand printing press."[6] There was no such book, of course, but the proposed title, and all it implied, was to serve him well in his poetry about the "group of incomplete geniuses"[7] he met and drank with in New York. These friends, or ones like them (for it will not do to insist too much on biographical parallels), come flickering to life, with customary Robinsonian indirection, in a group of poems centered around a saloon called Calverly's.

"We go no more to Calverly's," the first poem of the group begins, for strangers now inhabit the place, and four old companions who once rejoiced in song and drink are "cold and quiet." As James Dickey comments, the opportunities for bathos in such a situation are nearly limitless.[8] But Robinson redeems with his craft what might have been merely sentimental reminiscence. Characteristically, imagery of light symbolizes the fate of these four "light lives." The lights are dim in Calverly's now, and the speaker and the one companion who is left, "the remnant," cast no more than "twilight on a ruin" there. Like the saloon the dead men were ruined in this life, and wondering about their afterlife will only lead the survivors to madness, to the darkness of night illuminated only by the stars.

Just as characteristically Robinson does no more than hint at what the four were like, though in successive poems in *The Town Down the River* we learn more of three of them. But when they are remembered at all, it is not for what they have accomplished:

> No fame delays oblivion
> For them, but something yet survives:
> A record written fair, could we
> But read the book of scattered lives.

Reading this book of the grotesque is very difficult indeed, and Robinson makes it clear, here as elsewhere, that there are certain things we cannot know about such men. There can be only a page

> for Leffingwell,
> And one for Lingard, the Moon-calf;
> And who knows what for Clavering,
> Who died because he couldn't laugh?
> Who knows or cares?

No one, perhaps, may know, but the speaker of the poem, and anyone who reads it, must certainly *care* about these men. And having piqued the curiosity, Robinson begins to satisfy it in the poems that follow.

Of the three the lunatic Lingard is perhaps the least interesting. He is given to séances and table rappings and moon-gazing, and walks among the stars in full retreat from the mundane. In "Lingard and the Stars" an eager ghost raps out what he wants to hear:

> When earth is cold and there is no more sea,
> There will be what was Lingard. Otherwise,
> Why lure the race to ruin through the skies?

Overcome with gratitude at this promise of immortality, Lingard is yet sane enough to fear that it is a false promise. "I wish the ghost would give his name," he says, but then the séance is over, and he persuades Clavering to walk the midnight streets with him, while he communes with the skies.

Leffingwell's story emerges sketchily in an elegy made up of three sonnets, "The Lure," "The Quickstep," and "Requiescat." Apparently Leffingwell has committed suicide; certainly he has not lived the kind of life "mostpeople," to borrow Cummings' word, find respectable. In the first sonnet the poet separates his judgment from that of these other mourners at the funeral, whose perceptions are no more to be trusted than those of the Tilbury townspeople who so regularly misunderstand their fellow beings. Forget "your Cricket and your Ant," he tells them, for the chirp of gossip and the condemnation of the industrious who brand Leffingwell as "parasite and sycophant" hardly fathom his case:

> I tell you, Leffingwell was more than these;
> And if he prove a rather sorry knight,
> What quiverings in the distance of what light
> May not have lured him with high promises,
> And then gone down?

Again the light, again the lure, and again the race to ruin, for Leffing-well, like all the frequenters of Calverly's, "played and lost" at the game of renown. Now that the dirge is played and the burial per-formed (in the second sonnet), "we smile at his arrears," but cannot reckon what "his failure-laden years" cost him. Leffingwell may be a portrait of Joseph Lewis French, dilettante and congenital sponge who often "borrowed" money and clothing from Robinson, William Vaughn Moody, and others of their circle. Always on the brink of madness, French would appear (as, probably, in "Alma Mater") from out of nowhere, deliver a stream of invective against worldly injustice, promise to promote Robinson's reputation (he tried, unsuccessfully, to get him a Nobel prize), demand a dole, and be off again. "I had a rather dignified letter from French," Robinson once wrote a friend, "asking me for the gray suit that I am wearing." As the poet lay dying, French cadged one last five-dollar bill from Robinson; in earlier, more penurious days for Robinson, French had been content with a dime or a quarter.[9] Whatever the provenance of Leffingwell, however, in the third and final sonnet Robinson makes a plea against disturbing his ghost with speculation about his present whereabouts. "He may be now an amiable shade," enjoying himself in Hell, but "we do not ask," for if he is not allowed to rest in peace, Leffingwell will

> rise and haunt us horribly,
> And be with us o' nights of a certainty.
> Did we not hear him when he told us so?

Clavering, like Leffingwell and Lingard, is a man unaccommodated to the demands of this world. Obsessed by the past, and a hinted-at lost love, he composes metres (not poems) for Cubit, and steadfastly avoids commerce with the present. He drifts through life rudderless and without sails, and is bereft of illusions about himself. But Claver-ing is kind and loyal:

> I think of him as one who gave
> To Lingard leave to be amused,
> And listened with a patient grace
> That we, the wise ones, had refused. . . .
> I think of last words that he said
> One midnight over Calverly:
> 'Good-by—good man.' He was not good;
> So Clavering was wrong, you see.

Wrong, perhaps, but kind enough not to laugh at Lingard, and loyal enough to think the best of his friends.

The attitude of the speaker in "Clavering" progresses from near-certainty about its subject to nearly absolute uncertainty. "I say no more for Clavering," the first stanza begins, as the speaker puts down what can be said for sure: that Clavering drifted, that he saw

> Too far for guidance of today,
> Too near for the eternities.

Next, the narrator shifts from what can be said to what he now remembers, as five successive stanzas begin "I think of. . . ." A third change of attitude is reflected in the following three stanzas, when reminiscence yields to speculation: "I wonder" introduces these stanzas. But such thoughts and wonderings are without power to sum up the man within Clavering's shell:

> Why prate of what he seemed to be,
> And all that he might not have been?

Robinson provides carefully-hidden clues about Clavering, as about Reuben Bright and Leffingwell, Aaron Stark and Lingard. But these cryptic clues, even when deciphered, do not and cannot tell us everything about the motivations and depths of these men. They cannot be sounded, and he does not pretend to sound them, in New York or in Gardiner. But in these poems about Calverly's saloon and those who frequented it, there is an unmistakable poignancy, a tenderness toward those departed, that less often characterizes his portraits of Tilbury Town inhabitants. So "Clavering" ends:

> He clung to phantoms and to friends,
> And never came to anything.
> He left a wreath on Cubit's grave.
> I say no more for Clavering.

In all these poems Robinson leaves out more than he tells. But in all of them there is a thread of affection for those companions he must have thought of, from 1900 to 1916, as his fellow failures. Certainly, he likes and respects them more than the protagonist of "Old Trails," who cuts off his ties to these ghosts, gives up his early dreams along with his friends on Eleventh Street, fattens awhile, moves to Yonkers, and eventually "saunter[s] into fame." The white lights of fame beckoned all the regulars at Calverly's, but for them there was to be only twilight, moonlight, and the dark of oblivion. The protagonist of "Old Trails" succeeds because he has taken "a safer way," but Robinson prefers the failed idealists at Calverly's to this successful materialist, their dim light to his bright artificial "gleams." It is their case, as well as his own, that he pleads in "Dear Friends," when he repudiates the prevailing values:

> So, friends (dear friends), remember, if you will,
> The shame I win for singing is all mine,
> The gold I miss for dreaming is all yours.

Robinson's poems about Calverly and Lingard, Clavering and Leffingwell, testify to the poet's discovery of companions among the sometime brilliant failures who congregated in the bars of New York's Bohemia. To be sure, Robinson exerts imagination in bringing these characters to life, but there can be little doubt that his affection for Clavering, for example, has its origin in a particular friendship. There are poems of friendship, but not of heterosexual love: philia, not eros. Hagedorn's biography recounts Robinson's famous cautiousness toward women on the make, and his successful resistance even to such an accomplished seductress as Isadora Duncan.[10] When he does write of the women of the city, it is in sympathy or empathy rather than out of personal devotion. Two poems in particular, "Veteran Sirens" and "The Poor Relation," illustrate the point.

Veteran Sirens

> The ghost of Ninon would be sorry now
> To laugh at them, were she to see them here,
> So brave and so alert for learning how
> To fence with reason for another year.
>
> Age offers a far comelier diadem
> Than theirs; but anguish has no eye for grace,
> When time's malicious mercy cautions them
> To think a while of number and of space.

> The burning hope, the worn expectancy,
> The martyred humor, and the maimed allure,
> Cry out for time to end his levity,
> And age to soften his investiture;
>
> But they, though others fade and are still fair,
> Defy their fairness and are unsubdued;
> Although they suffer, they may not forswear
> The patient ardor of the unpursued.
>
> Poor flesh, to fight the calendar so long;
> Poor vanity, so quaint and yet so brave;
> Poor folly, so deceived and yet so strong,
> So far from Ninon and so near the grave.

Some have read this poem as a satirical portrait of ancient flirts in salon society, pitifully trying to stave off the ravages of age. On the other hand, Winters maintains that these sirens are prostitutes.[11] But whether they are the victims of their own foolishness or the victims of society, it is at least clear that Robinson sympathizes with their plight.

Their situation is contrasted with that of Ninon in the first and final lines of the poem. Ninon de Lenclos was a beautiful and rich Parisienne "who abandoned herself to epicurean indulgence . . . , renounced marriage, and had numerous lovers" among the most illustrious of seventeenth-century Frenchmen. Ninon was especially remarkable for preserving "her charms to a very advanced age": Byron cited her in *Don Juan* as one who never grew ugly.[12] Robinson's women are would-be Ninons: they seek the grandeur, the diadem, of ageless beauty, but are mastered by time. A series of adjective-noun paradoxes underlines their plight. They are "veteran sirens," experienced but hardly likely, any longer, to enchant Odysseus. For them time's "mercy" is "malicious" and indeed they suffer, yet they "may not forswear" the "patient ardor of the unpursued." True ardor cannot be patient, and no one calls to arouse in their breasts whatever real emotions they may yet be capable of feeling.

Perhaps it would be pleasanter, in their circumstances, not to think at all, but they must needs "fence with reason" and heed the cautionary injunction to "think a while of number and of space." How many years have they lived? How few are left to them? How much money do they have (will they have, will they need) to go on living?

Where in the world is a place for them to stay? Such are the suggestions of those innocent abstractions, number and space. They are indeed poor—in flesh which fights against decay, in vanity which bravely confronts mirrors, in folly which shields them from the truth. Theirs is a "maimed allure," another paradox, and they should, but do not

> *Cry out for time to end his levity,*
> *And age to soften his investiture.*

Time has treated these women frivolously, with levity—the word is' especially appropriate for its secondary meaning of changefulness—and it is age that will occupy the throne in their salon, not a reincarnation of Ninon.

The last stanza of "Veteran Sirens" demonstrates Robinson's sympathy for these women who can be subdued only in defiance of their will. In "The Poor Relation," however, the poet seems rather to identify himself with the plight of his title character. This woman, living alone in a New York apartment, abandoned by her relatives except for gifts of odds and ends, represents an urban and female counterpart to Eben Flood. They are both victimized by living too long, past the appointed time of their former friends and companions, and they both achieve a kind of dignity in their loneliness.

The poor relation is one of those rare Robinson characters who has discarded her illusions—about herself, about others' view of herself—and is yet able to survive. Once she had been a great beauty, and still, rarely, there are those visitors

> *who come for what she was—*
> *The few left who know where to find her—*

and she clings to them, but such visitors stay only a while, and then leave her alone in the apartment to "count her chimneys and her spires." She understands why their visits are short, and does not wish to bother them. Besides, there is one friend, one good ghost, one "truant from a tomb of years"—her own self, when young—who will stay with her; and so, like Eben Flood, she communes with herself in laughter and in song.

Two kinds of music are contrasted in the last four stanzas of the poem. On the one hand, there is the slender song the poor relation sings in concert with the ghost of her youth:

> *Her memories go foraging*
> *For bits of childhood song they treasure.*

In the final lines of the poem there is an elaboration of the metaphor which escapes sentimentality only because it has been carefully foreshadowed earlier:

> *Unsought, unthought-of, and unheard,*
> *She sings and watches like a bird,*
> *Safe in a comfortable cage*
> *From which there will be no more flying.*

The title contains a double irony. The poor relation is not financially desperate: her cage is a comfortable one. She is poor in the sense that she has almost no relations with other human beings, but rich in her own resourceful conjuring up of a youthful companion. The other kind of music, which contrasts vividly with her slender song, is that made by the world outside her windows, a music which reminds her cruelly of her mortality:

> *And like a giant harp that hums*
> *On always, and is always blending*
> *The coming of what never comes*
> *With what has past and had an ending,*
> *The City trembles, throbs, and pounds*
> *Outside, and through a thousand sounds*
> *The small intolerable drums*
> *Of Time are like slow drops descending.*

She can no more escape New York than could her creator; the "giant harp" and the "small intolerable drums" sang their siren song to Robinson. She is like him in other ways, too, notably in her basic and final isolation and in her unwillingness to discomfort others. Winfield Townley Scott visited Robinson at New York Hospital shortly after the operation that failed to save his life. A young man of twenty-five who had yet to fulfill his own promise as a poet, Scott came in awe and awkwardness to observe what he knew was a dying man. "I mustn't tire you, Mr. Robinson," Scott said. "It's not so much a matter of your tiring me as it is of my tiring you," Robinson replied.[13] In friendship, sympathy, and the moving empathy reflected in that phrase, E. A. Robinson brought to life in his poetry the men and women of the Town Down the River, just as his un-New Englandly "depth of understanding and altitude of passion"[14] gave quick breath to the people of Tilbury Town. So reticent in his own relationships, Robinson invested love and compassion in those characters who make up his book of scattered lives. If anything, he loved the New Yorkers more than the New Englanders.

NOTES

1. See for example Yvor Winters, *Edwin Arlington Robinson* (Norfolk, Conn., 1946), pp. 57–58, and Louis O. Coxe, *Edwin Arlington Robinson: The Life of Poetry* (New York, 1969), p. 161.

2. Hermann Hagedorn, *Edwin Arlington Robinson* (New York, 1938), p. 156.

3. *Ibid.*, pp. 356–357.

4. See Hagedorn, p. 235, for an account of Robinson's life style during the period 1905–1909, and Chard Powers Smith, *Where the Light Falls* (New York, 1965), p. 33, for a comment on his drinking habits somewhat later in life.

5. Coxe, pp. 158–159.

6. *Untriangulated Stars: Letters of Edwin Arlington Robinson to Harry de Forest Smith, 1890–1905*, ed. Denham Sutcliffe (Cambridge, Mass., 1947), p. 219.

7. Winters, pp. 6–7.

8. *Selected Poems of Edwin Arlington Robinson*, ed. Morton Dauwen Zabel, with an introduction by James Dickey (New York, 1966), p. xiii.

9. Hagedorn, pp. 290, 379.

10. *Ibid.*, pp. 228–232.

11. Winters, pp. 33–34.

12. Ebenezer Cobham Brewer, *Reader's Handbook of Famous Names in Fiction, Allusions, References, Proverbs, Plots, Stories and Poems* (Philadelphia, 1899), p. 757.

13. Winfield Townley Scott, "To See Robinson," *New Mexico Quarterly*, XXVI (1956), 178.

14. Winfield Townley Scott, "The Unaccredited Profession," *Poetry* (June 1937), p. 154.

The Metrical Style of E. A. Robinson

Robert D. Stevick

"Any poetry that is marked by violence, that is conspicuous in color, that is sensationally odd, makes an immediate appeal. On the other hand, poetry that is not noticeably eccentric fails for years to attract attention."[1] E. A. Robinson's observation on poetic reputation accounts as well as anything for his own years of obscurity. His subsequent fame derived from a number of causes, many of them, as the biographies and literary histories show, of a nonliterary kind; among them, though, was the presence of genuine poetic merit in many of his poems. But durability of reputation depends on both poetic merit and the equipment and tastes of readers. The ebb of Robinson's reputation during nearly two decades coincides with the rise of intensive (and often exclusive) interest in "new" poetry which Robinson, when taken out of historical perspective, does not give us. His verse is "traditional" in subjects, versification, symbols, allusions, sources, and formality; its familiar appearance is deceptively lulling, inviting the label "traditional" as adequate and final. But that label does not account for the qualities that distinguish his work from that of other "traditional" poets, especially his American contemporaries and predecessors. Studies of Robinson's "philosophy," his preoccupations and intellectual "content," his characters, his sources and verbal echoes, and similar matters have not identified fully his poetic merit though they are relevant and essential to determining it. The current revival of interest in Robinson's poetry, if it is to stand for more than further fluctuation in taste, should establish the nature and extent of Robinson's poetic worth by more enduring means than these were established by during the first flood of the poet's fame. Robinson's poetic worth can be reliably assessed through study of his style, I believe, and it is with some aspects of his style that I am concerned here.

Behind the familiar and smooth surface of Robinson's poems lies a technical repertoire from which derive in one way or another the qualities of his composition. In order to "rift this changeless glimmer of dead gray" in which he found American poetry (as he called it in the sonnet "Oh For a Poet"), Robinson fashioned for himself a distinctive style. Working alone and without a poetic "program," and experimenting with verse forms, subjects, and vocabulary uncommon in contemporary poetry, he sought a means of "winning the possible conjunction of a few inevitable words."[2] He achieved the quality of inevitability through a complex semantic interplay generated by word choice within a rigid and ordinary matrix of syntax and meter. His technique, the opposite to anything "sensationally odd," has when successfully executed a subtlety hiding the verbal excitement which we can infer from the poems—and from other sources as well—to have underlain it. What we regard broadly as style is the sum, or more usually the norm, of the technical procedures reflected in the texts of the poems.

That it is through study of style more than anything else that we can assess Robinson's poetic worth will (I trust) be granted from operational considerations for distinguishing his best poems. Some sonnets are outstanding, many are second rate. Some blank verse narratives remain practically unread while others have occasioned considerable study. Yet the similarities of most sonnets are more extensive than the differences among them, in respect to technique; the several long narratives are distinguishable in their plots and characters but not easily separated for structure and most technical aspects. Or, to take a specific case, critical consensus rates "Eros Turannos" as an excellent poem but no one would use "The Unforgiven" to build a case for Robinson's poetic stature, despite the extensive parallels in technical features of the two poems. Both poems belong to the same volume, *The Man Against the Sky* (1916).

Like "Eros Turannos," "The Unforgiven" has two characters, husband and wife, caught in a domestic tragedy of unsuccessful marriage. The discord arises from deception experienced by the characters before marriage as a result of Love's clouding their judgment. One is superior, the other inferior; the callous husband of "Eros Turannos" is matched in the other poem by the vindictive wife. Corresponding characters are described similarly. For example, the wife in "Eros Turannos" is "blind," a characteristic suggested repeatedly; the husband in "The Unforgiven" is also "blind" (stanzas 2 and 3) before his marriage. Both feel "fear" (stanza 4) as a result of their love. Both continue in indecision fed by pride and shrink from breaking off the marriage (stanza 6). Both have "striven"—one against "a god" (Love), the other against love; they "at first" found their mates "fair," thinking the other to be all they could ever desire (stanza 1). Both find that "Love" has ruled them (stanza 5) and, as prisoners, labor to retrieve their earlier "vision" (stanza 6). The inferior partners are passive, those who were desired for their attractiveness, who shatter the other's illusions by remaining as they have always been in actuality, and who make no effort to restore the temporary happiness that led to marriage. The abstract subject of each of the poems is the same—that Love is a tyrant. Because abstract- and character-subjects correspond, we may expect the narrative patterns to be similar, as they are in both scope of action and nature of the implicit "story." Both poems make extensive and similar use of feminine rhymes, both match rhyme patterns to syntactic patterns and play them off against the meaning and movement of the ongoing expression. The outsiders, the townspeople represented by the narrative voice, figure in both poems, with their own interpretation of the circumstances and with their own commonplace but mostly irrelevant wisdom. The two poems differ in length by only eight lines.

"Eros Turannos" stands as probably the finest example of Robinson's mature style for short poems. It combines his distinctive techniques of blending character portrayal, implicit narrative, and abstract, generalized statement, his sparing but careful employment of allusion, his indirect manner of providing a "hovering yet concentration of meaning,"[3] his considered use of regular and restrictive verse form, and a meticulous adjustment of all aspects of a poem in complex equipoise. "The Unforgiven" fails precisely where the other poem succeeds—in the intricate delicate balance of highly complex structure. We cannot trace the lack of adjustment to its source, since that lay in the irrecoverable process of composition; but we can enumerate loci of imbalance. The outsider's point of view is not integrated into the poem's structure, especially its dictional patterns, so that each expression will at every point manifest the characters' relations to each other and their relations to the townspeople. Achievement of that integration in "Eros Turannos" came only with extensive rewriting, as the manuscript[4] shows: the fifth stanza went through more drafts than did any other, and it was only when Robinson hit on "We'll have no kindly veil between / Her visions and those we have seen" that the integration was secured once for all. Also, instead of presenting a situation at an impasse for the husband and wife but rationalized by an outsider whose understanding (or misunderstanding) we are to take into account as providing part of the tension of the poem, "The Unforgiven" leaves a hiatus in the pattern by merely asking, "Who knows just how it will all end?" The image pattern of "Eros Turannos" provides, as Charles Cestre describes it, "an inevitable force of emotion . . . in spite of the lack of a story."[5] Again, the manuscript of the poem shows just how near Robinson came to missing the balance of images, especially when the second couplet of stanza 4 read: "And through it, like a trumpet, reigns / The crash of her illusion." Interestingly, it is also a musical instrument image in "The Unforgiven" (middle of stanza 3) that wrenches the otherwise compact and integrated image pattern of this poem.

The meter of "Eros Turannos" is superior also. That is not to say that the verse form abstractly considered is better than that of "The Unforgiven"; it is only to say that the metrical features are better adjusted to other aspects of the poem. In "Eros Turannos" the units of construction defined by rhymes coincide with the larger (and not necessarily the smaller) units defined by syntax. The *abab* lines typically contain balanced clauses; the feminine endings of the *b*-lines, which lack the fourth stress of the other lines, signal a stasis in sound, sense, and feeling, reinforcing the syntactic signals and breaking the tendency for the meter to jingle. The *cccb* lines then allow the expression to continue and accelerate through a much longer major construction until the last, short, feminine-ending line with its *b*-rhyme occurs, again terminating a stretch of the utterance. In "The Unforgiven" the ballad-like tendencies of meter and phrasing, on which some effects of both poems depend, are thwarted by the extra line in the second group in the *ababb* set. The nice symmetry of 2–3–2 lines per stanza does not counteract the imbalance of syntactic structures mapped as they are onto the *ababbab* rhyme scheme.

Finally, there is nothing in "The Unforgiven" that even approaches the adjustment of meter and diction achieved in "Eros Turannos." The effects of rhythm and rhyme create a suitable replica of colloquial

speech befitting the nature of the speaker of the poem. They also produce that paradoxical—and poetically superb—enhancing and disguis-
ing of word patterns. In the first three stanzas "him" is the unstressed
part of the feminine rhyme in all nine occurrences; in these stanzas
the positions of syntactic prominence concern the wife; the unstressed
but iterative occurrence of "him," however, subtly keeps the fact of
the relationship between husband and wife, which is the subject, before our attention. Moreover, the rhymes in these three stanzas, when
the repetition of sounds by rhyme brings them into our attention,
essentially summarize the substance of the stanzas: the ordinary exposition is recapitulated in "choose him," "refuse him," "lose him";
"sound him," "found him," "looks around him"; "allures him," "re-
assures him," "she secures him." While the symbolic counterpart of
the abstract statement is reinforced by these deliberate repetitions,
the abstract statement itself for the poem is emphasized by the same
rhyme device in the second half of the poem. The significance is again
recapitulated in "confusion," "illusion," "seclusion"; "should be,"
"could be," "would be"; the wife then has "striven" with a god, is
forced to take what the god has "given," and finally is "driven" blind
down to the sea.

Contrastive analysis of "Eros Turannos" and "The Unforgiven"
was introduced to establish the centrality of the study of Robinson's
style to the assessment of his poetic worth. Although the analysis has
exceeded the length necessary to make the point, ultimate economy
will accrue from it, first in the identification it provides of a number
of the aspects of Robinson's style. The style depends on complex and
subtle meshworks of word meanings evoked and fixed by syntax and
meter, such that the structure in which we comprehend the poem is
distinct from the ordinary discursive structure in which it necessarily
is written. The technique is in part dependent for some of its most
distinctive effects on an intellectual response as a reader is induced into
dismantling and re-assembling the text: it is dependent on quasi-
composition by the reader according to the poet's precept. The style
was developed early, in the short poems. The worth of Robinson's
poems lies in successful execution of his characteristic style—an intellectual, complex, delicate method of communication, deceptive in the
plain appearance of the words and verse forms, and unique in American poetry for its degree of cultivation.

The extensive analysis of the two poems also serves economy in
illustrating the crucial function of meter in Robinson's style. The

prominent place of rhyme in the metrical structure of the two poems will be only coincidental to the consideration of meter that follows; the general aspects of Robinson's style identified through the illustrative pair of poems could have been shown, though less efficiently, in some of the unrhymed "Octaves." It is with meter as a phenomenon of line structure of verse and with series of verse lines in Robinson's poems that the rest of this essay deals. Variations in Robinson's metrical style may serve as an index to his total style and the merit of his poems.

The metrical style that Robinson developed first is not easy to isolate from other aspects of his style. Diction is the aspect Robinson himself said most about, and it has been a recurrent, central topic in appreciative and critical writings about his poems: Robinson rejected archaic words, those that fall within conspicuously "poetic" diction, or those that in any other way did not belong to the standard cultivated lexicon of his own linguistic generation. Plainness of diction— something quite different from commonness—is part of his style. His typical subjects can be characterized similarly. So can his choice of traditional verse forms. And so can his characteristic syntactic constructions, at least in the earlier poems. His metrical style developed in consonance with and complementation to his diction, subjects, verse forms, and syntactic techniques.

In so far as it can be distinguished from other aspects of his style, Robinson's meter seems to rest on two principles. One is traditional foot-and-line scansion, for which "tetrameter," "iambic," and the like are appropriate descriptive terms. The other is not so simply described. It has to do with the line, but the quantitative aspect of a line can not be defined very well merely in terms of multiples of feet. The line has a quantitative measure—in terms of syllables or in terms of duration in spoken form—approximately equal to that of iambic pentameter, in his long unrhymed poems. Despite its inapposite connotations, "bulk" is somehow an appropriate term to help define quantitative aspects of the line not built of traditional stress-defined feet. For in countless lines and in strings of lines in Robinson's long poems, we do not have iambic pentameter unless we allow roughly thirty percent deviation from the abstract metrical pattern—far too much for "iambic pentameter" to be an economical or realistic label for the line structure.

The non-foot-line (if such an ungainly term may be permitted) is characteristic of the long poems written in unrhymed lines. In some ways, however, it is not very much unlike many of Robinson's lines in rhymed verse. The feminine ending is one departure from strict foot-meter lines that Robinson commonly used. An extra unstressed syllable here and there—by foot analysis—is another normal departure he used throughout his career. But the crucial difference between lines most typical of the two principles lies two steps further. First, the non-foot-line will not scan for metrical feet unless syllable count is only roughly approximate or unless word stress and phrase stress are frequently ignored—or sometimes both. (Let it be said immediately that occurrence of this kind of line does not imply bad verse.) Second, the line is defined by two means: its "bulk," together with syntactic features that set a boundary, that mark the terminal point of a line. Optionally but frequently the latter end of a line will scan as a rhythmically feminine ending.

The two principles of line structure are more alike than different. With both it is possible to produce verse that has the plainness that Robinson strove for in diction, subjects, psychological realism, and the rest. In "Captain Craig" the traditional principle dominates and we have probably the finest blank verse Robinson wrote in his long poems. "Ben Jonson Entertains a Man from Stratford" (in *The Man Against the Sky*) shows the duality of verse-line principles that became characteristic of the verse in the subsequent narratives. It is not easy to sight-read lines such as the following, because the metrical bases of the lines shift:

> *What he does*
> *Is more to you than how it is he does it,—*
> *And that's what the Lord God has never told him.*
> *They work together, and the Devil helps 'em;*
> *They do it of a morning, or if not,*
> *They do it of a night; in which event*
> *He's peevish in the morning. He seems old....*

The second line scans readily as iambic pentameter except for the feminine ending; it even tends to mechanical, patent pentameter of iambs with inclusion of the linguistically and stylistically superfluous "it is." Immediately following is a line for which iambic scansion stresses "the" with an effect quite contrary to normal speech, in a passage that is ostensibly not merely normal but specifically colloquial. The feminine endings of the second and third lines both mark line-end

and induce the impression of colloquial speech; at the same time they
condition a reader to elide, for metrical purposes, any unstressed syllable at the end of a clause or phrase. In the fourth line, then, the last syllable of "together" is metrically ambiguous until the line is completed
and analyzed; so is the stress pattern of "and the." The line contains
the third successive feminine ending. Lines five and six are simple,
regular iambic pentameters; line seven also has a syllable count of ten,
by *not* eliding the final syllable of "morning"; with consequent mechanical scansion, the sentence end contravenes the sentence-end
intonation in turn disturbing normal stress pattern for "He seems old,"
producing a stilted effect. The lines can be read effectively, to be sure.
The point is that they are not sight-read easily, and any effective oral
reading requires minimization of foot-meter and continual adjustment
of metrical features of two types of line structure. To illustrate the
point once more, let anyone try to read the last of the following lines
on the metrical basis established by the first two:

> his lark may sing
> At heaven's gate how he will, and for as long
> As joy may listen, but he sees no gate. . . .

There is no explanation ready at hand in the letters or biographical
records for the gradual shift in metrical style of Robinson's unrhymed
poems published in and after *The Man Against the Sky.* It is clear,
though, that the shift continued, and that the effects were cumulative.
In *Lancelot* (1920) there are many passages like the following in
their meter.

> I cannot use the word that you have used,
> Though yours must have an answer. Your two brothers
> Would not have squandered or destroyed themselves
> In a vain show of action. I pronounce it,
> If only for their known obedience
> To the King's instant wish. Know then your brothers
> Were caught and crowded, this way and then that,
> With men and horses raging all around them. . . .

The first three lines scan naturally as five iambs each, except for the
feminine ending in the second line. The fourth line begins with a
phrase that keeps syllable count but cannot be read naturally in iambs;
it too has a feminine ending. In the fifth line *obedience* counts as two

iambs contrary to the conditioned expectation that it too should be read as one foot with feminine ending. The phrase beginning line six, like that beginning line four, does not provide—in natural speech—an iambic pattern. It concludes with a feminine ending, in *brothers*, while *crowded* in the next line, phonetically identical in stress pattern, cannot be read with the same metrical pattern. In line eight we have once more normal iambic pentameter but with a feminine ending.

Plainness—an approximation of normal speech—is thus served, as mentioned earlier. But other effects follow as well. One is that a metrical base for the poetic utterance is dissipated. No sense of either elevation or profundity or even high dramatic feeling (which the context warrants) can be generated from the meter manifest in the expression. If Robinson determined to do without the magic, the supernatural, the nonrealistic elements of Arthurian legend (as he said he did), the narrative is in no less need of a style that attracts, that can move a reader; and since the narrative is in verse, the attractiveness of metrical aspects of style is no less necessary. Another effect (or perhaps a corollary of the first) is that the meter is unusable for qualifying, shaping, enhancing, or otherwise strengthening the expression. It is not to be expected, of course, that meter in long narrative verse should function to the full extent that it does in "Eros Turannos" and other of the best short poems; but it might be expected that it should have more than the peripheral value it shows in the narratives. Robinson also shifted from about 1915 to writing poetry of ideas—or attitudes, or social relations, or psychological experience, or political allegory. "Poetry of ideas" is a metaphor for something quite distinct from poetry; it is not something out of which poetry can be made (though the two are not incompatible) and it will not substitute for any of the component essential features of poetry. Whatever else it may have, poetry must have a continually clear metrical base manifested by stable principles of speech patternings; and the meter cannot be created by or replaced by conceptual patterns or syntactic patterns in and of themselves.

It is not clear whether the shift in metrical style and the shift in central substance of the poems stand in any causal relation. It seems more probable that as Robinson turned his attention to developing his ideas in narrative he gave less of his attention to metrical (and dictional) style. Or rather, perhaps, he sought richness of texture that his earlier verse had possessed in another component technique of his style. There is in fact another cumulative change in Robinson's style: it has to do with syntactic norms and deployment of units of meaning in sentences, and it is inextricably linked to meter.

The nature of meter is such that some elements of speech conventionally recognized as identical must be grouped together and that the groupings must form recurrent patterns. English has syllabic stress as a component, essential structural feature; the tradition of English poetry, within which Robinson squarely belongs, utilizes syllabic stress as the primary speech element whose measured recurrence forms the basis of meter. The changes in Robinson's metrical style described earlier consist of loosening the strict definitional rules for recurrence of stress at regular intervals that define metrical feet. The other change —the one in which change of syntactic norms is implicated—consists of loosening the rules for fitting the groupings into recurrent patterns larger than metrical feet. It has to do, in brief, with the way in which the poetic line (or set of lines) is recognized—apart from the way in which they appear on a page. In rhymed verse, with which Robinson began and in which he developed his principal stylistic skills, a line is defined by the recurrence of phonologically identical syllables; line length concomitantly serves to form patterns that recur. When he began writing unrhymed verse, Robinson followed traditional models and kept the identity of the line (a grouping of ten syllables, five stresses, etc. in this case) by so constructing his sentences that a clause boundary or a phrase boundary always occurred at the end of multiples of ten syllables, with five stresses on alternate syllables, as the norm; such boundaries might occur elsewhere as well, but they did not occur at regular intervals. In short, the only regular pattern larger than the foot that recurred was the one that we recognize in spoken verse as the line. The syntactic boundaries of clause and phrase, of course, are marked in speech by pitch configurations and timing features; in linguistic comprehension they mark the constituents of utterances that are construed as grammatical constructions. Robinson did not, as has been recognized, compose only in single "end-stopped" lines in the way exemplified by Marlowe, his predecessors, and those who write unreadable blank verse; the line was a metrical unit which, so long as it was continually defined, could enter into contrapuntal constructions involving purely syntactic units of sentences and/or major clauses.

Robinson developed his characteristic excellence of style, it was said, in rhymed verse or in blank verse that followed closely in the main tradition of excellent blank verse. The change, with respect to syntax and its relation to meter, like the other changes, also began with *The Man Against the Sky*; its effects became conspicuous only a little less rapidly than did those of the other changes. Let us consider two or three examples. Much of *Tristram* (1927) is written, as Robinson admitted, with more to give it wider appeal than most of his long poems had. The following passage begins very well, conjuring mood, a character's reflections on his plight, and situation, all at once.

> *Lost in a gulf of time where time was lost,*
> *And heedless of a light queen's light last words*
> *That were to be remembered, he saw now*
> *Before him in the gloom a ghostly ship*
> *Cleaving a way to Cornwall silently*
> *From Ireland, with himself on board and one*
> *That with her eyes told him intolerably*
> *How little of his blind self a crowded youth,*
> *With a sight error-flecked and pleasure-flawed,*
> *Had made him see till on that silent voyage*
> *There was no more to see than faith betrayed,*
> *Or life disowned.*

For about eight of the eleven and a half lines of this sentence, the sentence structure proceeds clearly; there is the forward reference of "words . . . that were to be remembered," and there is word play, but from point to point marked by major turns in the syntax the scope of constructions does not exceed limits for ready comprehension. But as the sentence goes on, from about line nine, the syntactic complexity increases such that linguistic comprehension requires all of one's attention and one must ignore—if not deny—the groupings of words as metrical lines. Meter no longer contributes to the effect of the utterance. Even more, the syntax and meter are not mutually sustaining; they begin to become mutually exclusive. In *Merlin* (1917) there is a particularly telling instance of syntactic complexity that interferes with the meter, yet paradoxically the meter can carry the sentence successfully if the syntactic tangles are not unraveled.

> *One shining afternoon around the fountain,*
> *As on the shining day of his arrival,*

> The sunlight was alive with flying silver
> That had for Merlin a more dazzling flash
> Than jewels rained in dreams, and a richer sound
> Than harps, and all the morning stars together,—
> When jewels and harps and stars and everything
> That flashed and sang and was not Vivian,
> Seemed less than echoes of her least of words—
> For she was coming.

The Glory of the Nightingales (1930) shows another aspect of syntactic strain.

> In the morning, in the light of a sun shining
> On a million little waves that flashed and danced
> With a cold primordial mockery there below him
> And beyond him, beyond sight or thought of him,
> Or of Nightingale, whose hospitality
> Was like a venomous food that a blind man
> Had eaten in his weariness, Malory looked
> Away into the distance and found only
> Distance.

In skeleton form this sentence says: In the morning, in the light of the sun, Malory looked into the distance and found. . . . It is only at the end of the seventh line, however, that the principal clause begins. To the second adverbial introductory phrase ("in the light of the sun") are appended the equivalent of six verse lines of modifiers. The relations among those modifiers are those of successive modification, some with only tangential or figurative semantic connection: there is no readily apparent relation between the phrases in, say, line six and those in line two, except for the chain that connects them. The syntactic structure is impeccable, when deliberately construed. It is of a kind, however (excessive left-loading is the technical linguistic term), that normally exceeds a hearer's or reader's capacity for comprehension when the passage is heard or read at a normal rate. It can be understood, but only under conditions that contravene meter, i.e., only when lineal sequence of syllables proceeding at a regular rate is set aside.

This essay is intended to praise Robinson, not to bury him. The method may have an unaccustomed indirectness, concentrating as it does on changes from Robinson's early style that lessened the worth of his later, long poems; but the method is not perverse. The principal point of the first section was to show the characteristic style of Robinson at his best—to show the technical repertoire he commanded and the intricacy and richness of poetic construction which he achieved when all aspects of his style were brought into perfect balance. The point, to say it another way, was to explicate the "hovering yet concentration of meaning" that Robinson achieved in his best poems, in his characteristic style. Handling of meter forms an indispensable part of his style. The principal point of the second section was to show changes in Robinson's metrical style. From these changes Robinson's earlier skill can be seen in relief, as it were, and the essentialness of rigorous metrical form for his style can be made the more apparent. Robinson's metrical style can be taken as an index to his best work and the changes in it may serve as an index to the changing quality of his later work. In the early poems—and in later short poems ("Many Are Called" is probably his best sonnet)—meter was firm and as carefully wrought as were any of the other aspects of the poems. It provided a control—and a discipline, no doubt—that helped create a specialized technique capable of producing excellent short poems, in which that technique was developed, but unsuited to long poems; he did not succeed in adapting it to long poems and indeed it is probably unadaptable for long poems of poetic quality comparable to that of the good short ones.

Robinson's poetry was never violent, conspicuous in color, or sensationally odd. Robinson himself never called attention to his style or published a rationale of his poetic technique. His worth and limitations developed through his steady dedication to the practice of poetry: his eccentricities of style gave rise at once to his distinctive good qualities and his worst qualities in poetry; they produced the delicately subtle, intellectual kind of aesthetic merit for which he is outstanding, and they left the fruitless exercises in the same method; they allowed him to come repeatedly to a kind of subject successfully, and permitted him to fall into formula or mediocrity. When Robinson's kind of excellence is ascertained, when his style is thoroughly explored, and when one discovers the number of finished poems of high merit that he published, Robinson's poetic worth is found to exceed that of his American predecessors and to have few rivals in degree and extent among his contemporaries. Robinson's poetry deserves the attention it does not contrive to attract.

NOTES

1. Joyce Kilmer quoting Robinson, in *Literature in the Making* (New York, 1917), p. 267.

2. *Selected Letters of Edwin Arlington Robinson*, ed. Ridgely Torrence (New York, 1940), p. 103.

3. Leonie Adams, "The Ledoux Collection of Edwin Arlington Robinson," *Library of Congress Quarterly Journal of Current Acquisitions*, VII (1949), 13.

4. The Lewis M. Isaacs Collection of Robinsoniana in the New York Public Library.

5. *An Introduction to Edwin Arlington Robinson* (New York, 1930), p. 46.

The Young Robinson as Critic and Self-Critic

Wallace L. Anderson

"I don't know anything about the poetry of the future," E. A. Robinson once said, "except that it must have, in order to be poetry, the same eternal and unchangeable quality of magic that it has always had. Of course, it must always be colored by the age and the individual, but the thing itself will always remain unmistakable and indefinable."[1]

In a like vein but somewhat earlier, Robinson had written to a friend, ". . . he [Goldwin Smith] thinks Tennyson is great because he can call 'hydraulics, astronomy, steam railways, balloons, etc.' by poetical names. . . . Nothing in the world tickles me quite so much as this prophetic analysis of the poetry of the future. When it gets to be great it will be very much like certain very smooth and inevitable places in Sophocles and Shakespeare. It will be great for what it is, not in spite of what it is."[2]

Strikingly similar as these two statements are, they were made in totally different contexts. The first was made in 1913 in an interview with William S. Braithwaite at a time when Robinson's poetry was about to receive increasing acceptance and even acclaim. The second statement was made fourteen years earlier, after the publication of *The Children of the Night*, in 1897, and just as Robinson was getting into the writing of "Captain Craig."

Underlying both statements is a critical position that Robinson held throughout his life: great poetry is individual, contemporary, and timeless. The poetry of the future, like that of the past and the ever-moving present, would be part of a dynamic tradition, constantly extended and modified by individual poets striving to present in artistic form something significant about the human condition. What additional characteristics great poetry would have other than its quality of magic, Robinson did not say. But it would be unmistakable—in the long run. This is the kind of poetry Robinson tried to write, and it was the long run he counted on. In his own mind, moreover, he had specific ideas of what he was looking for.

Robinson's public utterances were few and rather general, and he left behind no critical treatises. He did, however, have a sharp critical faculty which was respected by his contemporaries. In fact, he played the role of critic—sometimes asked, sometimes not—for a number of his fellow poets over a period of years. Josephine Preston Peabody, Hermann Hagedorn, Lilla Cabot Perry, and others sent their work to him for criticism. Robinson was at his best with a manuscript before him. Then he could point specifically to what was unmistakable and what was not. Several of these manuscripts are still extant. On the cover sheet of one, in Miss Peabody's bold script, is written "Violin Withheld by J. P. P. Corrected by E. A. Robinson!" Inside, in Robinson's microscopic "immoral fist," to use Moody's term, the manuscript is covered with Robinson's marginal and interlinear notes. Sometimes he questions ("Is *will* the word you want?"); sometimes he admonishes ("Be careful."); at other times he states flatly ("Wrong verb."). Robinson followed the progress of his friends' poems from manuscript to print. And his letters, both before and after publication of the poems, are filled with critical comments that reflect clearly the qualities he looked for in poetry—his own and others. Together these comments constitute his *Ars Poetica*.

Although some of Robinson's letters have been published, notably those to Harry de Forest Smith and, more recently, to Edith Brower, the bulk of his more than four-thousand letters are still in manuscript form in libraries and in private hands across the country. Recently gathered together, they are now being prepared for publication. When they are published, Robinson's role as critic will be fully revealed. Meanwhile the letters to Josephine Preston Peabody have been transcribed. In them we get a glimpse of young Robinson the critic in action. These letters, especially those from 1899 to 1902, are extremely significant, particularly when we take into account the poetic scene in general and Robinson's position at the time.

That the age was a barren one for poetry goes without saying. Standard accounts to the contrary, however, there was dissatisfaction with contemporary verse, and there was a desire for a new poet. The call for a new poet, heard in the latter years of the 1890s, became increasingly insistent with the approach of the twentieth century. The loss of the older established poets, national pride, rivalry with England, the Spanish-American War, and the turn of the century itself —all contributed to the mood of the times and the search for a new poet and a new poetry. The question was one of direction.

E. A. Robinson, as much as anyone, was aware that contemporary poetry was arid and irrelevant, and that a new approach was necessary to bring it into consonance with the modern spirit. As early as *The Torrent and The Night Before*, Robinson had been consciously moving in new directions. "When it comes to 'nightingales and roses,'" he wrote his friend Gledhill, "I am not 'in it' nor have I the smallest desire to be. I sing, in my own particular manner, of heaven & hell and now and then of natural things (supposing they exist) of a more prosy connotation than those generally admitted into the domain of metre. In short I write whatever I think is appropriate to the subject and let tradition go to the deuce."[3] With the addition of such poems as "Richard Cory," "Cliff Klingenhagen," and "Reuben Bright," *The Children of the Night* extended the line laid down by "Aaron Stark," "The Clerks," and one or two others written just prior to the publication of *The Torrent and The Night Before*. Although *The Children of the Night* was a marked improvement over the first volume, Robinson recognized it as only a partial formulation of what he was working toward.

The Children of the Night was published in December 1897. On January 15, 1898, Robinson wrote to Edith Brower, "I have been trying to get started on a piece of blank verse which, if it is ever done will be a book by itself—not a very big one, but still a book. If it goes on as it has been going it will be out some time in the middle of the next century; but I hope and rather feel that I am slowly getting it under control and that I shall be able to do it somehow. I doubt if many people will care to read it but that doesn't seem to make any difference; I've got to do it. And let me add—to relieve you of a possible uneasiness—that it is not 'preachy.'"[4] To Harry de Forest Smith, he wrote in February, "I'm doing some work but it is all in the way of an entirely new departure and I cannot bring myself to feel anything like sure of it. . . . Just now I am in a transition stage and realize that I ought not to print anything for five or six years, but it rather looks as if I should get out another book in about a year from now. It is in my system and must be expelled somehow."[5] By March 1898, on a different tack, he had thrown aside his "blank verse effusion" and was writing—in his head—"another of an entirely different sort." "This new book," he wrote to Edith Brower, "is going to be a wicked dose for Dr. Coan, and possibly the same thing for you; but I hope you may be able to stand certain parts of it."[6] It was in this experimental vein that Robinson worked from 1898 to 1901, composing the poems that eventually were published in *Captain Craig, A Book of Poems*, 1902.

It is a mistake to think, as some have done, that Robinson was discouraged about his work at this time. Quite the contrary. He was disturbed about things at home, and he was frustrated for a time because his financial situation forced him to take a job at Harvard. But his attitude toward his work was enthusiastic. In the main he was pleased with the reception of *The Children of the Night*, and despite the interruption of the job at Cambridge, this period must be considered one of Robinson's most creative. It was during this time that he composed "The Book of Annandale," "The Growth of 'Lorraine,' " "The Woman and the Wife," "Captain Craig," "Isaac and Archibald," "Aunt Imogen," "Twilight Song," "The Sage," "Erasmus," "The Wife of Palissy," and the half-dozen others that went into the completed volume. At first Robinson thought of them as three books, then as two, and finally, when it became apparent that "Captain Craig" was not acceptable by itself, as one volume. The heart of the volume, so far as Robinson was concerned, was "Captain Craig." Begun in the winter of 1899, it was completed by April 1900 but not published until October 1902. "A sort of human development of the octaves,"[7] the poem became an objective presentation of what Robinson had expressed subjectively in the "Octaves" in *The Children of the Night*. It was also "a rather particular kind of twentieth century comedy."[8] There is no doubt that "Captain Craig" was Robinson's major effort to meet what he considered to be the poetic demands of the new age. And it is in this light that his letters to Josephine Preston Peabody take on special significance, for they reveal the young Robinson as critic and as self-critic at a crucial time in his development.[9]

Though not much read today, Josephine Preston Peabody was a well-known and respected poet and dramatist during the first two decades of the century. Best known for *The Piper*, which won the

Stratford Play Competition in 1910, she was the author of six plays and six volumes of poetry. In 1894 she attracted the attention of Horace E. Scudder, editor of the *Atlantic Monthly* (who about the same time had rejected Robinson's prose sketches), and in that year published ten poems in the *Atlantic Monthly, Scribner's, The Chap-Book,* and *The Independent.* From that time on she published regularly in the magazines, collecting her poems in slim volumes from time to time. Her lively enthusiasm and sensitive nature made her appealing as a person, and these qualities are reflected in a number of short lyrics of delicacy and feeling. She loved Joy and Beauty and Life, and she wanted to be a Poet and Dramatist. Robinson's correspondence with her began in February 1899, shortly after the publication of her first volume of poems: ". . . I am very glad for a chance to make a personal acknowledgment of the pleasure I 'derived' from The Wayfarers," Robinson wrote. "They overtook me in Winthrop, Maine, at a time when I was trying to invite my soul by playing scales on a saxophone. They—The Wayfarers, not the scales,—helped me out amazingly" (February 8, 1899).[10] The fact that Miss Peabody was a mutual friend of Daniel Gregory Mason and William Vaughn Moody gave an added dimension to the correspondence.

Although Robinson published no critical essays as such, he did review in print at least one volume of poetry: Miss Peabody's *The Wayfarers.* The review is unsigned, and the circumstances leading to its publication are not fully known, but internal evidence in the article and in Robinson's letters confirms his authorship. Hitherto unnoted and not easily accessible, Robinson's review is printed here in its entirety.[11] It provides an excellent backdrop for the critical comments in the letters.

A Book of Verse That Is Poetry

Every critical reader of poetry, or of anything else, must involuntarily establish for himself a more or less definite standard whereby to discriminate between mediocrity and the real thing; and when this reader finds a modern poem that has in it more of the real thing than mediocrity, he feels that he has discovered something worth while. And he who discovers or in [any] way gets possession of *The Wayfarers,* by Miss Josephine Preston Peabody, cannot but feel that the real thing has been accomplished.

This does not necessarily imply that Miss Peabody has written a great book, or even a great poem; but it does imply that she has done something quite out of the ordinary. This may not, from the severer point of view, be startlingly high praise; but from the point of view of contemporary verse-making, it is practically equivalent to saying there is no writer in America to-day who is qualified to inspire Miss Peabody with any great amount of poetical awe. Her book may not commend itself to that exclusive majority which reads poetry "only for the thought;" but it is not, on the other hand, in any way to be identified with the rather distressing product of a school whose watchword is a self-confessed fallacy known as "art for art's sake"—whatever that may be. Art is a means to an end, and Miss Peabody is fortunate enough to know it. Consequently her work is neither form without substance, nor substance without form, but an artistic combination of the two—a combination which must occur whenever there is to be real literature.

These two things, however, are not in themselves enough to make poetry. There must be imagination and sympathy, there must be spirituality and wisdom. Miss Peabody's imagination is not of the pounding, pyrotechnic sort that has made so many ephemeral reputations for its victims; nor is her spirituality of that irrational, unsubstantial kind that causes so many lovely first editions to disappear from the mental gaze of mortals like colorless toy-balloons,—but she has imagination, and she has spirituality, and she has the other things.

The first and longest poem, from which the book takes its attractive title, contains much to praise and very little to condemn—nothing in fact beyond a few feminine vagaries of rhetoric which the author will outgrow. The following stanzas, which are no better than many others that might be chosen, will speak for themselves:—

XVIII.

She sat where all the high roads meet
    And all the striving ways are one.
The dumb sea crept unto her feet
    With lowered mane, his wrath undone.
The voice of all the worlds astir
    Sunk to the past at sight of her.
There was nought left but her blind eyes that gazed into
    the climbing sun.

XX.

She spake: "I am that One ye sought
    Through years that fade, through ways that wind.
I am that One for whom ye wrought

The lovely names ye thought to find:
'Life, the Revealer, when we reach
Her mother knees, shall smile to teach
Her soul to us.' And would I not, if I but knew! But I am blind.

XXI.

"Yet by the stranger gifts ye bring,
And by your alien prayers that throng,
I know I am not that ye sing,
The little dream that does me wrong.
You pray me that I show you what
My one name is: I know it not;
Only I know I am not Death, I am not Love, I am not Song.

XXIII.

"They dream I sit on high, afar,
A light to pierce all mystery;
Untroubled as a fixed star
That heeds no sorrow of the sea.
Yet stars make patient pilgrimage
Across the dark, from age to age;
And who would know me that I am, must take my hand and go
with me."

There are thirty of these stanzas in the whole poem, and all of
them are good. The closing one is particularly good, with just
enough of reminiscent flourish in it to give the desired culminating
effect without an overshow of consciousness:—

XXX.

I know not if the years be years,
As, great and small, we journey on,
Nor if the service of the spheres
And of the friendly needs [=weeds] be one . . .
Like singing harvesters, that fare
Weary and glad, we go where'er
She leads the way, with strong, blind eyes, that dare to
gaze into the sun.

As there is much to praise in this opening poem, so is there
much to praise in the seventy pages that follow it—though there
may be a little more to condemn in the way of occasional extrava-

gance and repetition. It is devoutly to be wished that the writer will in her next volume abjure such words as "glamourie" and "enringing" for instance. "Glamourie" may be a matter of taste, but "enringing," when used twice as a rhyming word in a small volume, is rhetorical crime. "Fade along the hush of air, Burden on the weed," may be all right, but certain disreputable and irreverent readers who are given to smoke pipes in silent places will almost inevitably misinterpret it. These, like many others that might be pointed out, are little faults, but they are the very faults which are likely to be magnified by the casual reader. Books of verse are not exactly novelties nowadays, and it behooves the writer of one to be wary in the printing of anything that may possibly give a totally wrong impression of the book as a whole.

But there is nothing to be misinterpreted or questioned in a poem like the following, in which there is a union of art and substance, of wisdom and imagination, that amounts almost, if not quite, to genius:—

Jongleur

Ah, ye that loved my laughter once,
  Open to me! 'Tis I
That shed you songs like summer leaves
  Whene'er a wind came by.
The leaves are spent and the year is old,
And the fields are gray that once were gold
Heart of the brook, my heart is cold—
  My song is like to die.

The windows look another way,
  The walls are deaf and stark.
Who heeds a glow-worm in the day,
  Or lifts a frozen lark?
Warm yourself with the days that were;
Follow the Summer, beg of her,
But never sadden us, Jongleur,
  Jongleur, go down the dark!

Poems like The Fishers, The Weavers, Canonized, Daphne Laurea, and the Envoy might be quoted as more powerful, more significant, but this little song is enough to illustrate the author's method of uniting something to say with an artist's ability to say it. The Envoy is unnecessarily modest, but "the wisdom of the one day more" will require a good deal of patience and hard work for its adequate poetical expression. If Miss Peabody is willing to do this work, and refuses to be flattered into doing too much of the kind of thing that usually follows the publication of a successful first book, her next appearance will be a literary event—without quotation marks.

Having established himself as critic at the outset of their relationship, Robinson continued the role of preacher-critic as his friendship with Miss Peabody developed. Sometimes playfully but also seriously, he pounded his critical pulpit. And Miss Peabody accepted the relationship in the same spirit, though not without demurrers and rejoinders when their critical judgments clashed. Prior to publication, she submitted to Robinson the manuscripts of her next two volumes of poems, *Fortune and Men's Eyes* (published October 1900) and *The Singing Leaves* (published in 1903 but written for the most part in 1901). The manuscript of *Marlowe*, a five-act poetic drama, she read to Robinson in New York in April 1901.

Robinson's concern with "the real thing," the artistic combination of substance and form, expressed in his review of *The Wayfarers,* is revealed more fully in his letters to Miss Peabody. Many of his comments deal with questions of diction, with the language of poetry, broadly defined:

"Stay-at-Home" [April 17, 1900]

Your "laughters have" in the song, does not satisfy me. It is strained and, I think, altogether out of harmony with the rest. "Laughter has" would be commonplace, but I am not at all sure that it is not what you want.... Whatever you do with the Stay-at-Home song, don't let it go into print until you can read it through without the ghost of a misgiving. The thing is too good to be sent out with "patches."

"Fortune and Men's Eyes" [April 17, 1900]

May I suggest that you be careful in your use of "o' ". It is always bad; and in "the greatest o' his day" it is needlessly awkward.

"Finches that *sing* small" is more musical and natural [than "sings small".]

"Pat as beer" jars somehow;—not because it is alcoholic but because the consonants are too thick. [JPP later changed it to "Pat as ale."]

"You look *palely*" would stagger a modern purist. Certainly you will take it out.

"Of baiting of a bear" is clumsy.

"Sweetened corse" is awful. Take it out.

Voice mixes unpleasantly with *visions*.

Rewrite line "I would I had not undertaken etc." It has not the ghost of rhythm.

"Belike" will make the judicious grieve.

Aghast. You have a tendency to make your directions to[o] "literary." Don't overdo it.

"Spell bound by a terrible recognition" has a ["]boarding-school sound." "Vaguely blue," likewise.

"The Violin Withheld" [April 17, 1900?]

Perfect is an overworked word. Don't use it if you can find anything else. It is not what you want here anyhow. [The first line of the poem in manuscript read "The perfect song unfolded, curve on curve." JPP changed it to read: "The Song, at last, unfolded, curve on curve."]

You must not say this too many times. ["Nigh to the central Heart, I understood; / And saw that it was good." Fifteen lines before JPP had written "Nigh to the heart of Light, I heard it send / Light pulsing without end." She dropped the offending two lines.]

This "and" lulls the music. ["With stranger ways, *and* threadbare and alone, / And shod so painfully." JPP let it stand. Apparently she missed EAR's point, which presumably was to omit the *and*, for she contemplated using *all* as a possible substitute.]

Make this a little thinner. [JPP had written "Of rose, that *hast* such lore from *brownest* earth." EAR wrote his comment below the line and underlined *hast* and *brownest*. In the revision JPP kept the *hast* but changed the line to read: "Of rose, that hast the lore from that brown earth."]

You can improve this. ["My Violin, if thou wert truly mine." JPP revised it to "My Violin, if I could call thee mine."]

Be careful how you repeat unusual words. If you will pardon me, this is a fault of yours. ["Of heart's desire, the utmost *urge* of want." No doubt Robinson had in mind JPP's repeated use of "enringing" and "glamourie" in *The Wayfarers*. In a letter dated August 9, 1900, he referred to the matter again: ". . . I haven't yet got over those *Enringings* in "The Wayfarers". The crass language I used on them in Badger's 'review' ought . . ." The remainder of the letter is missing.]

"Stay-at-Home" [May 9, 1900]

"Now the laughing's all gone by" is good enough to put an end to your misgiving, but is not, to my mind so good as "Now the laughing has gone by"—for it seems to me that the second arrangement adds somehow to the remoteness of all things pleasant. I doubt if I should ever have thought of your word, which is undoubtedly better than "laughter." [Here, too, JPP accepted EAR's recommendation:

> Now the laughing has gone by,
>   On the highway from the inn;
> And the dust has settled down,
>   And the house is dead within.]

"The Source" [May 9, 1900]

. . . you have improved the last line in The Source and . . . "reckoned for" is not of sufficient importance to cause you any great amount of hesitation; . . . You must be very ill indeed if you think seriously of taking "glow worms" from The Source and putting "motes ordainèd" in its place: you make me ask if you know Orpheus C. Kerr's "Preservèd Fish".[12] [The last stanza of "The Source" reads as follows:

> Then by the Source that still doth pour
> On star and glow-worm reckoned for,
> I will have more and ever more!]

"I Shall Arise" [June 11, 1900]

The expression "something had to die" gives me a feeling of unholy joy which I am sure you did not anticipate, and I feel confident that it will give the same thing to others. No, it is not slang at all; but there may be in it a subtle suggestion of "something had to come", and it makes me think of a dentist. [In this case JPP let the line stand:

> "And in such conflict, something had to die . . .
> It was not I."]

"The Wingless Joy" [June 11, 1900]

"Judas!" This is startling, but I think it is rather hazardous. I think transplanted cusswords of the second intensity are always rather hazardous. I think also that your second reference to J. would be strengthened by leaving this out.

I think you lost by repeating "unwisdom." It makes one think you are too conscious that it came so remarkably well the first time. It is not one of the words that will stand this sort of repetition.

"Return" [July 1900 ?]

. . . your Soldier Boy [="Return"] is very musical and pleasing. The only fault I have to find with it is that it may not be quite natural enough in its language. . . . Your singing facility seems to be hampered just a little by a certain antipathy of style, . . . I'll say nothing of a slight tendency on your part to conventionalize the old horse Pegasus, for that would be unkind.

"Grace" [July 1900 ?]

The *Grace* is highly satisfactory because it is so thoroughly natural. I should say "God give us heart to sing"; that is better than the other line for the simple reason that it says more and is just as musical. [JPP took EAR's choice.]

"The Fool" [January 31, 1901]

. . . I will go on now and tell you why I think your "fool" song must be fixed. As it stands, I think the third stanza completely spoils it.

> [Laugh, stare, deny. Because I shall be true, —
> The only triumph slain by no surprise:
> True, true, to that forlornest truth in you.
> The wan, beleaguered thing behind your eyes,
> Starving on lies.]

I hate to move to comparisons, but I must tell you that the five lines beginning with "Laugh, stare, deny" make me think of nothing on earth except Browning with cramps. The very complexity of the combination and of the punctuation is enough to show that you yourself are not satisfied with it, . . .

"Prince Charlie" [January 31, 1901]

The other two are wonderfully good, though I don't like your experimental assonance of *bear* and *despair* in II, or "sharpens" in the "Epitaph" [="Prince Charlie"].

> [O had you died upon the field
> That was so grim to plough,
> The tears had blinded every eye
> That sharpens on you now.]

If you stop your reader in these little things, which must be simple or nothing, you will make unnecessary trouble for yourself. . . . So you see I have treated you pretty well this time; and I hope you will give me a chance to do it again before long. It is a mystery to me how you write these things and get so much of the essence of poetry into them. But I won't worry about the mystery if you will only keep on writing them.

"Prince Charlie" [February 17, 1901]

When you tell me that you are going to keep "sharpens" because it expresses just what you mean, you compel me to pound my critical pulpit again and to call your attention to what I believe to be an Important Fact in poetry: viz. that the word which seems to express the required meaning most clearly and concretely is very often the last word that metrical language—particularly song language—will tolerate.

Such a pronouncement on the language of poetry makes a good place for a partial summary: avoid archaic language, the trite, the strained, and overstatement. Instead strive for naturalness, musicality, and economy of expression. The interest expressed here in the accommodation of sound to sense—the avoidance of jolts and jars—comes under the heading of tone and style. With all these matters Robinson was concerned in his own poetry as he strove to develop a style that was at once individual and universal. Other matters concerned him also: vagueness, form and structure, content. Back of them all was the question of how to write a poem that was both modern and a work of art.

In April 1900 Miss Peabody made the following entry in her diary: "E. A. Robinson exhorting me to drop 'philosophizing' and twittering at infinities and to write about things objective. Want to, but how can I without being D——d pessimistic?"[13] In Robinson's long letter of April 17, 1900, there is nothing to this effect. In the Josephine Preston Peabody Marks Collection in the Houghton Library at Harvard, the dated letter immediately preceding is November 27, 1899. Apparently some letters are missing. In all likelihood Robinson returned the manuscript of "The Violin Withheld" with the letter of April 17. On the cover sheet Miss Peabody had written: "This Ode has given me trouble; I'm so apt to fall into pigeon English when my 'mystical mind' gets talking! Can you suggest a better title?" Robinson's blunt reply on the manuscript itself may be the source of the diary entry. If not, it is certainly in the same vein: "The very title of the poem shows that you are playing with false ideas. Try to put away this decadent note entirely and let all the restless idealism go to the deuce for the next five or six years. Then you will treat it with a better sense of proportion."[14]

Robinson's comment on "restless idealism" is especially interesting in the light of his own espousal of idealism as "the only logical and satisfactory theory of life." It was his own restless idealism that he tried to express in a number of poems in his first two volumes, notably in "Two Sonnets" in *The Torrent and The Night Before* and in his "Octaves" in *The Children of the Night*. It might seem at first that he was denying his basic philosophy, but the context clearly indicates that it was the treatment that bothered him. This was a sensitive matter for Robinson himself. Harry de Forest Smith had criticized some of his early poems as "damned didactic" and Edith Brower apparently felt that at times Robinson was "preachy." In his own mind Robinson was sure that idealism ("spirituality and wisdom") and poetry were not incompatible; it was not philosophy but "philosophizing" in poetry that was bad. Robinson was trying to resolve the issue by using a more objective approach, and he was advocating that Miss Peabody do likewise.

The "decadent note" that Robinson found in "The Violin Withheld" Robinson himself did not completely escape. After the completion of "Captain Craig" he turned once more to poems he had roughed out earlier and to some new ones. In the main these were objective in nature, being dramatic and narrative pieces for the most part. In June 1900, however, perhaps stimulated by the knowledge that his "piece of deliberate degeneration," "Luke Havergal," had been selected to appear in Stedman's *An American Anthology*, he wrote to Miss Brower that he was working on a "symbolical" Twilight Song. He fretted over it during the summer, and in September he was still having difficulty. "I can't even straighten out a place in my Twilight Song,—which, by the way, has been called 'mistical,'" he wrote Miss Peabody. "It will be hopelessly obscure to the lynx-eyed, but as it was not written for them, I don't mind that very much. On the whole, however, I have come to learn that vagueness is literary damnation (nothing less); and I have determined that whatever I do in the future—excepting now and then an excursion into symbolism, which I cannot wholly throw off—will be tolerably intelligible" (September 14, 1900).

In matters of form and structure Robinson relied in part on a strong visual sense. He liked to see the shape of a poem, and frequently noted that he would be able to make a better judgment when he saw it typed or in print. His preference for a tight form with a clearly-articulated structure is also evident. His first reaction to "The Violin Withheld" was that it was "a total failure." Part of his dislike was related to its "decadent note" and "false ideas," but part of it was based on formal grounds. "This introduction is too abrupt—too much compressed—for what follows," he wrote on the manuscript. "If you could reduce the whole thing to half a dozen stanzas—or say a dozen—with the fourth line short three feet ('How far I go' for example) you would get a better result. . . . Do not think from this that I fail to appreciate the free melody of the 'irregular ode,' for I do; but in this case I don't like it. The form has, understandably, a tendency to lead one into the ways of rhythmical laziness, but I don't [think] that you are going to be lazy."

After the publication of *Fortune and Men's Eyes* Robinson went over the volume again, devoting parts of two letters to it. About "The Violin Withheld" he remarked: "I don't care so much for the poem as a whole, but as I read it now in type I find that I was wrong in calling it a failure" (November 29, 1900). He preferred "The Comfort" to "The Quiet" because it "has more body . . . and is better in that it is not so diluted. It seems to me that you are given to attach too much importance to mere length and I will make one more paternal suggestion that you beware of diffuseness. The play [*Fortune and Men's Eyes*] reads much better in print and the outlines come up with more clearness" (December 10, 1900). He congratulated her for having written "a real book," but concluded also: "The gist of my valuable reflections on the book is this: that your next work should be the writing of some lyrics—thirty or forty, more or less, mostly in quatrain stanzas and that you work a little harder (one cannot throw things from Cambridge to Yonkers) to keep out any possible vagueness of expression. I am hesitating whether or not to throw away my T. S. ["Twilight Song"] affair on this very ground, but all that does not keep me from preaching" (November 29, 1900).

Robinson's criticism of the irregular ode was based on something more than possible rhythmical laziness. He felt, at this time at least, that it was incompatible with the needs and direction of modern poetry. He had a similar aversion to the masque as a modern form. His summary statement to Josephine Preston Peabody, after reading the manuscript of *Fortune and Men's Eyes,* was a plea to write about things closer to home: "I hope . . . you may, in the course of a few years, find something of importance in the nineteenth century. There are all sorts of interesting things, though you may not think so" (April 17, 1900). Later in the year, waiting for the publication of William Vaughn Moody's *The Masque of Judgment* and Miss Peabody's *Fortune and Men's Eyes,* he wrote again to Miss Peabody, repeating his point in a different form: "If you people continue to be active you will help me through lots of dull seasons; so I pray you to keep at it, even though it be Marlowes and Masques. When Moody shakes himself free from traditions he will do big things; and it may be that he has done them already. And you are privileged to do the same thing on condition that you recover from your attack of Elizabethanism" (October 23, 1900).

Ironically the poetry of Moody and of Miss Peabody was being published; Robinson's was not. Moody's "Ode in Time of Hesitation," quickly followed by "Gloucester Moors," "The Brute," and "On a Soldier Fallen in the Philippines," attracted national attention. *The Masque of Judgment,* in the fall of 1900, and *Poems,* in January 1901, brought him to the forefront of critical attention. To some it appeared that he might be the new poet they were looking for. Like Moody Miss Peabody sent her poems out—to *Scribner's,* the *Atlantic Monthly, Poet-Lore*—and they too were promptly printed. *The Wayfarers* was followed by *Fortune and Men's Eyes,* October 1900, and by *Marlowe* in 1901. This slip of a girl, whose work Robinson had been criticizing, was even being mentioned as a possible fulfillment of the search for a new poet. "It is an understood thing that the lovers of poetry are constantly on the lookout for the coming great American poet," a reviewer wrote, "and if there is the slightest indication of power in any fresh aspirant for poetical fame, hope springs up that here at last is the poetical Messiah. It is too soon yet to greet Miss Peabody as the *long-expected one,* but such a poem as 'The Wingless Joy' reveals a strength and originality which readers of poetry should welcome with joyful acclaim."[15] Robinson, certainly another "fresh aspirant," also sent out his poems to the prestige journals and to others. In the four-year period between *The Children of the Night* and *Captain Craig,* the only new Robinson poems published were "The Corridor" and "Erasmus," both in the *Harvard Monthly.* The story of the journey of "Captain Craig" through five publishing houses, and one other house, is too well known to need repeating. Although Robinson had anticipated the possibility that the poem, his "Big Thing," might not receive immediate acceptance, either by the established old-time publishers or by the majority of readers, he did hope it might make its way with the more discriminating. As time passed, it became disconcerting to find that his work apparently stood little or no chance of publication.

Robinson's position was an anomalous one—a practicing poet whose work was unpublishable acting in the role of critic to poets whose work was obviously marketable. The irony and humor of it did not escape him, and his feelings were a mixture of envy and admiration toward his successful friends. The situation caused him to take a sharp critical look at his own work, completed and in progress. There is no question of Robinson's awareness of the contemporary poetic scene, his own consciousness of what he was doing, and the chance he was taking. Moody's Raphael and Uriel and Miss Peabody's Marlowe were, he knew, far removed from the Captain, Killigrew, and the learned Plunket. For Robinson the question was whether, from such unpromising material, he could produce a modern poem and a work of art—a kind of Aristophanic antimasque, individual, contemporary, and timeless.

Characteristically wary, he was both bold and defensive in his remarks about "Captain Craig." He knew the kind of attack he would be subject to, and he tried to protect himself beforehand. When he had completed "Captain Craig," he notified Miss Peabody "that the thing is 'done,'" and that he was "not altogether afraid of it." He hoped she did not suspect him of criticizing her "with any unconsciousness" of his "own failings," and then continued: "I fear I have tried to do too many things—tried to cook too many things in one dish—and I am a bit afraid that 'my readers' will not believe that I have tried very much to do anything" (May 9, 1900).[16] In September, after the manuscript had been returned from Scribner's, he wrote again to Miss Peabody: "In Captain Craig, I did whatever I liked; and I'm beginning to fear that the self consciousness in the thing, rather than the prosiness . . . will prove to be its worst obstacle. You will like it in places, but in other places <it> you will [go] crazy. Still it is very amusing and sometimes hilarious; and, as a whole, it is elevating —so Mr. Stedman says, though he doesn't care much for it" (September 14, 1900).

While "Captain Craig" was on the road, Robinson worked on the shorter pieces that he originally planned to publish as a separate volume. Some of these he sent to Miss Peabody and to others, soliciting criticism and responding in turn. He sent "The Old Maid," later retitled "Aunt Imogen," to Miss Peabody, with the remark: "I doubt if you will care for much for [= of] it, but I should like your opinion. Don't be afraid to pound it, if necessary" (October 8, 1900). Although she was critical in her response, she did not touch on one aspect that Robinson suspected was at least part of the reason that his work was unacceptable to contemporary editors: "I was most afraid you would descend on it for its prosaic quality. When it comes to this, I fear, I have a trick of skating along the ragged edge of the impossible and not infrequently of breaking through" (October 23, 1900).

As "Captain Craig" made the rounds of the publishers, Robinson's references to it changed. Referred to initially as "The Pauper" and "The Captain," it became "the long thing" and then "the Serpent" and "the Incubus." He wanted more than anything to get it off his hands, but he would not repudiate it. When it appeared for a time that Small, Maynard and Company might publish it, Robinson wrote to Josephine Preston Peabody: ". . . I am glad at any rate that you like it. I know well enough that the majority will not like it, and that is the thing that makes me fear that it may be a tour of something rather than a legitimate poem. I do not really think that either, for my definition of poetry includes almost everything. There is nothing new in this attitude, I know, but I'm afraid there is something new in my blank verse—maybe a little too new. But the thing is written, and I doubt if I change it very much. With all its crudities, or whatever you choose to call them, the book as a whole is pretty much what I intended it to be, and I am willing—if occasion requires any such performance on my part—to put my long-tailed name on the title page" (November 2, 1900). A few months later, he wrote again, reaffirming his belief in his "twentieth century comedy": "I am aware that the Captain is a pretty strong 'dose' to put forth in the name of poetry, but if I find poetry in him I don't know why I should pretend that I don't, or that I am afraid to stand by him." Then, with prophetic accuracy, he added: "He will be hooted at, if he is noticed at all, but if he does not survive the hooting he will soon disappear" (February 17, 1901).

When at last "Captain Craig" was published in 1902, Robinson's worst fears were confirmed. It was hooted at and for precisely the reasons he had predicted. The reviewer for the *Critic*, for example, wrote as follows:

> We can but feel that the volume might have been vastly better from an artistic standpoint had the author so willed it. While there is strength, and to spare, there is also a seemingly perverse carelessness, a frequent disregard of the niceties of form. Surely if a poet has aught to say—and Mr. Robinson has clearly proven that he lacks not in matter—he owes it to his readers, if not to himself, to dress his thought in attractive attire, and not let it go slovenly clad. Blank-verse that is little more than inverted prose chopped up into lines is continually elbowing passages that are shot through with real poetic fire in this disturbing volume.[17]

Robinson's self-criticism at this time is both a reflection of his sensitivity to contemporary standards of poetic judgment and a validation of his artistic integrity. "Captain Craig" has survived the hooting. Perhaps it is due to the unchangeable quality of magic that is at once unmistakable and indefinable.

NOTES

1. William Stanley Braithwaite, "America's Foremost Poet," *Boston Evening Transcript*, May 28, 1913, p. 21.

2. Letter to Edith Brower, May 16, 1899, in *Edwin Arlington Robinson's Letters to Edith Brower*, ed. Richard Cary (Cambridge, Mass., 1968), p. 93.

3. *Selected Letters of Edwin Arlington Robinson* (New York, 1940), p. 13.

4. *Letters to Brower*, p. 70.

5. *Untriangulated Stars: Letters of Edwin Arlington Robinson to Harry de Forest Smith, 1890–1905*, ed. Denham Sutcliffe (Cambridge, Mass., 1947), pp. 295–296.

6. *Letters to Brower*, p. 75.

7. *Ibid.*, p. 89.

8. *Untriangulated Stars*, p. 306.

9. In addition to Robinson's letters to Harry de Forest Smith and to Edith Brower, the letters to Josephine Preston Peabody are complementary to those written to William Vaughn Moody and to Daniel Gregory Mason. The letters of Robinson to Moody are in the Houghton Library at Harvard; see Edwin S. Fussell, "Robinson to Moody: Ten Unpublished Letters," *AL*, XXIII (1951), 175. The letters of Robinson to Mason are in the collection of Howard G. Schmitt, Hamburg, N. Y. Most of them were published by Mason: see *Yale Review*, XXV

(1936), 860–864 and *Virginia Quarterly Review*, XIII (1937), 52–69, and 223–240.

10. The letters of Robinson to Miss Peabody are in the Josephine Preston Peabody Marks Collection in the Houghton Library at Harvard. Citations are used with the kind permission of Mrs. William S. Nivison and the Harvard College Library.

11. *Literary Review* (Boston), III, No. 1 (January and February 1899), 12–13.

12. Robinson is referring to "the Deacon stern and true" in R. H. Newell's humorous national anthem facetiously attributed to "John Greenleaf W————." The first stanza reads:

> My native land, thy Puritanic stock
> Still finds its roots firm-bound in Plymouth Rock,
> And all thy sons unite in one grand wish—
> To keep the virtues of Preserv-èd Fish.

Like Miss Peabody's "motes ordainèd," the anthem was rejected by Orpheus C. Kerr because of its "sectional bias," which rendered "it unsuitable for use in that small margin of the world situated outside of New England."

13. *Diary and Letters of Josephine Preston Peabody*, ed. Christina Hopkinson Baker (Boston and New York: Houghton Mifflin Company, 1925), p. 131.

14. The original title was "The Violin Not Mine."

15. "American Poetry of the Past Year," *Poet-Lore*, XIII, No. 1 (1901), 123.

16. In a similar vein Robinson wrote to Moody: "It ['Captain Craig'] is pretty good stuff in its way, but I am not altogether certain that it has unity, which is the thief of time and the damnation of men. . . . During the past year I have invented a unity of my own, which you will have a chance to inspect when the book is out. I call the book funny, but you may call it prosaic. I call it funny because it begins with a line that will not scan (so I am told) and ends with a brass band." Letter to Moody, May 2, 1900, in Fussell, p. 177.

17. *Critic*, XLII, No. 3 (March 1903), 232.

Robinson's Road to Camelot *

Charles T. Davis

E. A. Robinson wrote no poem on the quest of the Holy Grail. He had
his reasons for selecting Merlin, Lancelot, and Tristram as characters
who might profit from his special kind of ironic elaboration and for
repressing an interest in Galahad. One reason may be an overwhelm-
ing affection for the imperfect man, an abiding sympathy for the
struggling human figure who can achieve only partial or temporary
satisfaction in a hostile or indifferent world. There was, it is true,
nothing in Robinson's experience to sustain a perfect Galahad who
achieved a direct and total vision of the mysterious vessel of God.
Much source study in Robinson has been governed by the principle
of the holy quest—by the conviction that somewhere there is a sacred
book, or person, or system of ideas, or set of experiences which will illuminate all, flooding even the obscure relationship existing between
an author and his work. But the fact is that Robinson's work does not
lend itself easily to this approach. His categorical denials of many influences (including that of Robert Browning and Josiah Royce) that
critics have sought to establish is sufficient warning that there can be
no simple explanation of the works on Arthur and his court, no straight
road to Camelot.

Determining the sources of Robinson's Arthurian poems is a terrifying problem if we have to confront, without assistance, the whole
Arthurian tradition. Fortunately Robinson has helped us, though he
had not intended to do so. We can follow the progress of his work

* I am indebted to the Houghton Library, Harvard University, Cambridge,
Massachusetts, for the permission to quote from unpublished letters of Edwin
Arlington Robinson, and I wish to thank the staff of that library for their assistance.

on the Arthurian poems in his correspondence, largely still unpublished. Of particular value to us are the letters written to a New York poet, Louis Ledoux, and his wife, Jean, whom Robinson often referred to humorously as "Les Ledoux." The letters addressed to other friends at this time, Laura Richards and Lewis Isaacs, for example, though they may record accurately the number of lines written during a summer at the MacDowell Colony in Peterborough, New Hampshire, are not nearly so rich in the references to Robinson's reading—to the books Robinson has borrowed or wishes to borrow, to other versions of the particular Arthurian theme which is engaging him. We have at hand, too, the technique of analysis which students of sources customarily employ: the comparison in literary works of the selection and ordering of episodes, of the details of characterization and background, of the emphases in the development of theme, and of the characteristics of the diction and imagery. The aim of such an analysis is to establish the probable existence of a source—and "probable" and tenuous the source remains until we can demonstrate the author's access to it. We have the advantage today of beginning with a quite specific notion of what the range of Robinson's opportunity was to consult sources. The sense of range may well be, if anything, too restricted—inevitably so with an insatiable reader like Robinson.

If there were a sacred book for Robinson's Arthurian poems, it would be Malory's *Morte D'Arthur*. We know when Robinson began serious work on *Merlin*,[1] his first Arthurian piece, by a postscript in a letter to Jean Ledoux, in which he said simply: "I took away the two volumes of Malory."[2] The time was April 18, 1916. Robinson did not think of returning the books until 1924, when he wrote with some embarrassment to Ledoux, apologizing for still having the books in his possession.[3] There has seldom been a more profitable loan.

Robinson's *Merlin*, which relies less upon *Morte D'Arthur* than his *Lancelot*[4] does, reproduces the basic dramatic situation which Malory presents and resolves, with almost unseemly dispatch, in the first chapter of Book IV.[5] Here Merlin becomes infatuated with Nimue, one of the damsels of the lake, leaves Arthur's service after uttering final prophecies, accompanies his wily beloved to the lands of Benwick and Cornwall, and achieves permanent entombment under a great stone through his lady's enchantment. Though we recognize that Robinson has altered many of the details, we see that he has followed Malory's bare design for the early action in *Merlin*. In

Robinson's poem Merlin retires from Arthur's court, gives up his strange power and authority, yields to sensual enjoyment with rather more grace than Malory's wizard displays, and finds a burial of a kind within the castle and the grounds of his lady, now called Vivian, who dwells in the enchanted forest of Broceliande. Robinson proceeds from this point to project the bold idea of Merlin's resurrection and of his sad return to neglected responsibilities. For this fortunate addition there is no precedent in Malory.

Malory supplied Robinson with something more—easier perhaps to overlook because we assume it so readily. I am referring to the pattern of human relationships in the king's court, so elaborately worked out even before Malory touched the "matter of Britain": Arthur's affection for Lancelot and Bedivere; the enmity of Gawaine and his brothers for Lamorak, in prowess the third knight of the land, behind Lancelot and Tristram; the curious status of Dagonet, the fool-knight; and, preeminently, the love of Lancelot and Guinevere.

The devotion to *Morte D'Arthur* becomes even more evident in *Lancelot*. Robinson derives the entire plot of his narrative form from Books XX and XXI.[6] We have the plotting of Gawaine's brother and half-brother, Agravaine and Modred, the latter the illegitimate son of the King; the trap to expose Lancelot and Guinevere, in which Colgrevance and Agravaine are slain; the Queen's death sentence and her rescue by Lancelot and his knights, at the expense of the lives of Gareth and Gaheris, other brothers of Gawaine; the long war between Arthur and Lancelot, spurred on by Gawaine's hatred; the intercession of the Pope and the return of Guinevere to Arthur; the renewal of war between Arthur and Lancelot in France; the war's sudden termination and the final battle in the West, in which Arthur and Modred perish; and the commitment of Lancelot and Guinevere to the religious life. The details of the familiar story are all in Robinson's *Lancelot*, and they are as exciting there as they are in *Morte D'Arthur*. The problem here for the student of sources is to account for the material which is not Malory's, which remains considerable, as we shall see, despite Malory's impressive contribution.

It is *Morte D'Arthur*, too, which is a primary source for Robinson's *Tristram*. This is a claim which requires proof because of the popularity of Joseph Bédier's reconstruction of the celebrated romance. Bédier in *Le Roman de Tristan et Iseut*[7] made a synthesis of episodes which had come from the works of early writers like Thomas, Béroul, and Gottfried of Strasbourg, and Robinson, whose French was good, undoubtedly knew it. He never referred to it in his correspondence, however, and he seems to have derived almost nothing from it. Robinson's *Tristram*[8] has none of the French work's rich associations with nature (for example, the close affinity existing between animals and people evident in such episodes as "La Voix du Rossignol"), none of the otherworldly magic (which appears not only in "Le Philtre" but in "Le Grelot Merveilleux"—the charming episode of Iseut's dog and its wonderful little bell), and little of the primitive, distorting violence which erupts constantly in the pages of Bédier. Robinson's indebtedness may be limited to the name "Andret," one of the four villainous barons who plague the life of the French Tristan. "Andred" in Robinson's narrative is the conspirator and traitor who kills ultimately Tristram and Isolt.

In October 1925 Robinson wrote to Jean Ledoux, after a summer of hard work on *Tristram*: "I use the version in which Tristram doesn't see Brittany again."[9] The statement implies some knowledge of the various forms of the romance. Tristram does not return to Brittany in *Morte D'Arthur*, but this twist of the plot is only one of several characteristics of the narrative, pointing to a grounding in Malory. Others would be the reference to Tristram as a knight of the Round Table and as a defender of the weak and the oppressed; the prominence of Joyous Gard, humorously referred to in a Robinson letter as "Lancelot's country house";[10] the use of Lancelot's friendship for Tristram; and the intrusion of the mysterious Queen Morgan. Now it is true that the Tristram materials are scattered in *Morte D'Arthur*, that we have nowhere in a compact and continuous form a narrative which is comparable to the climax of the great love between Arthur's first knight and his queen with its destructive effect upon Arthur's kingdom. We establish indebtedness by the details of the narrative, and we find some support for our claim in the recollection that Malory was close at hand for Robinson. There are no clues in *Morte D'Arthur* to suggest the ultimate shape which Robinson would give to the old love tale. For these we must look elsewhere.

Though we see much raw matter from Malory in the three Robinson Arthurian poems, and in the fragment *Modred*, originally in some form a part of *Lancelot*, but published separately nine years afterwards, we feel that the poems are clearly Robinson's. He has not attempted reconstruction, with the intention of capturing the spirit of an earlier time, as Bédier has done in his *Tristan*. We admit that there is a fine art in such reconstruction, in which an important part of the essential vigor of a work is the echo of the language, the attitudes, or the manners which are found in its models. We think of William Morris' Arthurian poems in this connection, of "Sir Galahad, a Christmas Mystery," "King Arthur's Tomb," and "The Defence of Guenevere"[11] (despite Gawaine's odd appearance as the Queen's chief prosecutor), and of the Arthurian pieces of Edgar Lee Masters.[12] It is Masters, known for his meticulous description of character and its development within an American community, who is, interestingly, most scrupulous about accuracy of details. One of the stanzas of "The Death of Sir Lancelot":

> He was the kingliest, goodliest knight
> That ever England roved
> The truest lover of sinful man
> That ever woman loved.[13]

is almost a direct transcription of Sir Ector's eulogy in Book XXI of *Morte D'Arthur*.[14] Masters' impulse to produce a precise record was obviously not limited to Spoon River.

Related to Robinson's artistic purpose is an interesting request which Robinson made of Louis Ledoux in April 1916: "Will you be good enough to send the names of the author and publisher of your book called The Arthurian Epic, and so oblige the prospective author of an immoral poem?"[15] Robinson's request reflects a genuine desire to gain perspective on the abundance of Arthurian literature and to discover especially how Tennyson's *Idylls* related to the tradition. The "immoral poem" is *Merlin*—but why "immoral"? The matter concerned him more than a little, because he returned to it in a later judgment upon his own poem: "The thing seems to me to be interesting and, on the whole, entirely moral. It all depends on the point of view" (July 30, 1916).[16] The best explanation is that Robinson has compared his project with Tennyson's idyll "Merlin and Vivien,"[17] in which the wizard's sensual weakness leads directly to his own destruction. There is in Tennyson none of Robinson's glorying in sensual experience in which a starved and tired Merlin finds a brief happiness which seems long overdue. What is suggested by the whole statement to Ledoux is a curious mixture of motives: Robinson's desire, for one thing, to ground his project in the fertile soil of the Arthurian tradition and his pride, for another (and we must call it that), in the uniqueness of his proposed poem, in its challenge to conventional moral opinions.

Now Robinson was not interested in the whole Arthurian tradition. The poet went to Malory for facts, but he discovered the source of his general attitudes in the nineteenth, not in the fifteenth, century. What obviously impressed him was the way certain nineteenth-century artists looked at the Arthurian stories, gave them form, and evaluated the characters participating in the action. Tennyson, more than any other writer of his time, established standards here. His great influence was not a product merely of the wide popularity of the *Idylls* or of the impressive range and unity of the work, though these facts are important; it came from the critical reception given to the *Idylls* by scholars like MacCallum, who, writing at the end of the nineteenth century, looked upon Tennyson's poems as the high point in modern achievement and as the realization of tendencies at work in most modern versions of the Arthurian stories.[18]

Robinson had read Tennyson's *Idylls* in the 1890s—probably during the Harvard years, 1891 to 1893, and certainly by 1894, when he had returned to Gardiner. In a letter to a Harvard friend, George Latham, later to teach English with distinction at McGill University, Robinson praised the "art" of the *Idylls*;[19] at another time he referred to "Guinevere" as the "greatest of all the *Idylls*."[20] There is little doubt too that Robinson was familiar with the Arthurian pieces of other nineteenth-century authors. He knew the whole of Arnold's work which he had read with affection since his high school days and with a real sense of identification with the English author. And this affectionate concern included Arnold's *Tristram and Iseult*.[21] He studied carefully Swinburne's *Tristram of Lyonesse*[22] at the time he was writing his own *Tristram*, though he had probably read it before. He examined the work of one other Arthurian of the nineteenth century as a part of the preparation for *Lancelot*. In late spring of 1917 Ledoux received this note from the MacDowell Colony: "Will you let me have your copy of Hovey's Lancelot play (I don't remember the name of it, but it isn't *The Birth of Galahad*)."[23] What Robinson asked for was the second of the dramas, *The Marriage of Guenevere*, in Richard Hovey's ambitious and incomplete series, *Launcelot and Guenevere*.[24] Robinson's own creative need transformed a play about court intrigue before and immediately after Guenevere's marriage into a "Lancelot" play.

The model for Robinson's own Arthurian project did not come

from Arnold, Swinburne, or Hovey; clearly it came from Tennyson. The influence of Arnold and Swinburne was limited to *Tristram*, the last of Robinson's Arthurian poems. It is doubtful that Robinson acquired anything from Hovey which he had not already received from Tennyson, and I suspect that he would discover much in *The Marriage of Guenevere* which would annoy him—for example, the ignorant idealism of Guenevere's brother, Peredure, and the proliferating subtleties of Roman conspiracy in Arthur's court.

Tennyson is the crucial source for Robinson among nineteenth-century writers, though it is difficult to measure the extent of influence. The *Idylls* provided the example of a tightly-unified structure which was large in scope and which was both poetic and dramatic. There was social significance in Tennyson, too, with his vision of the construction of a noble, civilized order under Arthur, achieving triumph despite the existence of a flaw, the threat of unbridled passion, which would lead ultimately to decline and destruction. Robinson had the nineteenth-century yearning for the big work, the impulse which had produced previously two long, talky narratives—one, "The Night Before,"[25] a melodramatic monologue which was a decided failure; the other, *Captain Craig*,[26] highly original and displaying a genuine sense of dramatic form. Robinson, in 1916, conceived of his Arthurian project on a large scale, projecting a trilogy of poems. With *Merlin* barely completed (November 1916), Robinson wrote to Jean Ledoux about his writing schedule: "Next Monday I'm going to begin writing *Launcelot and Guinevere*, which ought to keep me quiet for some time—with Tristram and Isolt in pickle."[27]

Robinson did not talk a great deal about an integrating principle for his poems—something more considerable than the background of Arthur's court—but this did not mean that one was lacking. From 1910 on Robinson in his poetry had edged toward a more open statement of his feelings about contemporary society. His letters, especially those after 1916, included often worried, gloomy observations about the state of western civilization. One of these comments was attached to the description of a performance of Wagner's *Tristan* in February 1921, which he had written to Jean Ledoux, then in China: "For a few hours I fancied that our so-called civilization might not be going after all—though of course it is. The whole western world is going to be blown to pieces, asphyxiated, and starved, and this, for a few centimes."[28] Robinson, the poet, was seldom so direct, but the undercurrent of discontent became stronger in the middle 1920s and produced the frankly political Dionysian poems ("Dionysus in Doubt" and "Demos and Dionysus").[29] The Arthurian poems are imbued too with the feeling of the impending disintegration of the social order, but the feeling becomes something more, fortunately. Robinson, like Tennyson, found an attitude toward civilization to be artistically useful. In the *Idylls* we see both the building of the courtly and idealistic society and its destruction; in all of Robinson's Arthurian poems we sense only an inevitable movement toward chaos, with only flashes here and there of what once was an organized, generous way of life, and we are not certain that we believe these when we see them. Robinson's intention, his pervading artistic principle, is more complicated than this— a point which he took some pains to explain to Jean Ledoux after he had finished a draft of *Merlin* (July 1916): "You may still call me an evangelist of ruin when you read it, but you mustn't forget the redemption—even if you don't see it."[30] There is a notion of redemption in Robinson's poems, and it is all Robinson's, with his special emphasis upon realization of the individual self. But Robinson's beginnings are in the *Idylls of the King*: it is Tennyson who gave Robinson the conception of the large poem based on Arthurian matter and filled with suggestive implications about the state of modern society.

Tennyson influenced Robinson's characterization much more, perhaps, than the American poet was prepared to admit. Robinson was most conscious of the uniqueness of his women in *Merlin* and *Lancelot*, but he permitted his men to follow rather closely patterns established in the *Idylls*. He designed and redesigned the portrait of Vivian, striving to make it less obvious and to give it greater subtlety of line. He was deeply dissatisfied with previous Gueneveres, even Tennyson's, and grumbled to Jean Ledoux: "I don't know whether I deserve a crown or a foolscap for trying to make Guenevere interesting—a feat that hasn't to my knowledge been accomplished heretofore—but she must have had a way with her or there wouldn't have been such an everlasting amount of fuss made over her."[31] Merlin and Lancelot are quite another matter.

In the *Idylls* Merlin gains a new glory—a recognition which the nineteenth century seems to have reserved for him, perhaps as a consequence of its preoccupation with the expression of force in the material world. Tennyson's seer is "the most famous man of all these times," and one

> *who knew the range of all their arts,*
> *Had built the King his havens, ships, and halls,*
> *Was also Bard, and knew the starry heavens;*[32]

Tennyson adds that "the people call'd him wizard,"[33] but Merlin, weighed correctly, is the architect of a kingdom. This is Robinson's Merlin too, "Who made kings and kingdoms, / And had them as a father. . . ."[34] Tennyson's wizard is undone by Vivien, an artful minx in league with King Mark of Cornwall and moved by a malice which seems inspired by the envy of a lower form of nature for a higher one. Tennyson's imagery is revealing in this respect in its heaping up of animal references to describe Vivien's sure progress. The threat to Robinson's Merlin is essentially the same, defined by effective allusion to fishes, frogs, and snakes, but his Vivian has more dignity. She holds a love of a sort for Merlin and responds to a deep and genuine need in him.

Robinson did not know, apparently, the works of important continental writers on the figure of Merlin. One of these works, Karl Immermann's *Merlin, Eine Mythe,*[35] published in 1832, presents quite a different portrait of Merlin. The poem is an ambitious metaphysical exploration which makes much of the curious circumstances of Merlin's birth, as a child sired by the Devil and born of a maiden. Tennyson's conception of the wizard and Robinson's, after it, are not touched by this form of speculation.

We sense Robinson's debt to Tennyson too in *Lancelot*. In the *Idylls* Lancelot is Arthur's first soldier—a courtly lover and a gentle, generous knight. These fine qualities pale before the emerging picture of a torn and wracked man, caught up by an internal moral struggle. It is a gaunt and disillusioned Lancelot who says after the death of the fair Elaine, who has loved him well, but futilely:

> *For what am I? What profits me my name*
> *Of greatest knight? I fought for it and have it;*
> *Pleasure to have it, none; to lose it, pain;*
> *Now grown a part of me: but what use in it?*
> *To make men worse by making my sin known?*
> *Or sin seem less, the sinner seeming great?*
> *Alas for Arthur's greatest knight, a man*
> *Not after Arthur's heart!*[36]

Lancelot stands in the Robinson poem as a man similarly divided, and as he ruminates upon the prospect of a last meeting with the Queen, in Arthur's castle, he questions his own identity in the same bewildered way:

> And who is he?
> Who is this Lancelot that has betrayed
> His King, and served him with a cankered honor?
> Who is this Lancelot that sees the Light
> And waits now in the shadow for the dark?[37]

As we recognize the unmistakable model for Robinson's Lancelot, we should acknowledge Robinson's alterations too. The conflict in Tennyson's character is between the attractions of sin and the consciousness of it—a more negative and less complicated business than having the desire to betray, on the one hand, and the sense of the Light, or the way to divine truth, on the other. The difference suggests the intensification of moral turmoil in Robinson's hero.

Though Robinson considered *Tristram* to be a third poem in an Arthurian trilogy, related by cross-references and by theme to *Merlin* and *Lancelot*, he was quick to admit something special in his attitude toward *Tristram*. He wrote to Jean Ledoux about it in August 1925: "The key and color of the thing are altogether different from those of *Merlin* and *Lancelot*, and may cause some readers to suspect that I'm getting a little tired of hearing too much about my New England reticence—which may be partly true."[38]

Robinson did not discuss his sources, but we shall see that these have been radically changed too. For one thing, we are no longer aware of a reliance upon Tennyson, since the easy, worldly, free-lover of *The Last Tournament* has nothing in common with Robinson's intense Tristram. For another, there are new sources, fresh and persuasive interpretations of the love tale which complement the factual information which Robinson retained from Malory. First among these, and most powerful in its influence upon Robinson, is Wagner's *Tristan und Isolde*, but there are contributions as well from Arnold's "Tristram and Iseult" and Swinburne's *Tristram of Lyonesse*.

Wagner's *Tristan* had Robinson's enduring love. The poet's affection was not limited to the music or to the emotional lift which he felt at a good performance of the opera. He knew the libretto thoroughly and he complained when the words were lost in the music. He delighted in comparing performances, and he had a sharp eye for small details. After one performance at the Metropolitan in the winter of 1921, he wrote a strong objection to Jean Ledoux to a concluding bit of stage business which had changed Isolde's final position—perhaps in the interest of false gentility: "Instead of falling down on Tristan, where she belongs, she lays herself carefully about three feet away from him with her head at his feet."[39] Robinson even knew something of Wagner's state of mind when he was composing *Tristan*. We should expect a consequence of some sort from this devoted concern, and we find it in the form of Robinson's *Tristram*.

The opera presents a story of the explosive awakening of passion in Tristan and Isolde, a violent transformation from hate to love, and this is followed by a reversal of values in which the world of daylight responsibility and knightly honor becomes illusory and unreal, and the nocturnal world of love becomes genuine and permanent. Beneath the change in the lovers is the yearning for death which they know will bring ultimately fulfillment and peace. Robinson tells a similar story. His Tristram and his Isolt awake belatedly to love, moved not by drinking a philtre, a device which Robinson deplored, but by the simple discovery of each other, prevented earlier by a stubborn blindness. We find in this passage Robinson's substitute for the magic potion:

> Tristram, blind
> With angry beauty, or in honor blind,
> Or in obscure obedience unawakened
> Had given his insane promise to his uncle
> Of intercession with the Irish King
> And so drawn out of him a slow assent,
> Not fathoming or distinguishing aright
> Within himself a passion that was death,
> Nor gauging with a timely recognition
> The warfare of a woman's enmity
> With love without love's name.[40]

There is the promise of a reversal comparable to that in Wagner's *Tristan*:

> He knew too late
> How one word then would have made arras-rats
> For her of all his uncles, and all kings
> That he might serve with cloudy promises
> Not weighed until redeemed.[41]

And the reversal comes in the love idyll of Joyous Gard, not, as in the opera, in the dark garden of Mark's castle at Cornwall. Robinson's Tristram, like Wagner's Tristan, announces the retreat of the everyday world:

> We are the last that are alive, Isolt,
> Where the world was. Somewhere surrounding us
> There are dim shapes of men with many names,
> And there are women that are made of mist,
> Who may have names and faces.[42]

Perhaps we have more tolerance for the lovers in the opera when their rapture is conveyed in Act II by the constant repetition of their names. But tolerance is stretched in Robinson's *Tristram* when the same repetition of names occurs and when the word play on "twilight," "shadow," "death" and "long" does not sustain the repetition with the conviction of Wagner's music.[43]

Robinson's reversal of values is less permanent than Wagner's. In the opera the lovers do not compromise with the sketchy daylight world but proceed immediately to confirm their rejection in death. In the poem Isolt is prepared to come to terms with the misty forms of reality, though she has rejected practical possibilities before and though Tristram continues to do so. Her cautious observation

> There is your world outside, all fame and banners,
> And it was never mine to take from you[44]

suggests a different resolution for Robinson's poem, though it is not one which changes the fate of the two lovers.

We have no great emphasis upon treachery or villainy in either version of the Tristram narrative. True, Melot, Mark's kinsman, gives Tristan his mortal wound in the opera, and Andred, one of Mark's barons, murders Tristram and Isolt in the poem, but death seems to be the necessary consequence of the total commitment to love. Mark is not for Wagner and Robinson the destroyer of good knights, the coward and some-time buffoon which he is in *Morte D'Arthur*; nor is he the bestial predator which Tennyson has made him. Wagner ennobles him as a generous and just monarch, deeply attached to his nephew Tristan. Robinson dignifies him as a man, self-indulgent, sensual, and fallible, but retaining a measure of fairness. More important, he struggles vainly to understand a problem which is, he admits, beyond him.

If we regard Wagner's *Tristan* as a source for the inner life of Robinson's poem, we must look to Arnold's "Tristram and Iseult" for a clue to the outer frame. Iseult of Brittany, the Iseult of the white hands who is Tristram's wife, not the dark Irish beauty who holds his love, has the last word in Arnold's poem. She is an innocent creature, mild and long-suffering, who finds a lonely peace caring for Tristram's children and preserving other remnants of life which he has left behind. Though she does not display sympathy or achieve understanding, Arnold's white Iseult had a special value for Robinson. She is not the duped victim of a maiden marriage, as she is in Swinburne's *Tristram of Lyonesse*; nor is she the vindictive, rejected wife whose malice changes the color of the sail of the Cornish ship bearing the Irish Iseult to the ailing Tristram.

Robinson sought to improve upon his source. His Isolt of Brittany, like Arnold's, is a woman of the commonplace world, not a being set afire by a passion which withers all else, and like Arnold's heroine, Robinson's remains behind to order what is left. She represents the mundane half of Tristram's life, which is not made to disappear or to become distorted because Tristram chooses to deny it. Robinson's bold addition to Arnold's strategy is to bring to the neglected wife a genuine understanding of her husband's errant action; she sees it finally as a part of the complex motion of life.

One other area of agreement between Robinson and Arnold is worthy of a brief comment. Robinson wrote to Laura Richards, a member of a prominent Gardiner family, a writer, and a loyal friend of his, that "he had always seen a dark haired Isolt." "Iseult," he added, sounded "yellow."[45] His preference in hair, not the name, follows Arnold's. I should add that it echoes that notorious law in romantic narratives, which we can see just as well in Hawthorne's fiction as anywhere, that blondes are innocent, true, and wholesome, and that brunettes are alluring, worldly, and dangerous.

We can say always when we comment upon Arnold's influence upon Robinson that the two poets were very much alike in spirit—with their lingering devotion to romantic tradition, their concern for poetic statement which would challenge as well as sing, and their strong sense of moral purpose. But there is little harmony of this kind linking Swinburne and Robinson. When Robinson in the course of writing about Tristram asked Louis Ledoux for a copy of "Swinburne's melodious poem on the same fellow," he is careful to explain that he wished the book so that he might avoid "possible collisions."[46] I can think of only one reason to doubt the adequacy of Robinson's statement, and this has to do with a special quality of Robinson's language in *Tristram*. Though Robinson developed elaborate image patterns in earlier works—in references to light and darkness, fire and ashes, houses or castles and gardens, he has nowhere relied so heavily upon sea imagery. His references are not descriptive merely, for they tend to be symbolic. The sea is the movement of life, reflecting, at one moment, despair and acute unhappiness, and, at another, delight and ecstasy, but these impressions are illusory, since the sea, finally, is indifferent to men's fortunes. It comprehends them all and stands for ceaseless change. Robinson's use of the sea is very close to Swinburne's in *Tristram of Lyonesse*, in which Fate is defined in terms of a pattern of ocean figures. We are less aware of the sequence in Swinburne because it must compete with other elaborate sets of figures describing the nature of love and the beauty of the protagonists. In Robinson's poem, with a background of a less florid diction, the sea images stand out with prominence. Swinburne's practice, perhaps, suggested to Robinson one way, at least, of enriching his poetic language.

We see that the literary sources of Robinson's Arthurian poems arrange themselves into two meaningful groups—in the first, we find the single work that offered to Robinson a vast store of plots, characters, and situations, Malory's *Morte D'Arthur*; and in the second we discover the nineteenth-century interpretations of Arthurian matter that aroused Robinson's admiration and served as useful precedents and examples for his own highly original work. We are left with Robinson himself, to discover sources, if any, in his earlier production. This sort of investigation is particularly rewarding for Robinson because he was a writer who returned constantly to the same themes, often altering them only slightly.

Actually, there is much that is old in the Arthurian poems. The theme of *Merlin* resembles that found in a prose play, *Van Zorn*,[47] which Robinson had worked on from time to time, from 1906 to 1913 and which he published in 1914. The main character in this curious play is a mysterious millionaire, Van Zorn, who holds himself to be an agent of destiny and who interferes with the lives of the people around him so that they might achieve their individual goals. His meddling is all to the good because no one in his pathetic world, except a self-deprecating writer of comic fiction, is able to make the correct decision about his own future. To perform his duty, Van Zorn denies love—or at least the possibility of it—and influences his friend Farnham, a painter, to reject marriage, presumably because it will spoil his art. We have, in fact, a functioning Merlin figure in modern dress who matches his intelligence and intuition against the stupidity of the contemporary world. There is even in Otto Mink, the writer, with his wit, and his song and dance routine from *Pinafore*, a character not unlike the Dagonet of Robinson's *Merlin*.

No such interesting precedent exists for *Lancelot* and *Tristram*, but even here we feel the force of Robinson's earlier work. The poet insists that Lancelot, like Captain Craig, must undergo hardship and humiliation before he attains the promise of peace, and the peace, unattractive and bleak for many readers, is a consequence of the acceptance of the realities of a difficult world. Isolt of Brittany follows this pattern too, acquiring her equilibrium after the hard trial of Tristram's neglect and the shock of his death. Robinson's attitude toward love in *Tristram* can be seen as a part of a general shift in his intellectual position in the 1920s. He was in retreat from what he considered to be the restrictions of his New England background, and he was genuinely disturbed by the Prohibition Law, a tribute to an over-eager American conscience. He gave a new importance to the emotional world of the individual and to his capacity for enjoyment. In a discussion of the theme of "Demos and Dionysus" he wrote in August 1924 that he had treated life in general "from the Dionysian as opposed to the bee-hive point of view."[48]

Though love acquires a sensual power in *Tristram* which is new in Robinson's work, it does not change in any fundamental way old views toward the basic problems of human existence. We can see in Robinson's Arthurian poems an extension of those in *The Torrent and The Night Before* and in *The Children of the Night*. There, we may recall, man is shackled by the weaknesses of his own nature—by selfishness, indifference, and stupidity, limitations that create a twilight world more akin to death than life. Hope exists in the confidence that the Light will come. How? We don't quite know. Robinson suggests somewhat tentatively that improvement in man's estate rests in God's love and in art. If we turn our eyes to the Arthurian scene, we shall discover that man's vices have become something more malignant than "sin's frail distress."[49] Selfishness is now vulgar self-indulgence; indifference, now treachery and disloyalty; and stupidity, the criminal neglect of urgent responsibilities. What stands as a dyke holding back the flood of destruction is art—Merlin's, indeed, and Arthur's—and love—any form of it, not exclusively God's. Here it is preeminently the nobler passions of an Arthur not twisted by Gawaine's hate or of a white Isolt who attains ultimate understanding on a lonely beach in Brittany. In Robinson's Camelot we have no pure Galahad and no Holy Grail; we are left, when Camelot has vanished in flames, only with the figure of a battered Lancelot who possesses the hope that in the darkness "the Light" would come and the confidence that "There are worlds enough to follow."[50] We are impressed, finally, with the consistency and continuity in Robinson's art, and we lose any sense of its varied and motley origins. Robinson has erected the towers of Camelot on familiar ground, perhaps, even in New England, well within the walking range of men of his own time, and of later times.

NOTES

1. *Merlin* (New York, 1917).

2. Unpublished letter of Robinson's to Jean (Mrs. Louis) Ledoux, April 18, 1916, from a typescript in the Houghton Library.

3. Unpublished letter of Robinson's to Louis Ledoux, July 24, 1924, from a typescript in the Houghton Library.

4. *Lancelot* (New York, 1920).

5. Eugène Vinaver, ed., *The Works of Sir Thomas Malory* (London: Oxford University Press, 1954), pp. 91–93.

6. *Ibid.*, pp. 818–883.

7. *Le Roman de Tristan et Iseut*. Renouvelé par Joseph Bédier (Paris: L'Edition d'Art H. Piazza, 1962).

8. *Tristram* (New York, 1927).

9. Unpublished letter of Robinson's to Jean Ledoux, October 16, 1925, from a typescript in the Houghton Library.

10. *Ibid.*

11. *The Defence of Guenevere and Other Poems* (London: Ellis and White, 1883).

12. In *Songs and Satires* (New York: Macmillan, 1916).

13. *Songs and Satires*, p. 154.

14. *The Works of Sir Thomas Malory*, p. 882.

15. Unpublished letter of Robinson's to Louis Ledoux, April 18, 1916, from a typescript in the Houghton Library.

16. Unpublished letter of Robinson's to Jean Ledoux, July 30, 1916, from a typescript in the Houghton Library.

17. *The Works of Alfred Lord Tennyson* (Boston and New York: Houghton Mifflin Company, 1904), IV, 180–216.

18. Mungo William MacCallum, *Tennyson's "Idylls of the King" and Arthurian Story from the Sixteenth Century* (Glasgow: J. Maclehose and Sons, 1894).

19. Unpublished letter of Robinson's to George Latham, October 10, 1894, Houghton Library.

20. Unpublished letter of Robinson's to George Latham, June 6, 1894, Houghton Library.

21. *The Poetical Works of Matthew Arnold*, ed. C. B. Tinker and H. F. Lowry (London: Oxford University Press, 1950), pp. 130–156.

22. *Tristram of Lyonesse and Other Poems* (London: Chatto and Windus, 1882).

23. *The Birth of Galahad* (Boston: Small, Maynard and Co., 1898).

24. *Launcelot and Guenevere, A Poem in Dramas*, 5 vols. (New York: Duffield and Co., 1907).

25. In *The Torrent and The Night Before* (Cambridge, Mass., 1896), and in *The Children of the Night: A Book of Poems* (Boston, 1897).

26. *Captain Craig* (Boston and New York, 1902).

27. Unpublished letter of Robinson's to Jean Ledoux, November 7, 1916, from a typescript in the Houghton Library.

28. Unpublished letter of Robinson's to Jean Ledoux, February 2, 1921, from a typescript in the Houghton Library.

29. In *Dionysus in Doubt: A Book of Poems* (New York: The Macmillan Company, 1925).

30. Unpublished letter of Robinson's to Jean Ledoux, July 30, 1916, from a typescript in the Houghton Library.

31. Unpublished letter of Robinson's to Jean Ledoux, August 26, 1917, from a typescript in the Houghton Library.

32. In "Merlin and Vivien," *The Works of Alfred Lord Tennyson*, IV, 186.

33. *Ibid.*

34. *Collected Poems of Edwin Arlington Robinson* (New York, 1954), p. 259.

35. Karl Immermann, *Merlin, Eine Mythe* (Düsseldorf: J. E. Schaub, 1832).

36. In "Lancelot and Elaine," *The Works of Alfred Lord Tennyson*, IV, 270.

37. *Collected Poems*, p. 383.

38. Unpublished letter of Robinson's to Jean Ledoux, August 3, 1925, from a typescript in the Houghton Library.

39. Unpublished letter of Robinson's to Jean Ledoux, February 2, 1921, from a typescript in the Houghton Library.

40. *Collected Poems*, p. 602.

41. *Ibid.*

42. *Ibid.*, p. 679.

43. See the exchange between Tristram and Isolt in *Collected Poems*, pp. 676–677.

44. *Collected Poems*, p. 695.

45. Unpublished letter of Robinson's to Laura Richards, July 24, 1926, Houghton Library.

46. Unpublished letter of Robinson's to Louis Ledoux, June 14, 1925, from a typescript in the Houghton Library.

47. *Van Zorn: A Comedy in Three Acts* (New York, 1914).

48. Unpublished letter of Robinson's to Lewis Isaacs, August 20, 1924, Houghton Library.

49. In II of "Two Sonnets," *Collected Poems*, p. 89.

50. *Collected Poems*, p. 436.

The Transformation of Merlin

Nathan Comfort Starr

The sage and enchanter Merlin, especially as we find him in Edwin Arlington Robinson's poem *Merlin*, is a striking example of the change and development in the Arthurian legend from the very beginning. During the twentieth century he has been more originally portrayed than ever before. First, however, let us briefly survey his past history.

He first appears in Nennius' *Historia Brittonum* (c. 800) as Ambrosius, a boy born without a father, who reveals miraculous powers of divination to King Vortigern. Geoffrey of Monmouth's *Historia Regum Britanniae* (1136) expanded Nennius' account, re-naming the boy Ambrosius Merlinus, and telling of Arthur's birth, who was conceived through Merlin's enchantment. The seventh chapter of Geoffrey's *Historia* consists of the prophecies of Merlin, a confusing series of predictions, many of dire disasters. Geoffrey also wrote the *Vita Merlini*, which describes the strange career of a Merlin not associated with Arthur, the so-called Caledonian Merlin, Merlinus Silvestris. Both of these works by Geoffrey foreshadow the dimension later found in the twentieth-century seer. Successive re-workings of the *Historia Regum Britanniae* by Wace and Layamon add greatly to Merlin's importance as Arthur's adviser.

In the thirteenth-century Vulgate romance, *L'Estoire de Merlin*, the seer is even more important. As a two-year-old child he had dictated to the clerk Blaise an account of Joseph of Arimathea and the Holy Grail. He is responsible for the early nurture of Arthur, and had proposed to Arthur's father, Uther Pendragon, the establishment of the Round Table. After Arthur is chosen king by the test of the sword in the anvil Merlin advises him to marry Guinevere, and plays an important role in wars against the rebellious kings and the Saxons. Eventually he meets Viviane, who induces him to reveal his secrets of magic and imprisons him in the forest of Broceliande.

Malory, who based the *Morte D'Arthur* in large part on the Vulgate romances, enhanced Merlin's function as a seer and magician by a number of important prophecies, including a prediction of his own end. He gives valuable advice to Arthur, takes him to a lake where he receives the sword Excalibur, and shows great skill as a shape-shifter. Malory's account of Merlin's imprisonment by Nyneve is lively and circumstantial.

> Then the lady and Merlyon departed. And by weyes he shewed hir many wondyrs, and so come into Cornuayle. And all wayes he lay aboute to have hir maydenhode, and she was ever passynge wery of hym and wolde have bene delyverde of hym, for she was aferde of hym for cause he was a devyls son, and she cowde not be skyfte of hym by no meane. And so one a tyme Merlyon ded shew hir in a roche whereas was a grete wondir and wrought by enchauntement that went undir a grete stone. So by hir subtyle worching she made Merlyon to go undir that stone to latte hir wete of the mervayles there, but she wrought so there for hym that he come never oute for all the craufte he coude do, and so she departed and leffte Merlyon.

The contrast between this imprisonment and that of Robinson's Merlin could scarcely be more striking. The later seer is "imprisoned" by the fascination of an unusually gifted woman, not by enchantment.

After the publication of the *Morte D'Arthur* the fortunes of Merlin suffered in the general decline of the Arthurian legend until the return of Malory to favor in the nineteenth century. Even so, Merlin was not distinguished. The ill-tempered old humbug of Mark Twain's *Connecticut Yankee* was a grotesque figure, and even Tennyson's Merlin, in the *Idyll* "Vivien," was a learned old fool, at the mercy of a predatory, shallow wanton. He seemed to have been imprisoned more by Tennyson than Vivien. In a welcome revision of the traditional story, however, he was released from bondage by the publication of Robinson's *Merlin* in 1917.

Before we go further it is well worth noting that at least three writers after Robinson's time also greatly increased Merlin's importance. Robinson seems not to have influenced any of them; in all likelihood they were the inheritors of the exploratory, expansive temper of the time, especially of inquiries into the mysterious capacities of the human mind. At any rate a new Merlin has come into the legend.

Charles Williams, in his distinguished cycle of Arthurian poems, *Taliessin through Logres* (1938) and *The Region of the Summer Stars* (1944), describes Merlin as a supernatural force acting for Christian ends. He and his sister Brisen, the son and daughter of Nimue (a striking change from the old relationship), live in the wood of Broceliande, where inchoate forces are working for the creation of forms. Merlin is called Time (compare Robinson's Merlin, and Time) and Brisen is Space. Merlin helps Arthur come to the throne and is the means by which Galahad is conceived. Most important of all, it is his mission to assist Arthur in establishing the holy kingdom of Logres. In Williams' poems we are conscious of a vastly enlarged world, not only of sense, but of the region of the summer stars, of the "Third Heaven," the abode of "the feeling intellect," as the author says in a borrowing from Wordsworth.

Laurence Binyon's *The Madness of Merlin*, published posthumously in 1947 and never completed, was based mainly on Geoffrey of Monmouth's *Vita Merlini*. That being the case, Binyon's Merlin, Merlinus Silvestris, is not the usual enchanter. His world is vast and terrible. Even as a boy he was set apart. His sister Gwyndeth says of him:

> *I remember how, but a boy,*
> *Suddenly he would seem a stranger among us.*
> *As if he had wandered out in a strange land*
> *Seeing us no more; and then as suddenly*
> *His spirit would return to the use of the body;*
> *But to none told he ever in what land he had been.*
> *Now, as I guess,*
> *It was some blinding vision from above*
> *Estranged the world to him.*

Like Geoffrey's, Binyon's Merlin is ridden by terror. He does not have the solace of Christianity as in Williams, or the "Light" which shines, even though faintly, in Robinson's Camelot. Yet again these Merlins are kin, members of the doomed band of men who see too much.

Finally there is C. S. Lewis' Merlinus Ambrosius, in his novel *That Hideous Strength* (1947), a tale of England after the Second World

War, in which malign spirits from outer space try to degrade and destroy mankind. Merlinus has lain buried for many centuries in a state of suspended animation, but finally rises and joins in the destruction of the evil force. Lewis explains that he is able to give his aid to a small group of dedicated Christians because he represents immemorially old supernatural power, "Atlantean" magic. Again this Merlin is far removed from the conventional magician and seer. Like Williams' Merlin his ancient home might well have been the region of the summer stars.

Let us return, however, to Robinson. His concept of the poem *Merlin* and the world-view which it embodied ensured great breadth for the story. It was written during the First World War, a disaster which caused Robinson again and again to express apocalyptic premonitions of doom facing the world. The tale of Arthur and the tragic fall of his kingdom had gripped his imagination since boyhood; now the destruction of Camelot seemed to him all too like the decay of twentieth-century civilization.

Arthur's realm was tottering to its ruin, rent asunder by the selfishness and violence of the knights of the Round Table and by the cancerous adultery of Lancelot and Guinevere. Merlin finds himself almost immobilized by divided loyalties to Arthur and Vivian. Lancelot and Guinevere cannot give up their love, and Arthur is powerless either to acknowledge or correct the situation. Robinson's description of Arthur's agony of mind is deeply moving.

> . . . he saw giants rising in the dark,
> Born horribly of memories and new fears
> That in the gray-lit irony of dawn
> Were partly to fade out and be forgotten;
> And then there might be sleep, and for a time
> There might again be peace. His head was hot
> And throbbing; but the rest of him was cold,
> As he lay staring hard where nothing stood,
> And hearing what was not, even while he saw
> And heard, like dust and thunder far away,
> The coming confirmation of the words
> Of him who saw so much and feared so little
> Of all that was to be. No spoken doom
> That ever chilled the last night of a felon
> Prepared a dragging anguish more profound
> And absolute than Arthur, in these hours,

> Made out of darkness and of Merlin's words;
> No tide that ever crashed on Lyonesse
> Drove echoes inland that were lonelier
> For widowed ears among the fisher-folk,
> Than for the King were memories tonight
> Of old illusions that were dead forever.

Arthur's helplessness finds its counterpart in the entrapment of Merlin between two obligations: his new-found identification with youth and beauty in Vivian and his position as Arthur's adviser. Arthur sees clearly the disastrous conflict in Merlin.

> "Men change in Brittany, Merlin," said the King;
> And even his grief had strife to freeze again
> A dreary smile for the transmuted seer
> Now robed in heavy wealth of purple silk,
> With frogs and foreign tassels. On his face,
> Too smooth now for a wizard or a sage,
> Lay written, for the King's remembering eyes,
> A pathos of a lost authority
> Long faded, and unconscionably gone;
> And on the King's heart lay a sudden cold.

Merlin's authority, his occupation, like Othello's, is gone. He is like the person in Robinson's "The Man Against the Sky," published the year before *Merlin*:

> ...mounting with infirm unsearching tread,
> His hopes to chaos led,
> He may have stumbled up there from the past,
> And with an aching strangeness viewed the last
> Abysmal conflagration of his dreams. . . .

Robinson's preoccupation with men faced by agonizing difficulties, losses of direction, failures of will, and paralyzing disillusionments finds powerful expression in his treatment of Merlin, giving him a dimension he almost never had before. Like Annandale

> Astray
> Out of his life and in another life;
> And in the stillness of this other life
> He wondered and he drowsed.

Yet Merlin's problem is vaster than Annandale's and his vision is more searching. Like Clavering he saw "too far for guidance of today"; yet unlike him he never saw "too near for the eternities." Robinson stresses Merlin's prophetic vision. In speaking of the Grail to Arthur he says,

> "I saw
> Too much, and that was never good for man.
> The man who goes alone too far goes mad—
> In one way or another."

And after Vivian leaves him for a time he tells himself,

> "The man who sees
> May see too far, and he may see too late
> The path he takes unseen."

Of all the characters in *Merlin* Vivian is the most original. She is a believable and intelligently conceived woman, no vulgar wanton as in Tennyson, no ambitious amateur in magic as in Malory, but an unusually fascinating and capable person, entangled in a difficulty far more troublesome than a love affair between a young woman and an older man. Vivian is no longer simply a seductress, finally extracting the secrets of Merlin's magic and condemning him to a perpetual imprisonment. Like Dalila she is involved in a national emergency. While Merlin lingers with her Arthur has to meet terrible difficulties in his crumbling kingdom without the counsel of his trusted sage. Arthur has been fully warned of Merlin's fate.

> Ten years ago
> The King had heard, with unbelieving ears
> At first, what Merlin said would be the last
> Reiteration of his going down
> To find a living grave in Brittany:
> "Buried alive I told you I should be,
> By love made little and by woman shorn,
> Like Samson, of my glory; and the time
> Is now at hand."

The tragic dimension of the story and the dilemma of Merlin himself—another Samson—is revealed in the twin imperatives of Broceliande and Camelot. Contrary to the opinion of some critics the two strands unite to make a single story of the conflict of virtually irreconcilable forces.

Like her predecessors Vivian is determined, against all the pressures from Camelot, to get what she wants. Again like her sisters, this seems not to be sensual delight—though she is by no means insensitive to it and appreciates physical attractiveness enough to make Merlin shave his beard—rather it is Merlin's *wisdom* that she seeks. But in a departure from earlier versions it is not his incantations that she wishes; like her predecessors she is a relentlessly ambitious woman, but unlike them she has a good mind which she wants to improve. As she says to Merlin,

> "When this great Merlin comes to me,
> My task and avocation for some time
> Will be to make him willing, if I can,
> To teach and feed me with an ounce of wisdom."

Vivian's lively, original mind is evident throughout the poem. She has a degree of self-knowledge which puts her far above her predecessors. As she says, she is cruel and cold and likes snakes. Volatile as quicksilver, she has no set, inflexible attitudes. Though the first visit of Merlin frightens her, she receives him with frankness and informality. Expressing hatred easily—she hates King Arthur and she poisons those she hates—she is also capable of giving Merlin a kind of love he has never known, adoration for his greatness, and deep affection. To her Merlin is a means of self-realization in the fullest sense. As she says,

> "In an age
> That has no plan for me that I can read
> Without him, shall he tell me what I am,
> And why I am, I wonder?"

Later in Merlin's first visit she gains a deeper perception.

> "You are the wisest man that ever was,
> And I've a prayer to make: May all you say
> To Vivian be a part of what you knew
> Before the curse of her unquiet head
> Was on your shoulder, as you have it now,
> To punish you for knowing beyond knowledge.

> You are the only one who sees enough
> To make me see how far away I am
> From all that I have seen and have not been;
> You are the only thing there is alive
> Between me as I am and as I was
> When Merlin was a dream. You are to listen
> When I say now to you that I'm alone.
> Like you, I saw too much; and unlike you
> I made no kingdoms out of what I saw—
> Or none save this one here that you must rule,
> Believing you are ruled. I see too far
> To rule myself. Time's way with you and me
> Is our way, in that we are out of Time
> And out of tune with Time."

Possibly Robinson's greatest achievement in creating the character of Vivian lies in providing Merlin, as never before, with a woman who can not only satisfy the craving of his lost youth for beauty but who can also stimulate him intellectually. This stimulation is shown in passages like the one just quoted and in Vivian's angry reproach when Merlin tells her he must return again to Camelot. It is apparent also in practically every exchange between the two, in the deference which Merlin pays to a creature of mind as well as body.

There is another aspect of Vivian that makes her very real, and likable: her common sense. Merlin's "imprisonment" is not an imprisonment at all; Vivian tells him quite clearly that he is not supposed to dance attendance upon her. He should roam by himself as he pleases in complete freedom. What better way to complete Merlin's infatuation?

For a man who never married and who apparently never had a fully-satisfying love affair Robinson knows a great deal about women. The ladies in his Arthurian poems, Vivian, Guinevere, and Isolt, usually outshine the men. It is not that Merlin is weak by comparison: he is simply less original, less various, less flexible than Vivian. She is a very real person. The sage's imprisonment through incantation is gone; his "jailer" is a woman of flesh and blood—and mind.

Now as to Merlin himself. The gate-keeper Blaise, when Merlin reproaches him for the "vicious" and noisy gate to Broceliande replies,

> "There's a way out of every wilderness
> For those who dare or care enough to find it."

The irony of this remark is immediately apparent. Merlin was indeed free to leave Broceliande when he wished; what he could never escape from was the "wilderness" of his dual obligations. This conflict, unlike Vivian's single purpose, adds great intensity to Robinson's Merlin. Early in the poem Gawaine says of him, in Broceliande, that he "wears the valiance of an ageless youth / Crowned with a glory of eternal peace." Yet Gawaine was wrong on both counts; his judgments were too capricious to be trusted. Merlin's "ageless youth" was factitious; his "eternal peace" a mockery.

The poignance of Merlin's dilemma, combined with the vivid originality of Vivian, gives new breadth and depth to the legend. It might be easy to assume, from the theme of Nemesis in the poem (as Arthur said of Merlin, his "Nemesis had made of him a slave") that the sage does nothing but let events take their course. This is not the case. He acts vigorously a number of times. After his first visit to Broceliande, for example, he reproaches Arthur as "a slack, blasted, and sad-fronted man"; he also warns the King against Modred, and bids him not to let his enemies take the Queen and kingdom. Moreover, he is a free agent; he leaves Broceliande when he wishes, and he returns to Camelot the last time in agony of mind to do what he can for Arthur's realm. When he tells Vivian of the dangerous state of affairs in Camelot she reproaches him bitterly in a powerful scene. Merlin is in despair. Yet his place is in Camelot.

> A melancholy wave of revelation
> Broke over Merlin like a rising sea,
> Long viewed unwillingly and long denied.
> He saw what he had seen, but would not feel,
> Till now the bitterness of what he felt
> Was in his throat, and all the coldness of it
> Was on him and around him like a flood
> Of lonelier memories than he had said
> Were memories, although he knew them now
> For what they were—for what his eyes had seen,
> For what his ears had heard and what his heart
> Had felt, with him not knowing what it felt.
> But now he knew that his cold angel's name
> Was Change, and that a mightier will than his
> Or Vivian's had ordained that he be there.
> To Vivian he could not say anything

> But words that had no more of hope in them
> Than anguish had of peace: "I meant the world . . .
> I meant the world," he groaned; "not you—not me."

Later Merlin comes to terms with his destiny, in what is perhaps the most moving passage in the poem, a soliloquy charged with the imminence of death, indeed with the burial of his "poor blundering bones," and yet also illumined by courageous acceptance of what must be, and by the "light" which leads him:

> "... let the man
> Who saw too much, and was to drive himself
> From paradise, play too lightly or too long
> Among the moths and flowers, he finds at last
> There is a dim way out; and he shall grope
> Where pleasant shadows lead him to the plain
> That has no shadow save his own behind him.
> And there, with no complaint, nor much regret,
> Shall he plod on, with death between him now
> And the far light that guides him, till he falls
> And has an empty thought of empty rest;
> Then Fate will put a mattock in his hands
> And lash him while he digs himself the grave
> That is to be the pallet and the shroud
> Of his poor blundering bones."

Robinson gives a remarkably inclusive picture of Vivian and Merlin. Vivian is all concentration: her movement is centripetal. Her problem is her identification with Merlin here and now. Merlin represents the opposite: his movement is expansive, centrifugal. Yet he needs Vivian, and her concentrative force struggles against the wider obligation to Camelot—and indeed also against the promise he sees in the "Light" of the Grail. Merlin's mind is far-ranging, deeply contemplative and metaphysical. As he speaks with Dagonet the King's fool, Merlin goes far beyond the bounds of his own earthly needs to insist on

> "... an eternal will, strangely endowed
> With merciful illusions whereby self
> Becomes the will itself and each man swells
> In fond accordance with his agency."

Merlin, who "saw too much," perceives the impending tragedy of
Camelot; he sees, moreover, the permanence of that earthly passion
which meant life and strength to him. With prophetic insight he
speaks to Dagonet of Vivian.

> "In time to be,
> The like of her shall have another name
> Than Vivian, and her laugh shall be a fire,
> Not shining only to consume itself
> With what it burns. She knows not yet the name
> Of what she is, for now there is no name;
> Some day there shall be."

In his moments of prophetic vision Merlin rises above the harsh-
ness of ordinary life. At these times he is an instrument of metaphysical truth far beyond conventional behavior or mere incantation.
He knows "beyond knowledge," says Vivian. Here one finds a reminder
of Merlin's far earlier and almost forgotten predecessors: the seer of
Geoffrey's *Prophetiae Merlini* and Merlinus Silvestris of the *Vita
Merlini*. In both of these works Merlin transcends the bounds of
ordinary conduct in a wildly confusing series of disasters and predictions. In the *Prophetiae* the seer foretells "Woe to the perjured nation,
for whose sake the renowned city [Winchester] shall come to ruin."
With a flash of recognition we remember the scene in which Merlin
and Dagonet talk of the doom of Camelot.

> The wizard shivered as he spoke, and stared
> Away into the sunset where he saw
> Once more, as through a cracked and cloudy glass,
> A crumbling sky that held a crimson cloud
> Wherein there was a town of many towers
> All swayed and shaken, in a woman's hand
> This time, till out of it there spilled and flashed
> And tumbled, like loose jewels, town, towers, and walls,
> And there was nothing but a crumbling sky
> That made anon of black and red and ruin
> A wild and final rain on Camelot.

In the *Vita Merlini* Myrddin, who goes mad after the death of his
three brothers in battle, takes to the woods, and asks that a house be
built with many windows, through which he can see the stars and
discover what will happen to the kingdom. Like Robinson's Merlin,

therefore, his remote ancestors see farther than ordinary men and are the prophets of great and often terrible events to come.

Merlin sees far because this is Robinson's way of looking at the world. It is a deeply penetrating view, unique in the history of the Arthurian legend. Robinson was determined, so far as possible, to get at the reality of experience. And for him reality was not simply the data of the senses: it was the totality of human perception. Readers have often been tempted to ponder the critical cliché: was Robinson a realist or a romanticist? Such Solomon's judgments are futile. If one thinks of dogmatic literary classifications one could say that he was both, like Melville and Thoreau and Conrad. Yet in a wider sense he is a realist. For him reality necessitated an expanded comprehension both of the world of sense and the world of idea, whereby he achieved a stereoscopic view of great depth and clarity.

In the more formal sense Robinson's awareness of reality makes him completely de-mythologize the legend. Merlin has no incantations that Vivian wishes to learn; the Holy Grail is not the sacred vessel of the sacrament but rather a kind of ethical guide, a "Light." It will be remembered that in like fashion Robinson completely eliminated the magic love-potion in his version of the Tristram story. His people are moderns: in all his poems they are easily recognizable as parts of our own experience.

A further dimension to Robinson's reality lies in an awareness of sensuous beauty not often found in his poetry. Broceliande is an earthly paradise in contrast with the gloom of Camelot. Merlin's arrival at Vivian's domain is described with delicate sensitivity.

> The birds were singing still; leaves flashed and swung
> Before him in the sunlight; a soft breeze
> Made intermittent whisperings around him
> Of love and fate and danger, and faint waves
> Of many sweetly-stinging fragile odors
> Broke lightly as they touched him; cherry boughs
> Above him snowed white petals down upon him,
> And under their slow falling Merlin smiled
> Contentedly, as one who contemplates
> No longer fear, confusion, or regret,
> May smile at ruin or at revelation.

Broceliande is indeed a very garden of pleasant delights for the embattled Merlin, and the beautiful Vivian is its mistress. Robinson describes her vividly.

> "More like a flower
> Tonight," he [Merlin] said, as now he scanned again
> The immemorial meaning of her face
> And drew it nearer to his eyes. It seemed
> A flower of wonder with a crimson stem
> Came leaning slowly and regretfully
> To meet his will—a flower of change and peril
> That had a clinging blossom of warm olive
> Half stifled with a tyranny of black,
> And held the wayward fragrance of a rose
> Made woman by delirious alchemy.

Merlin finds himself lapped in a world of luxurious sensation.

> Fatigue and hunger—tempered leisurely
> With food that some devout magician's oven
> Might after many failures have delivered,
> And wine that had for decades in the dark
> Of Merlin's grave been slowly quickening,
> And with half-heard, dream-weaving interludes
> Of distant flutes and viols, made more distant
> By far, nostalgic hautboys blown from nowhere,—
> Were tempered not so leisurely, may be,
> With Vivian's inextinguishable eyes
> Between two shining silver candlesticks
> That lifted each a trembling flame to make
> The rest of her a dusky loveliness
> Against a bank of shadow.

In passages such as these Robinson explores another dimension of reality, the world of subtle sense impression and suggestion.

The truth of the imagination, capable of reaching into areas beyond the reach of logic, the acute awareness of the world of sense made animate by people who reason as well as feel—all these make *Merlin* a remarkably successful poem. It is not simply its originality which makes it likely to endure; Arthurian literature is filled with ill-conceived excursions off the beaten track of the legend. Apart from its originality, apart from a modern interpretation which strips the story of its old insistence on magic, Robinson has given us a poignant account of a doomed love, acted out by living people. The tragedy of the story of course is the impending fall of Camelot. No less moving, possibly even more so, is the pathos of Merlin's love for Vivian. It is an old story, but one that never loses its power. Merlin wrenches the heart in ways that Lancelot almost never does, for he has so much more to lose, psychologically, than Lancelot. To Merlin the experience of love was an unexpectedly demanding reversal. He who had been the prophetic sage, no expert in the ways of women, now had to become a lover. Lancelot always had been the servant of Venus. Yet the shattering emotional change Merlin undergoes never destroys his nobility, or the devotion of Vivian. They act out their loyalties and their disillusionments in a world which constantly suggests a dimension greater than Camelot.

Imagery and Theme in *Lancelot*

Christopher Brookhouse

Of Robinson's three Arthurian poems—*Merlin* (1917), *Lancelot* (1920), and *Tristram* (1927)—the first two are, by their theme of national destruction, part of each other, and historically they are part of the basic Arthurian narrative while the Tristram story has had an independent life of its own. In this essay, aside from a few remarks on *Merlin*, I wish to concentrate on *Lancelot*.

Malory's *Morte D'Arthur* is Robinson's primary source for *Lancelot* and to a lesser extent for *Merlin*. However, I would not emphasize Robinson's borrowing of plot and incident, generalities of characterization, or historical information as much as certain feelings about history that Robinson and Malory shared. Both writers lived in times of national change. Malory witnessed the political and social changes of fifteenth-century England. He participated in the Wars of the Roses, for which he spent periods of time in prison, where he died. Robinson published *Merlin* the year America entered World War I and *Lancelot* two years after the armistice. For both Malory and Robinson the destruction of Camelot is the symbol of historical change and national disaster. Moreover, I think Malory's understanding, interpretation, and treatment of Camelot's fall interested Robinson because Malory stressed the dualism of the flesh and the spirit, the secular world of men and their pursuits against the world beyond, a world announced by the Grail. This dualism is clearly present in Robinson's *Lancelot*.

Of course Robinson also differs from Malory. Robinson chose to select and not surround. Malory combined nearly all of Arthurian legend into his prose romance; Robinson selected two major figures,

Merlin and Lancelot, and omitted any emphasis on material which treated finding the Grail, that is, the Galahad portion of Malory.

Robinson's Merlin is an observer of the secular world, although an unwilling one; he had left Arthur's world for Vivian until Arthur recalled him to Camelot in time to see the beginning of its destruction. Robinson's Merlin becomes a sort of anti-romantic seer unblest, a man who foresees Camelot's ruin and his own doom but is powerless to change the course of destruction, the will of fate.

> "I saw too far,
> But not so far as this. Fate played with me
> As I have played with Time; and Time, like me,
> Being less than Fate, will have on me his vengeance.
> On Fate there is no vengeance, even for God."

Merlin almost seems to be a symbol of the poet himself, of Robinson brooding on the western world rushing into war.

Merlin is more "medieval" than *Lancelot*. Robinson's emphasis on fate makes it so. The medieval stories of Camelot's ruin contain a similar fatalism, a belief that no matter how fine and extraordinary knights and kings could be, their very participation in the secular world marked them for destruction. Generally the medieval writer would have hesitated putting fate above God as Robinson has Merlin do, yet in medieval writing a feeling exists that all the Boethian and Christian explanations of fate and the irrational could suddenly break down. Robinson does break them down in *Merlin*, and the poem is deeply moving and evokes spiritual terror.

Lancelot takes the reader back to Camelot's ruin. Now, however, national catastrophe results from what men do with their own world, in particular what Lancelot, Guinevere, Gawaine, and Arthur do. There is no Merlin to be an observer and seer; Robinson gives us active participants who bring their world down upon themselves.

In terms of action, much more happens in *Lancelot* than in *Merlin*; but neither poem describes action: instead Robinson records it through conversations and monologues. The place, setting, and time become crucially important in underscoring what is spoken. Setting, temporal and spatial, becomes a metaphor through which the reader enters the mind and the world of Lancelot, Guinevere, Gawaine, and Arthur. Also Robinson selects and repeats many images, such as color and hue, darkness and light, to expand and sustain his emphasis on character and moral responsibility within the major figures of the poem.

Section I takes place in the King's garden, which means Arthur's garden, and suggests a false, mortal paradise. Lancelot and Gawaine confront each other, standoffish and sarcastic at first, then, as their conversation centers on Lancelot's desire to leave Camelot and follow the new Light which has turned him from Arthur's world, they become serious and respectful of each other. Lancelot, speaking of the Grail quest, says:

> "When I came back from seeing what I saw,
> I saw no place for me in Camelot.
> There is no place for me save where the Light
> May lead me; and to that place I shall go."

Gawaine replies:

> "You are a thing too vaporous to be sharing
> The carnal feast of life. You mow down men
> Like elder-stems, and you leave women sighing
> For one more sight of you; but they do wrong.
> You are a man of mist, and have no shadow."

The opposition of Lancelot and Gawaine is established. Gawaine loves the "carnal feast of life," the secular world, while Lancelot, who is shadowless in the light of this world, seeks a world beyond this one, beyond Camelot, and beyond Guinevere too. But Lancelot is still in the King's garden, is yet a part of Arthur's world, and has not taken his leave from Guinevere. She enters now and approaches Lancelot and Gawaine:

> Guinevere,
> With many questions in her dark blue eyes
> And one gay jewel in her golden hair,
> Had come upon the two of them unseen.

Guinevere's worldly beauty is suggested by the color of her eyes and hair, and the jewel she wears; even her unseen approach is symbolic; it is as if she suddenly comes into Lancelot's consciousness where before there was only his desire to leave Camelot.

Section II is an extraordinary balance of present time in the garden and Lancelot's memories of first seeing Guinevere, falling in love with her, and betraying his loyalty to Arthur; of light and color, the golden light of Guinevere, the fading light of afternoon, and the fading light of Arthur's world; of Lancelot's will struggling to escape from Camelot and yet held back by his love for Arthur's queen.

When the section opens, there is still sunlight:

> The flash of oak leaves over Guinevere
> That afternoon, with the sun going down,
> Made memories there for Lancelot, although
> The woman who in silence looked at him
> Now seemed his inventory of the world
> That he must lose, or suffer to be lost
> For love of her who sat there in the shade,
> With oak leaves flashing in a golden light
> Over her face and over her golden hair.

Guinevere is in shade but not in darkness, there are shadows in the dying afternoon, but sunlight too; there is yet the world of Camelot, sensuous and beautiful in its degree, against another world beyond. Lancelot makes Guinevere understand his intention to follow the true, everlasting Light toward another world; and when she hears his intention she pales, the earthly colors of her life fade in the brightness of the Light Lancelot follows.

> Blood left the quivering cheeks of Guinevere
> As color leaves a cloud; and where white was
> Before, there was a ghostliness not white,
> But gray; and over it her shining hair
> Coiled heavily its mocking weight of gold.

Robinson weaves images of light and darkness through their remaining conversation about the change in Lancelot and the danger of Modred to the kingdom. During this time the afternoon recedes into night:

> "... some far-off unheard-of retribution
> Hangs over Camelot, even as this bough
> That I may almost reach, hangs overhead,
> All dark now. Only a small time ago
> The light was falling through it, and on me.
> Another light, a longer time ago,

Was living in your eyes, and we were happy.
Yet there was Modred then as he is now,
As much a danger then as he is now,
And quite as much a nuisance. Let his eyes
Have all the darkness in them they may hold."

Lancelot for all his knowledge of the future, "the darkness of a
darker night" soon to be, is fixed between following the Light and
remaining one more day with Guinevere. She still touches him with
her beauty, the blue and gold of eyes and hair.

Lancelot's memory wandered
Into the blue and wistful distances
That her soft eyes unveiled. He knew their touch,
As he knew the great love that fostered it,
And the wild passionate fate that hid itself
In all the perilous calm of white and gold
That was her face and hair. . . .

At the end of the second section, Guinevere mentions that Arthur
has gone hunting, which offers Lancelot one more chance to be with
her. In Section III Lancelot, alone now, considers the circumstances
and his decision to accept Guinevere's invitation. He is forthright
about his responsibility for adulterous love, and about himself looking
back once more to the old life, the world of earthly colors and vanity.

"Who is this Lancelot that has betrayed
His King, and served him with a cankered honor?
Who is this Lancelot that sees the Light
And waits now in the shadow for the dark?" . . .

"God, what a rain of ashes falls on him
Who sees the new and cannot leave the old!"

Arthur's absence is a trap. Lancelot and Guinevere are caught, she
is condemned to the stake, and rescued by Lancelot, who kills Gawaine's brothers in the process. Sections IV and V contain reports of
these events brought to Arthur, Bedivere, and Gawaine as they wait
in Arthur's chamber in the "grim light of dawn." Time has shifted:
it is the bleak morning out of which events grow and entwine to bring
about Camelot's ruin. Gawaine is the force rising now to struggle with

Lancelot. The events are humanly caused; the issue is not fate but moral responsibility and the corruption of judgment. Lancelot, unable to resist following Guinevere one more time, must rescue her; and Gawaine, always rash and the follower of the "carnal feast of life," cannot swerve from his revenge on Lancelot for slaying his brothers. Arthur himself, who was a more forceful figure in *Merlin*, is reduced to

> . . . a sick landlord shuffling to the light
> For one last look-out on his mortgaged hills.

In Sections VI and VII Lancelot and Guinevere are secluded at Joyous Gard, ironically the castle connected with Tristram's tragedy. Lancelot and Guinevere express their sorrow over the war with Gawaine and the uselessness of human slaughter; both accept responsibility for the deaths they have caused. In Section VI Guinevere says:

> "—why dishonor Time
> And torture longer drawn in your slow game
> Of empty slaughter? Tomorrow it will be
> The King's move, I suppose, and we shall have
> One more magnificent waste of nameless pawns,
> And of a few more knights."

The sarcasm of Guinevere's "I suppose" speaks the general tone of the sixth section, the tiredness and fatigue felt by Lancelot and his knights for the war, by Guinevere toward Lancelot's continuing the war, and by Lancelot toward himself. The emotions of tiredness and wearing down are concentrated in imagery of rain and mist. The rain, which continually falls outside on Joyous Gard, inside washes away the old light, the worldly colors, and beauty of Guinevere. Furthermore, she herself sees the forms of men at war reduced in the darkness to shapes of lesser life:

> . . . and like another mist,
> All gray, came Guinevere to Lancelot,
> . . . and she saw faintly where she gazed,
> Like distant insects of a shadowy world,
> Dim clusters here and there of shadowy men
> Whose occupation was her long abhorrence.

At the end of the sixth section, Lancelot meets with the Bishop of Rochester and agrees to return Guinevere to Arthur at Camelot.

Section VII develops the depth of Lancelot's feelings about leaving Guinevere. The imagery of rain and mist continues to enforce the power of the section, and Robinson also uses imagery of fire, ripeness, and decay. Fire suggests Lancelot's old desire for Guinevere as well as the punishment from which he rescued her. Sitting by himself while the rain falls on Joyous Gard, "where now there was no joy," Lancelot

> . . . saw no more. Now and again he buried
> A lonely thought among the coals and ashes
> Outside the reaching flame and left it there,
> Quite as he left outside in rainy graves
> The sacrificial hundreds who had filled them.

Then Lancelot tells Guinevere he, not she, is responsible for the deaths of men filling the graves.

> "They died because
> Your world, my world, and Arthur's world is dying,
> As Merlin said it would. No blame is yours,
> For it was I who led you from the King—
> Or rather, to say truth, it was your glory
> That led my love to lead you from the King—
> By flowery ways, that always end somewhere,
> To fire and fright and exile, and release."

Guinevere desperately wants to go with Lancelot to France, to "have yet one morsel more of life," but Lancelot rejects her wish. The language of his rejection is amazingly powerful. Robinson's imagery defines Lancelot's sorrow for Guinevere, his own loneliness, and the approaching destruction of Arthur's world. Almost every literal detail becomes symbolic.

With words that recall the earthly garden in which the poem opened, Lancelot tells Guinevere:

> "Could we go back
> To the old garden, we should not stay long;
> The fruit that we should find would all be fallen,
> And have the taste of earth."

Guinevere begs again to be taken to France. Lancelot, refusing, holds her in his arms:

> And there was no sound then of anything,
> Save a low moaning of a broken woman,
> And the cold roaring down of that long rain.

Then Lancelot is left alone, the rain covers everything, and the fire of memory and desire goes out:

> All night the rain came down on Joyous Gard;
> And all night, there before the crumbling embers
> That faded into feathery death-like dust,
> Lancelot sat and heard it. He saw not
> The fire that died, but he heard rain that fell
> On all those graves around him and those years
> Behind him; and when dawn came, he was cold. . . .
> He was not sure of anything but the Light. . . .

In Section VIII the danger of Modred as the force of doom to Arthur's kingdom is openly presented. Gawaine and Lancelot make peace with each other, and Gawaine, attended by Lancelot, dies. Besides serving to introduce Modred's rebellion, the section is important because of Gawaine's self-admitted failure.

> "Be lenient, Lancelot; I've a light head.
> Merlin appraised it once when I was young,
> Telling me then that I should have the world
> To play with. Well, I've had it, and played with it. . . ."

Robinson also uses Gawaine's death-bed speech to emphasize again that Modred is Gawaine's half-brother, which recalls the adultery of Arthur, Modred's father. This detail, which stresses that the moral failure of men causes their eventual destruction, is restored to the Arthurian story by Robinson in contrast to Tennyson, who mitigated the circumstances of Modred's parentage.

In Section IX Lancelot arrives too late to help Arthur's cause; Arthur and Modred are dead, and Guinevere has ridden west to the nunnery at Almesbury. Caught one last time between the secular

world and following the Light into another world, Lancelot follows
Guinevere.

> [He] rode on with his memories before him,
> Before him and behind. They were a cloud
> For no Light now to pierce. They were a cloud
> Made out of what was gone. . . .
>
> . . . .
>   He found the queen,
> But she was not the Queen of white and gold
> That he had seen before him for so long.
> There was no gold; there was no gold anywhere.
> The black hood, and her white face under it,
> And the blue frightened eyes, were all he saw. . . .

Ironically Guinevere, not Lancelot, has abandoned the secular world.
Lancelot, acting suddenly more like Gawaine, asks Guinevere this
time to go to France.

> "There is France left," he said.
> His face flushed like a boy's. . . .

Guinevere firmly rejects his plea, and again ironically, considering
their positions in Section VII, she forces him to leave her and follow
the Light. When Lancelot says good-bye to her, his perceptions imply
once more the fading of the earthly garden of Arthur's world.

> He crushed her cold white hands and saw them falling
> Away from him like flowers into a grave.

And also the loss of the golden artificiality of the world of men contrasted to the natural world:

> He closed his eyes, and the white face was there,
> But not the gold. The gold would not come back.
> There were gold fields of corn that lay around him,
> But they were not the gold of Guinevere. . . .

At last Lancelot follows his vision, but less by his own will, which
wavered between the old and the new, than by Guinevere's.

Robinson's own vision in *Lancelot*, where he brings us not just up
to but beyond the destruction of Arthur's world, is of a private, spiri-

tual salvation. This answer may have been what first attracted him to the Arthurian material and to Malory, for this solution has long been implicit in the Arthurian story, and especially in Malory, who confronted the chaos and failure of worldly undertakings with the spiritual vision of the Grail. By the same reasoning Tennyson's treatment of Arthur was perhaps less acceptable to Robinson. In Tennyson the Grail search disrupts the worldly business of men. Tennyson's Arthur is an ideal who operates within this world. In *Lancelot* Robinson reduced Arthur to a very imperfect king and a very imperfect man, and reduced the scope of the Arthurian story to concentrate on Guinevere and Lancelot, both human and imperfect, both in part morally responsible for the end of Camelot, but who find a private salvation in withdrawal from the material world, endurance, and spiritual vision beyond the garden of this life.

A Crisis of Achievement: Robinson's Late Narratives

Jay Martin

> "... You are like a book with pages in it
> You have not read, and cannot read in the dark.
> Some of us would be happier in the dark,
> As you have been, and cannot be again. ...
>   There is no cure for self;
> There's only an occasional revelation,
> Arriving not infrequently too late."
>   Matthias at the Door (1931)

The Town Down the River (1910), Robinson's first volume in eight years, appeared five years after Theodore Roosevelt had "fished" him (as the poet put it) "out of hell by the hair of the head," and so enabled him to write the poems comprising this volume. Before the poet had been saved through the influence and aid of the President, his characteristic themes had closely resembled those of regional New England writing in the 1880s and '90s. Having experienced personal disaster, he had seen crisis generalized in the life of his family, community and nation. Like writers as different from each other and from him as Sarah Orne Jewett and Henry Adams, Robinson subjected the assumptions of the New England past—about the value of progress, work, success, gentility, the prospects for local integrity and felicity, and at last belief in the usefulness of the past itself—to calculated, critical examination. Continuing this scrutiny in The Town Down the River, such poems as "Miniver Cheevy" satirized both the mechanical present and the nostalgia for the past which Robinson hated in rural New England.

But he had not rid himself of his own past, or of personal agony over his relation to it in the present. 1910 ushered in a decade during which Robinson experienced a series of personal crises related both to the way he defined himself as a poet and to the kind of poetry he wrote, and brought on by the recognition he was being accorded. Roosevelt fished the public man out of hell; but the acclaim which followed plunged the poet into a hell of personal crisis. Indeed, he virtually ceased to be a poet, since, as I shall say, the beliefs through which he had defined himself as a poet seemed more and more unsatisfactory to the person. Enabled to write poetry by appointment to a sinecure in the United States Customs Service for the Port of New York, he found that he had lost interest in verse. He yearned, instead, for popular recognition and commercial success. Although acclaimed as a major poet by Roosevelt in *The Outlook* and by other critics following *The Town, The Man Against the Sky* (1916), and *Merlin* (1917), he had spent most of the decade between 1905 and 1915 attempting to write novels, sketches, and plays. He had questioned conventional values in America; yet men of convention were calling him their poet. He had created anti-heroes like Captain Craig as vehicles for irony and satire; yet Captain Craig was more and more taken as a new kind of modern hero. He had rebelled against the genteel tradition, its standards and its aims; yet rebellion against the genteel was taking place on a wide front. He had defined his ego (and esteemed his work) through what he opposed; but now, suddenly faced in middle age with acceptance, and finding that he yearned for it, he was obliged to define himself anew through what he had accomplished. In short, the historical accidents which saved him as a poet now threatened him as a person and brought him to a real crisis of self. Speaking generally, Erik H. Erikson calls this the *"crisis of generativity,"* which occurs "when a man looks at what he has generated, or helped to generate, and finds it good or wanting, when his life work as part of the productivity of his time gives him some sense of being on the side of a few angels or makes him feel stagnant."

I call it the crisis of achievement; for it occurs with a special force in the lives of American writers, particularly poets, in whose careers aesthetic achievement normally precedes popular acceptance by a number of years. When it comes, such acceptance provokes in the writer personal responses which have affiliations to both the ways by which Americans have traditionally defined their poetry and the roles of their poets and the way that the poet has defined himself in relation to his fellows—now, in a real sense, his audience.

Robinson, born in December 1869, was a third child, whose birth almost cost his mother her life. Through curious indifference or conscious antagonism, his parents left him unchristened—in a Christian society, lacking name or "true" identity—for six months and only finally agreed to name him through the drawing of names placed in a hat by vacationers at a summer resort. Mrs. Robinson rewarded the woman who suggested Edwin by adding Arlington, after the Massachusetts town whence the woman came. Thus, casually, and it must have struck the young boy, brutally, he was named. Moreover, as he grew up, both his older brothers seemed destined for success, one as a doctor and the other as a businessman, while Edwin from the first showed the difficulty which he was having in establishing his own identity; he suffered through acute embarrassment, which sometimes resulted in what he afterwards felt was offensive social behavior, and always in reluctance in speech. By the time he was five he was convinced that he was "never going to be able to elbow [his] way to the Trough of Life" and interpreted the scriptural "Suffer little children" as an admonition for his punishment. These, and many other personality traits, hint at a death-wish, a desire for the extinction of identity, as did his belief, derived somewhat later from his brother's medical books, that he had "lock-jaw, lupus, leprosy, cancer, elephantiasis, Bright's disease, and falling of the womb, all at once."

Certainly, to the end of his life, Robinson harbored an oedipal hostility toward his father, who, he felt, had abandoned his sons to their personal disasters. He spoke to the physician and poet Merrill Moore of his resentments against his father in a parable—probably originally a dream—about three men who had fallen into a well. "We are lost and shall never get out," they cry. But someone—the tormenting father-figure, it is clear—lowers a thread to them. "Here is our chance," one—Robinson himself—cries; and though the others deride him, he takes hold and is drawn upward, with the others clinging to him. "But just as they reach the surface, one man doubts and they all drop, sinking under the water." When such nightmares still obsessed Robinson in old age, it is easy to guess at the pain which he suffered as a young man and to understand the difficulty which he had in establishing a stable identity.

By the time of his late adolescence, temporizing over his identity and providing himself a moratorium through remaining in high school for a year after graduation to study Horace and Milton, he began to define himself as a poet whose eminence could be secret and therefore untested by the conventional standards of success which otherwise threatened him. Writing poetry, he hinted much later in an article in the *Colophon*, was then a way of avoiding time, and thus the ideas associated with it of work, achievement, and commercial success represented by his brothers. Poetry, it would eventually turn out, would involve him deeply in the very investigation of himself that he was trying at this point to avoid. For now, however, it saved him, as he intimated to a friend, from "getting acquainted with one's self, [for] if one gets too well acquainted there is likely to be trouble." Even as late as his twenty-fourth year, still living in Gardiner, he told a friend: "Here I am, shut in by myself with only one or two people in town that I care two snaps of my finger for (and who, in turn, care about as much for me) with no prospects." He would be, he added, a "penniless *gent*": a poet, a gentleman figure whose identity would rely on his avoidance of conventional modes of self-definition. Like Hawthorne who, Robinson knew, had experienced a similar solitary moratorium in a nearby Maine town before achieving recognition as a writer, he defined himself through his romantic conception of the poetic role.

This claim for an identity distinguished precisely by its opposition to conventional society provided Robinson with the values, attitudes, and definitions which drove his poetry between *The Torrent and the Night Before* (1896) and *The Town Down the River*. But by 1910 a complex of societal drives which had lain dormant while he remained in obscurity combined to threaten the belief in private distinction through which he had given himself identity.

The first of these drives consisted in the separation in America between wealth and culture. Celebrating on the one hand material progress, the accumulation of wealth or power, Americans on the other raised the artist to a position of prominence as a seer or sage who could preserve culture for a civilization whose chief goals tended otherwise to abrogate wisdom, sensibility, or reflection. This paradox of American culture had become, indeed, a major subject for the very writers whom Americans placed in the position of sage: Emerson, Lowell, Bryant, Whittier, Hawthorne, Holmes, Whitman, and Howells. By the mid-nineties all were dead but Howells. Never before, however, had the abyss, and the tensions, between civilization and culture been so absolute. From all quarters the cry, reminiscent of that in the 1830s, for the appearance of new sages—those "prophet-voices that appealed so powerfully to the moral consciousness of the generation before our own"—was heard. "How we have longed," one critic wrote, "for the indignant words of protest that our Whittier or our Emerson or our Lowell would have voiced had their lives reached down to this unhappy time." Robinson, too, had shared and voiced this sentiment. In a sonnet published in 1894, he called "for a poet— for a beacon bright / To rift this changeless glimmer of dead gray." He, certainly, had "indignant words" to utter. Whitman-like, he might put the "little sonnet men," false poets, and their false civilization to flight. Whitman-like, too, it would turn out that he was calling for what he himself hoped to be. "Beware of cleverness; think of nothing but greatness," he warned a friend—and himself—in 1897. That he sent copies of his first volume, in which his sonnet was included, to such recognized arbiters of public taste as Edmund Clarence Stedman and Richard Watson Gilder suggests the submerged presence in Robinson of a desire to be a seer for his culture. Moreover, following Howells, he moved to New York City to discover material appropriate to this aspiration—"the biggest conglomeration of humanity and inhumanity that America affords," as he grandly described it to William Vaughn Moody, for a time Robinson's rival for the role of sage.

Robinson, the evidence accumulated after 1910 shows, was particularly susceptible to the dangers involved in assuming this role. The desires for a position, material success, social status, and fame through whose suppression he had defined himself as a poet now revived chillingly and drove him to worship these strange gods. By 1910 he yearned for recognition, an altogether different basis of identity than self-definition through what the self opposes. "If only [the critics] had said something about me!" he told a friend. "It would not have mattered what. They could have called me stupid or crazy if they liked. But they said nothing. Nobody devoted as much as an inch to me. I did not exist." More and more he came to define himself by his reception. Indeed, even after tangible critical recognition—first in being treated at length in Amy Lowell's *Tendencies in Modern American Poetry* (1917) and later in winning two Pulitzer Prizes—he still yearned for a popular sale and admitted that he wrote *Tristram* "with my eye to the public" (and to a third Pulitzer Prize, which indeed resulted). He felt compelled to produce a volume every year. Increasingly a fear of poverty oppressed him, so much that even during his last illness when Ridgely Torrence spoke of the view from his hospital window, Robinson declared surprisingly that he didn't dare look out: "I found that when I did, I could see the corner of Welfare

Island and I couldn't stand it. Think of the old men down there, think of what is going on, the suffering, the crowded, dingy quarters, the loneliness." The best description of the changes occurring in Robinson after his recognition comes from his friend Chard Powers Smith: "With me he grew just a touch formal, socially correct. He made conversation on trivial matters, showed less humor; his chuckle became artificial. At the same time he spoke cautiously, choosing his words with care, and he would qualify comments with 'You mustn't repeat that,' or 'I wouldn't want to be quoted on that.' ... He knew I admired *Merlin*, and in June 1930 he gave me a first edition of it. I pushed it across the table for him to inscribe, and when he pushed it back he said, 'You can sell that for fifteen dollars if you want to.' He was immediately flustered by the unintended affront. It was simply on his mind that everybody wanted to get something out of him."

A second unforeseen element increasingly important around 1910 to Robinson's changing sense of his vocation related to the way that Americans conceived not of the social function of the writer but of the very nature of literature. The Puritan tradition, whose influence persisted, distinguished absolutely (as Thomas Hooker put it) between the "quaintness of language" which serves only "to please the niceness of mens palates," and "the substance and solidity of the frame . . . which pleaseth the builder"—that is, between aesthetic form, extrinsic to or ornamental in the work, and the logical, the moral truths about reality which it conveys. The result of this, of course, was that Americans asked their writers for both amusement and edification; but by refusing to understand or accept a relation between aesthetic form or language and the structure of reality, Americans forced intuition and cognition, perception and reality apart and, for the most part, obliged their writers to choose one or the other and write either poems without content or poems without context. Moreover, by 1910 Americans were no longer defining reality as God's universal design, but as the material reality of society, technology, and commerce, and asking their seers to edify them about this. On a higher level, even some of Robinson's close friends were deeply interested in scientific materialism. By 1910 his old friend Lawrence Henderson, for instance, had arrived at the conclusions which he presented in his Lowell lectures and later in *The Fitness of the Environment: An Inquiry into the Biological Significance of the Properties of Matter*, where he announced that "the whole process of cosmic evolution . . . is pure mechanism."

Now Robinson's early poems, as I have said, derive from the complex of emotional and intellectual opposition to material reality by which he had defined himself. His poems were saturated with his personality: he had, in truth, no other subject than his identity. Of all his poems, he wrote as late as 1927, only "Captain Craig had an external original," the "other people are entirely imaginary"—which was to say, himself. All his poems deal with the interior life, the identity which he had created; outer forms remained for him insubstantial and unstable. "You won't find much in the way of natural description," he remarked truly of his early work.

Thus around 1910 Robinson found himself accepted by discerning critics as a leading American poet while remaining unable to write the kind of literature his audience (and so now he) most desired. He was, as William Stanley Braithwaite was soon to announce in the Boston *Transcript*, perhaps "the leading poet in a nation of ninety millions of people," yet he was unknown to all but a few of his countrymen. He knew what "the age demanded," but could find no way to satisfy it; and unlike Pound he was not yet prepared to redefine those demands to accord with his sense of self. In consequence of his utter inability to resolve the conflicting demands of society with self, he suffered an intense crisis of achievement. Between 1902 and 1911 he drank heavily; and while alcohol concealed the tensions in his personality, it provided him no continuous reassurance that they did not exist.

In an attempt to resolve this dilemma through writing, he virtually gave up poetry for experiments with drama, just as Henry James, impelled by a similar paradox, had done during his own crisis of achievement in the mid-nineties. Robinson had spoken of writing a dramatic "trilogy [not] for the stage but altogether for the shelf" as early as 1904. These plays were to be "in my own particular blank verse, with a spatter of rhyme here and there." After the sensational success on stage of Moody's *The Great Divide* (1906), it appeared that the poet-turned-playwright might win the popular esteem which seemed necessary to Robinson. Before 1910 he had written two dramas, later published as *Van Zorn* (1914) and *The Porcupine* (1915). Receiving little encouragement and in a frenzy of indecision in which he revived the aims which had earlier led him to attempt a book of prose sketches called *Scattered Lives* in the manner of New England regional writers, he spent the next two years futilely attempting to turn his plays into novels. Yet he seemed only to sink further from popular acclaim. By the summer of 1911 Scribners had rejected the novelized *Van Zorn* as "too difficult and too far off the popular key," and (he told Hage-dorn) condemned it as "morbid, depressing, lacking in humor (oh, hell!) and god knows what else." Nonetheless, by this time, plunging on, he had already written three chapters of a novel based on *The Porcupine*. This too was rejected by several publishers; at last, in 1913 he declared his novels "extinct."

Still almost entirely avoiding poetry, where his conflicts of personality were focused—publishing no poems in 1911 or 1912 and only one in 1913—by this time he had already returned to drama and was hard at work on a comedy. He referred to it as his "Jack and Jill" play and detected in it "a real odor of the stage." "Since my violent reform of two months ago," he wrote to Hermann Hagedorn in 1912, "the playwriting devil has been after me with a red-hot iron." He had planned one play and had two more brewing, and he intended, he declared, to write at least a half-dozen, "for I am really bitten this time. I have been bitten all my life for that matter." Clearly he was writing under compulsions which he could not suppress. He complained to Kermit Roosevelt in early 1913 that he should "have the good sense to go back to poetry," but he could not yet either abandon his hopes for popularity or resolve the crisis of his personality through poetry. He told his friends all through this period that he knew he was throwing his life away on prose, but he could not do otherwise.

At last, in March 1913, he admitted reluctantly to John Hays Gardiner (and to himself) that "there is no immediately popular impulse in me": "When I come down out of myself and try to write for the crowd, I perpetrate the damnedest rubbish that you ever heard of, and I seem to have no guiding hand to let me know what I am doing." He would need to go back to himself, his poetic personality, to know what he was doing. Finally, in a resolution strikingly like James's decision* to "take up my *own* old pen again," Robinson told Gardiner: "At last I can see light again, and I am going to write another book of poems; and then I shall know to some extent what I am about."

---

* Though James's career provides an instructive parallel to Robinson's, I should make clear both that to my mind, they are far from identical, and that Robinson himself by no means understood the similarities between his own and James's development. He read the novels which James produced after his own crisis of achievement before he went through that crisis himself, and dismissed them, calling *What Maisie Knew* "the most amazing piece of preciousness that I have ever encountered," and later adding: "Avoid the *Sacred Fount*." Their careers did not, of course, coincide, and Robinson found a resolution of his own.

II

He might have said "what I am." For in returning to poetry he was reluctantly seeking to resolve the crisis of self to which, increasingly, acceptance and his desire for acceptance had brought him. He had failed to satisfy anyone, himself least of all, with his efforts to amuse an audience or to delineate material reality; and, like James, he was thus obliged to press further into the reality of self.

A full account of Robinson's efforts along these lines between 1913 and 1921 would include close examinations of the two different directions which Robinson took toward resolution. In the first he emphasized the mythic mode of reality beginning in *Merlin* (1917), and continuing in *Lancelot* (1920) and *Tristram* (1927). By temperament and experience Robinson was unsuited to deal imaginatively with the myth existing most responsively in the American mind, the Whitmanian myth of the Adamic man. W. R. Robinson has well summarized the character of Robinson's world: "no open road, no infinite vistas, no spacious America exists in the world as he imagines it; the frontier has closed. His scene is always a tightly contained space—a closed room, an oppressive community, an inescapable self, a universe forever doomed to be what it now is." His decidedly un-Adamic characters tend far more to reverse the state of Adam; each, like Fargo in *Amaranth* (1934), exists "as the last man alive, and without fear." Indeed, his characters have been compared to Beckett's and are remarkable anticipations of those characters in novels of the fifties and sixties who affirm either their lostness or what David Noble calls "the sinful brotherhood of mankind."

The myths which Robinson used in his Arthurian poems were more appropriate to his temperament and continued his tendency to oppose American myths. Unable to write a *Huckleberry Finn*, he could yet attempt a *Connecticut Yankee in King Arthur's Court*. Even so, at their best his Arthurian poems would remain insubstantial, a *Mont-Saint-Michel and Chartres*. Once, at the MacDowell colony, a young critic informed Robinson that his work was not sufficiently vivid, being all blacks and browns and grays. "Those are pretty fast colors," Robinson remarked. So, for all their lyric heraldry, Robinson's Arthurian poems remain distinctly unmythic: they have the substance, but not the thrust, of myth.

Robinson's alternate mode of resolution appeared in *The Man Against the Sky* (1916) and, in more limited fashion, in succeeding volumes of short pieces beginning with *The Three Taverns* (1920). To some extent, of course, such poems in these books as "Mr. Flood's Party" (1921) and "New England" (1925) constituted a return to the mode of the opposing self characteristic of his earliest poetry. But at their best the poems in these volumes merely assume a vague material reality and proceed at once to assert the reality of transcendence. He is not so much mythic as symbolic; not so much concerned with what enables man to exist as what presses him to endure. Like Henry Adams, who had attempted to synthesize material necessity and physical law with the ego and the freedom of the imagination, Robinson here writes a synthetic poetry balancing the scientific materialism of the nineteenth century with the twentieth-century science of mind to disclose new evidences of human motivation and to make a teleology based on the dogged persistence of the human effort at understanding.

Robinson might have written his major poems in this mode during the remainder of his life, since it potentially offered him a resolution for his personality crisis, essentially a crisis of imaginative integrity. Through this mode, clearly, he was able to circumvent the tensions of his identity by denying the priority of self through creating a cosmology of transcendence, the effort at understanding uniting all men. In his own way he was following the line of development common in the careers of most nineteenth-century regional writers: beginning in rebellion and proceeding to acceptance—of historic process (like Edward Eggleston), of mysticism (like Hamlin Garland or Mary Wilkins Freeman), or of romantic transcendence (like George Washington Cable or Sidney Lanier). Robinson, coming somewhat later than these, with needs more intense, continued all three impulses:

> Between me and the sunset, like a dome
> Against the glory of a world on fire,
> Now burned a sudden hill,
> Bleak, round, and high, by flame-lit height made higher,
> With nothing on it for the flame to kill
> Save one who moved and was alone up there
> To loom before the chaos and the glare
> As if he were the last god going home
> Unto his last desire.

As is characteristic of this mode, Robinson's opposing self disappeared and to his friends' surprise he even began to talk nostalgically of the period between 1865 and 1914.

But Robinson did not continue wholly, or in his major work, to emphasize the reality of transcendence. He was truly, perhaps, not inclined temperamentally* to do so, but had only been driven to this mode by a need somehow to integrate his ego. After the publication of *The Man Against the Sky*, however, two events, one communal and the other personal, brought him to face directly the question of identity, and to suffer a revived crisis of achievement.

The first event was what Robinson called "the Great War." World War I, many people, young and old, felt, destroyed the institutions, the ideas, and even the sensibility of the period 1865–1914. Edith Wharton, for instance, pointed to the "successive upheavals which culminated in the catastrophe of 1914" as impelling her to write *A Backward Glance*, her autobiography; for she was obliged by it to attempt to save, through literature, what had been lost through history, the past which the war had sheared from the present.

Robinson's response was very different: he experienced the war as a release. He mildly and sympathetically criticized Thomas Sergeant Perry for clinging to his "Victorian memories": "He knew, like many others, that the Great War had carried away with it the world that he had known, and in which he had best belonged; he knew also that time was at his heels, and that the new world would somehow take care of itself without him. He was undoubtedly more at home with his Victorian memories than with his twentieth century questionings and apprehensions. . . ." Deeply affected by the war, Robinson possessed anew the "twentieth century questionings and apprehensions" which he had begun to raise in the mid-nineties; and he would make a new order of the disorder which was now, again, vividly before him.

A year after the end of the war, with the changes which it accelerated everywhere apparent, Robinson was encouraged by friends to prepare a volume of his collected poetry. By its very nature, for any poet, this task is retrospective; and for Robinson in 1920, feeling his poetic powers not only undiminished but even liberated by social change, and continuing to be compelled to write, the second crisis of achievement which it directly instituted was particularly intense. For he was thus obliged to consider, through a close inspection of the work he had accomplished, what he might yet achieve. "The crisis of generativity," as Erikson writes, "offers [the person] either promise of

* Early in his life, before these needs were manifest, he had confided to a friend that from Josiah Royce's lectures on "Absolute Idealism" he had gotten "absolutely nothing."

an old age that can be faced with a sense of integrity, and in which he can say, 'All in all, I would do this over again,' or confronts him with a sense of waste, of despair."

Robinson was neither contented nor in despair. At first hesitant to undertake a collected volume, he soon began thoroughly to revise his early works. Early in 1921 he asked a friend to "tell me which of the poems you dislike most," adding: "I am tempted to make a pretty thorough job of it, and yet, if I do so, I'm afraid there won't be much left." He rejected some poems as beyond revision or unsuited to carry his new sense of his poetic self, and revised the rest heavily. Even *Captain Craig* (1902), the poem best representing Robinson's sense of self during the first phase of his work, had been considerably altered as early as 1915, when Robinson began to undertake a new self-definition. He now spoke of his early poems as "grilling exercises" which only prepared a foundation on which to make a new style, and he predicted ironically (but with psychoanalytic accuracy) that his collected poems would be manufactured from "the gray fibre of E. A. R.'s unhappy soul." Even though he rearranged the chronology of his work, placing *The Man Against the Sky* first to suggest that the mode there achieved provided the perspective by which his whole work, now revised, was to be judged, the *Collected Poems* (1921) is, rather, the first product of his second crisis of achievement, which would lead him to a new definition of personality and reality in nine long narrative poems. Yet as the *Collected Poems* were completed for the press, he still hesitated at the prospect of the change implied in his harvest. It might be a "neat finish," he wrote, "if I were to be struck by lightning this summer at Peterborough." But he would go on.

III

The first poem in this series he fittingly titled *Avon's Harvest* (1921). Though he referred to it as his "metrical dime novel," and so hinted at the connections between this period and the time when he had sought to resolve his crisis through fiction, *Avon's Harvest* was by no means a return to the dilemmas which Robinson had then found no means of solving. Avon sits with the narrator in the library. "He calls it that, you understand," Avon's wife explains, "Because the dictionary always lives here." Once inside this room where the dictionary "lives," and where men live in words, Avon locks the door.

All of the heroes of Robinson's late narratives are similarly locked into the solitary room of self, equipped with language; they are locked out of time and caught in the twinkling maelstrom of the consciousness, where language alone can unlock the door to the self's secrets. As Avon describes the compulsions which possess him, the narrator "Essayed the dictionary on the table, / Wondering if in its interior / There was an uncompanionable word / To say just what was creeping in my hair." The story which he tells of this encounter—the poem itself—is his demonstration that in the lexicon of consciousness he has found the proper words.

We should remind ourselves that by 1921, when *Avon's Harvest* appeared, Henry Adams' *Education* (1918), Sherwood Anderson's *Winesburg, Ohio* (1919), and Freud's *Beyond the Pleasure Principle* (1919)—books dealing with the life of the imagination—had all recently come out. Published in the same year as *Avon* were Yeats's *Michael Robartes and the Dancer*, Lawrence's *Psychoanalysis and the Unconscious*, Freud's *Group Psychology and Analysis of the Ego*, Pirandello's *Six Characters in Search of an Author*, and Proust's *Guermantes Way*. But the following books had not been published when Robinson's narrative of the mind appeared: Joyce's *Ulysses*, Lawrence's *Fantasies of the Unconscious*, Eliot's *The Waste Land*, Cummings' *Enormous Room* (all in 1922), nor had Stevens' *Harmonium* (1923), Freud's *The Ego and the Id* (1923), Rilke's *Duino Elegies* (1923).

Robinson's exploration of the self in a series of narratives beginning in 1921, then, was related to a world-wide movement in literature and stood near its inception. In common with other American poets, though earlier than the rest, he thereby helped to make what Louis L. Martz calls "the poem of the mind" the essential form of modern poetry.

He learned to do so not from fellow poets or from the psychoanalytic studies that Freud and his co-workers were publishing—he told an interviewer "that psychological observation in his poetry was accidental"—but in resolution of his own identity; his poem of the mind resolved at last the tensions rising from his crisis of achievement, partly concealed and partly circumvented, lasting between 1910 and 1920. The resolution of his crisis of achievement was in the new kind of poem he learned to write. The narrative poems were the personality he had made, and to preserve it he was driven to produce

them in a steady stream. Near the end of his life he remarked to
Esther Bates: "People ask me why I do not do the short poems any
more. I can't. They don't come any more." He was silent for a few
moments, then he said again, sadly, "They don't come." On his own,
and on native grounds, he discovered what Henry James had learned
much earlier. Reviewing a Howells novel, James had announced that
the subject characteristic of American writing was the ability of the
writer to *perceive* whatever his subject may be. Howells, he says, "reminds us how much our native grown imaginative effort is a matter of
details, of fine shades, of pale colors, a making of small things do great
service." American writers, he strikingly remarks, "have to take what
we can get"—themselves, in the act of perceiving what else than self
might be perceived around the rim of self.

By taking perception of self as his subject Robinson turned the
conflicting elements of his own identity into materials for poetry.
Earlier defining his ego by what it opposed (that is, what the self
saw) and later by what it transcended (what it knew), he now defined the ego by the process through which it saw or knew reality.
He thus redefined his place in the tradition of the American sage; not
Emerson or Whitman, but Hawthorne and Emily Dickinson—at this
period being rediscovered and reappraised—became his models for (in
James's phrase) "our native grown imaginative efforts." Echoing
James's remarks, "I tread a narrow path," Robinson wrote a friend,
". . . but I do a considerable amount of observing." This led him, he
said, to analyze "human nature from many points of view."

Now he took a step beyond this to understand human nature as
consisting in a succession of points of view. In moments of individual
crisis, he saw (for he had learned this of himself), the whole lifelong sequence of perception or knowledge defining the self might be
compressed and epitomized. Seeing this, Robinson could resolve the
dilemmas inherent in the American separation of reality and truth.
For he could thus assert that the truth of reality was the process whereby it was lodged in the mind and ultimately in the whole personality.
Language, as the key which opens the door of self—the room where
the dictionary "lives"—is thus one with reality: both create and disclose the process of mind which is the personality. In consequence
Robinson invented an aesthetic form in which the renderings of language and material phenomena are identical; both have meaning only
in the context of the mind's reality. "I have about come to the con-

clusion that timidity is the besetting sin of the American mind," he wrote to Edith Brower. "We can face germs and Germans, but we get behind the nearest tree at the approach of anything that really is." Robinson's inability to deal with "germs and Germans" allowed him to redefine the poet's activity as the saturation of personality, that which "really is." His decade-long personal crisis of achievement thus became the subject for the major poetry he was thereafter to write. Again and again he would project his own crises of achievement into characters obliged, in a similar extremity, to give up the security of the phenomenal world and confront, as Robinson had done, the process of mind where resided the only meanings which the phenomenal could have. Neither what allows man to exist (the theme of "Captain Craig"), nor what forces him to endure ("The Man Against the Sky"), nor "what will suffice" (Wallace Stevens's theme), but what gives existence, endurance, and sufficiency to human life—the engagement of mind with itself—was the subject Robinson now took as his own. He would neither explore, like Williams, "not ideas, but in things"; nor even, as Conrad Aiken described Robinson's mode, "not things but the ideas of things," but instead the individual on whose personality people, beliefs, institutions, and emotions had had decisive effects. He was not interested primarily in the truths discovered by his characters or himself—he persisted in telling students that only his poetry, not his "philosophy" (if he had one) was important—for like Hawthorne, he knew that too much truth could destroy the ego's flexibility. Like Zoë's sword (in *King Jasper*) truth may destroy. One day Robinson appeared in his friend Ridgely Torrence's apartment. "A man just called on me who wanted to tell me the whole truth," he said. "He ought to be killed!" Truths live for the seeking of them, the effort at knowing which creates, for a moment, a heroic image of self.

Robinson's early "grilling exercises" in composition and his revisions of the *Collected Poems* now issued into a poetry remarkable both for its variety and compositional precision. Done partially with an eye on Tennyson's work, his Arthurian poems had taught him narrative design, which he could now put to experimental uses. "As a rule," he wrote L. N. Chase, "I see the end of a thing before I begin it (if I don't see it then, I am likely never to see it) and the rest of the process is simply a matter of how the thing goes." Increasingly skillful in architectonics, he learned to focus his poems on the progress of the characters, on "how the thing goes."

He made them go, primarily, by developing compositional methods adequate to render the flux of speculation and conjecture, of changing minds, unstable identities. Amy Lowell mistook this for his attempt to "voice the contradictory elements of the American character"; but Robinson himself voiced the proper corrective in warning a student in 1931: "nothing of an infinite nature can be proven or disproven in finite terms . . . and the rest is probably a matter of one's individual ways of seeing and feeling things." From New England culture and regional writing he had absorbed the habits of what C. H. Foster calls "New England doubleness"; now he fully made this a principle of his composition. Stylistically, the habit of altering perspectives allowed him to join the streaming varieties of experience: the elegiac and ironic, the anguished and mirthful, the colloquial and formal, the obscure and banal. This was certainly not contradiction, nor quite even what Mark Van Doren described as Robinson's ability to see "life in that profound perspective which permits of its being observed from two angles at once." Rather, his style defines character through its sequence of responses, incongruous but for their continuity in one being, where neither contradiction nor incongruity —only ambiguity—exists. Emerson had argued for the incompleteness of logical propositions by pointing out that "we cannot strongly state one fact without seeming to belie some other." But Robinson is on the one hand radically anti-dialectical in his refusal to recognize logical relations between phenomena, while on the other he is remarkably unitive in accepting the sequential hum of responses as providing a genuine unity of the self. His type of "poem of the mind," therefore, was dramatic, not meditative, not devoted single-mindedly to the integration of memory, understanding, and will; these faculties, in Robinson's work, number only three of the affective responses possible to the insatiable self. The "doom" for Robinson's characters, as Penn-Raven remarks in *Roman Bartholow* (1923), "is to see . . . . / Your doom is to be free."

IV

A sufficient number of figures resembling Captain Craig appear in Robinson's late narratives to allow us to measure the distance which he has come since his early poems. In *Roman Bartholow* the Craig figure is bifurcated into the analyst and the wise man. Penn-Raven, who has restored Roman Bartholow's joy in life, is a "resident saviour" and as the poem opens is preparing to depart: "There would be always locusts and wild honey / Enough somewhere." Umfraville, who will replace Penn-Raven (as conjecture follows logic), has some of Craig's Christ-like attributes and speaks in his accents. He describes himself:

> *Say it was one who laughed when others laughed*
> *And thereby kept a sorry craft afloat*
> *That else had foundered or been strangely missing;*
> *Say it was nature's inadvertency*
> *Confessed in one on whom there were few men,*
> *And fewer women, to look humanly,*
> *And one that only dogs could ever love;*
> *Say it was one who lived again the past*
> *In books, where there were none to laugh at him. . . .*

Fernando Nash, the hero of *The Man Who Died Twice* (1924), is another such figure, in his present incarnation,

> *an inferior mystery that had yet*
> *The presence in defeat. At a first view*
> *He looked a penitent Hercules, none too long*
> *Out of a hospital.*

So in appearance is Malory in *The Glory of the Nightingales* (1930), "a man scratched, a gentleman gone down, / And going still." Dr. Quick in *Talifer* (1933) is another, though somewhat chastened; but the Tavern of the Vanquished in *Amaranth* (1934) is populated almost solely by Craigs—"philosophers who delve and starve / To say again what others have said better," "divines / Who long ago lost their divinity," "deceived inventors" who grope for bridges "Between their dreams and their discrepancies"—

> *And with all these there are as many others*
> *As there are lives that are not to be lived—*
> *Not here—but should have been, or many of them,*
> *And well enough, had they been lived elsewhere.*

But in these narratives the focus is no longer on the wisdom residing in the man alienated from ordinary convention—"the abhorred iconoclast," as Craig names himself—nor is it even in what such a man can teach another. Indeed, the "abhorred iconoclast" is no longer the sole reservoir of wisdom: he is simply one of the many ways of knowing with which the main persons of the narratives must be engaged. Robinson has redefined the character who best represented his own resolution of identity as only one facet of man's sequential self.

The search for that multiple self, in these poems, has extraordinary variety. *Avon's Harvest,* where the narrator watches Avon obsessively consolidate his life's multiplicities into one compulsion, was followed, in succeeding poems, by multiform explorations of the entanglements of motives, people, and emotions possible for the self to experience and so to become.

The limits of such becoming are dramatized in *Cavender's House* (1929) and *Amaranth. Cavender* is the closest of all the narratives to being a strictly meditative poem. Twelve years before the poem opens, Cavender, suspecting his wife Laramie of infidelity, pushed her off a cliff in a rage. Since that time he has lived tormented by the uncertainty that she had really been unfaithful. Now, by an act of will, he returns to his house—the dark house of self—where he seeks understanding through his memory of that time:

> *It was not time and dying that frightened him,*
> *Nor was it yet the night that was around him;*
> *It was a darker night, and one within him,*
> *That others not himself were not to know.*

"Cavender, you are locked in a dark house, / Where you must live, or wreck your house to die," he later tells himself. For the moment, he believes it is his wife speaking, since his meditation has driven his imagination to recreate her so that he may seek knowledge of himself through her and one by one review the self-doubts which have led him back to this dark house. Like Matthias in a later poem, Cavender is an egotist, "the sort that owns and gloats," yet he has never, until now, understood what his ego is. Laramie, the projection of his own ego, insists that she cannot answer his question—as Robinson explained to Edith Brower, "she can tell him nothing that he doesn't know—though she does tell him things about himself that he didn't quite know that he knew." He must give up the question and explore instead the process of knowledge and the nature of his self. Still tormented by his need to justify his actions, he yet begins to understand that he, not she, is responsible for the desire to be justified which has possessed him. Accepting his own guilt, not so much for

Laramie's death as for the self-ignorance which caused it, he begins, as the poem ends, to open his dark house to understanding,

> *coming like a stranger, slowly,*
> *Without a shape or name, and unannounced—*
> *As if a door behind him in the dark,*
> *And once not there, had opened silently,*
> *Or as if Laramie had answered him.*

If *Cavender's House* ends with the prospect of imagination generated by meditation, *Amaranth*, which Robinson called "my nightmare poem," dramatizes a wild phantasmagoric adventure which ends at the rim of understanding. *Cavender* is gothic and ratiocinative in tone and form, resembling tales by Poe and Hawthorne, while *Amaranth*, fantastic and surreal, has overtones of *Mardi* and *Pierre* and is a Dantean journey through the vividly-lighted rooms, streets, and houses of the mind. There the traveler Fargo meets the crowd of misfits who have lost their souls by losing faith in their vocations and thus faith in themselves. He himself has come, for the second time in his life—much like his creator—to a crisis of achievement, and he has destroyed all but one of his paintings. But he has only circumvented his crisis—again, like Robinson—for ten years, and his memory of his work mixes with his suppressed yearnings for true achievement. He falls into a sleep and dreams:

> *"Where have I seen all this before, I wonder,"*
> *Said Fargo to himself; and Amaranth,*
> *Appearing, answered:*
>   *. . . "You were here before,*
> *But you had then your zeal and ignorance*
> *Between you and your vision of it now.*
> *Since you are here to stay, you will see more:*
> *You will see memories that you may have felt,*
> *And ecstasies that are not memories yet. . . ."*

Fargo wanders through the levels of his self—Freud's *New Introductory Lectures on Psychoanalysis* was published in 1933—ego, superego, and id, exploring aspects of himself by projecting them as personages, even seeing his own wish for "disaster and extinction" made visual in "soiled and uncouth shapes, and . . . lewd faces /

Watching him with a glee that had no mercy." He passes through representations of alienation, faithlessness, egotism, despair, and the pleasure-principle—I am here schematizing as this brilliantly-realized nightmare does not—in preparation for looking into the eyes of Amaranth. If Amaranth symbolizes reality, it is one, Fargo has come to learn, which consists in the whole sequence through which he has gone. In Amaranth's eyes, then, he will see the process of his own remaking, his revivified self. Finally, in the light of dawn, while "the world around him flamed amazingly," Fargo sees the shadows of his dreams fading. "You are wiser now / For your return," Amaranth says, "You will not come again." Forms of his own imagination, they have now become part of his memory and provide the basis for whatever understanding he will achieve.

Between the limits of self-investigation—through memory which leads to imagination and imagination which creates understanding—dramatized in these poems, Robinson's other narratives operate in ways almost as different from one another. Fernando Nash, whose life-history is reported in *The Man Who Died Twice*, has experienced a crisis of achievement similar to Fargo's and burned his symphonies. His vision of his own failure grows from the same sensibility through which his achievement came, and destroys it. For twenty years he has lived in "the Valley of the Shadow," with the extinction of self. But at the last, only a year before the narrator sees him playing the drums in a sidewalk Salvation Army band, Nash experiences, inwardly, a symphony such as had only once or twice been written. Precisely because he no longer has the creative energy to write it down, he now experiences his music as a process—not as an achievement, as a signal of the self's status, but as a sign of being. The symphonies which are written down perish while the symphony of the mind still sings vividly before him and allows him, by losing the self in the process of self-making, to achieve his identity. He "found his whole fragile armor of negation / So tattered that it fell away from him."

The focus of the poem, of course, is ultimately not on Nash, but on the narrator, an empiricist and determinist, whose philosophy Nash brings radically into doubt. "How do you know," Nash responds to his empiricism, ". . . What have you done to know? / What have you been that you should think you know?" But Nash himself becomes an aspect of the narrator's altered mode of knowing. For while the narrator remarks that his tale itself offers "more . . . than the confirmable," in the narrator's experiencing of it the tale has undeniable truth. Thus he concludes: "So I believe,"

> Though at first,
> And many a time thereafter my persuasion
> May well have paused and halted, I believe
> Today that all he told me for the truth
> Was true.
>
> .   .   .   .
>
> I believe him
> Today as I believed him while he died,
> And as I sank his ashes in the sea.

The Man Who Died Twice, then, is an epistemological parable of the shift of the narrator's sensibilities from phenomena to the process of knowledge. *King Jasper* (1935), the last and the weakest of these narratives, seems to be pushing toward the same conclusion. Robinson called this poem his "treatise on economics": the idea for it came to him during the "bank holiday" following the inauguration of Franklin Roosevelt in March 1933. Clearly enough, he was attempting to dramatize the persistence of knowledge—the truths of the self—however knowledge may be suppressed by the societal ignorance of states, nations, communities, and institutions. But probably from reluctance in treating the theme in contemporary terms and from a sense that the material itself was inferior for his kind of poetry, he treated it allegorically. Thus, through Zoë, knowledge, alone endures the cataclysm which consumes capitalists and communists alike, nothing is affected by her endurance. At the conclusion "Nothing alive / Was left of Jasper's kingdom. There was only / Zoë. There was only Zoë—alone."

Four of Robinson's narratives, however, have the encounter with truth abundantly, and very differently, as their subject. These are *Roman Bartholow, The Glory of the Nightingales, Matthias at the Door* (1931), and *Talifer*. All deal with marital relationships. Malory, the main personage of *The Glory of the Nightingales*, begins, like the narrator of *The Man Who Died Twice*, as a character who has established ego-strength (but also rigidity) through belief in scientific materialism: "Man, even if not divine," he asserts, "is mechanism," and the imagery of his thoughts is taken directly from the *Origin of Species*. Still, this belief, combined with his compulsive fixation on killing Nightingale, has preserved him. By the end of the poem, however, both his materialism and his compulsions are wiped from him by experience; and he begins again with a self released, possessing

> . . . the lonely joy of being alive
> In a good servitude, and of not being
> Obscurely and unintelligibly wasted.

While Matthias—the successful man who, Robinson remarked, "assumed that he was perfect until he discovered that he wasn't"— seems opposite to Malory in status, he is identical to him in self-delusion. Egotistical, believing (as Timberlake remarks) that if he "stumbles the world trembles," and complacent in his simple world view, he tells his anguished wife Natalie:

> "The trouble with you,
> And me, and a few millions who are like us,
> Is that we live so long to know so little,
> And are not willing then to know ourselves.
> Where are the mysteries in us that require
> So much dramatic fuss?"

No less than King Jasper's, Matthias' simple reality is a delusion. His friends and wife—Garth, Timberlake, and Natalie—die, each, as he passes through the dark Egyptian rock of extinction, leaving Matthias further intimations of the defects in his knowledge. He has not yet been born and, at the door of death, is turned back to begin life, "to search the darkness in him." Like Cavender, he projects at last what he has come to know into a voice outside him:

> "You have not yet begun to seek what's hidden
> In you for you to recognize and use.
> There's more of you for you to find, Matthias,
> Than science has found yet, or may find soon."

Before he can close the door of death behind him he must open the door of self. He begins only with "memory / Guiding him as it might." But he begins to live.

Talifer, of course, is the comic episode of the marriage-group, an evidence of the range of Robinson's powers in dealing with the varieties of self-experience, here with the lightest of touches. Talifer rejects

Althea, a woman richly endowed with life-spirit, for the beautiful Karen, a woman of intellect whom Dr. Quick characterizes as an "ivory fish." "Let her be boiled or frozen," he says wittily (and wickedly), "Her feminine temperature, if she has any, / Would feel no change." Quick spirits her off to Oxford, where she studies philosophy and Greek and has "Dons following her like dogs, and ancient sages, / With a last gleam of evil in their eyes, / Watching her and forgetting their arthritis," while Talifer and Althea marry.

The history of Robinson's crisis of achievement which I have traced out here is epitomized in *Roman Bartholow*, a poem which he began to plan in 1910 during his first crisis. Not until 1921, following the publication of his *Collected Poems*, however, could he actually begin its composition. *Roman Bartholow*, therefore, spans the whole period of crisis I have described and was the forerunner of all the narratives which Robinson would compose in reflection of his solution of it. To my mind, moreover, it was the major product of his crisis, the best of his narratives.

Structurally the poem has the pattern of the double crisis common to most of these poems and best named in the title of *The Man Who Died Twice*. A year before the poem begins, Roman Bartholow experienced a sickness of mind relating to his ancestral heritage. Having lived all his life in his father's house—"Built years ago by one [of] glowering faith / In gold on earth and hope of it in heaven"—and identifying his self with his father's achievement, he married, only to see the coldness of his father repeated in his wife. This reinforcement of his suppressed differences from his heritage threw him into despair. "You are not the son of any father," Penn-Raven, an analyst-figure, convinces him, renewing his joy in life by removing responsibility from him. This, it soon becomes clear, is a delusion, a mere circumvention of the crisis of his personality. He has simply made Penn-Raven a substitute father. Still, from the first, even when most joyous, Roman has intimations that he has not filled, only buried, his emptiness of self:

> . . . now, with all this morning light upon him
> He looked about him with a life renewed
> Upon a world renewed, and gave himself
> Less to remembering an obscure monition
> Than to confessing an assured renascence,—
> Albeit his whim was once or twice to fancy

> *That if he stamped upon the footworn flags*
> *Beneath him, he should hear a sullen ring*
> *Of buried emptiness, like that wherein*
> *His endless and indignant yesterdays*
> *Had held him.*

The "buried emptiness" still remaining in his reconciliation with himself is made apparent when Penn-Raven seduces Roman's wife Gabrielle; once again the father-figure, in a new guise, punishes him and tears away his circumventions to drive him truly to himself. This poem is not so much a poem of the mind, where his conflicts may be hidden, as a poem of the personality, where they must break out.

None of Robinson's late narratives is obscure. They deal with few characters in simplified settings and use transparent symbolism in an all-out effort to focus on the experience important to one personality, and thus to make the whole poem a crystalline symbol of the manifestation of personality. What vagueness they possess is used with precision to suggest the complexity of relations which make that experience, and may make it meaningful. Only the compositional quality is dense, as the personality responds on all its levels to the flux of its experiencing. In no other Robinson poem is this quality of compositorial density so unremitting. Roman's past, his apparent reconciliation with it, his suppressed fears concerning the integrity of this resolution, and his present and remembered relation to Gabrielle, Penn-Raven, and Umfraville—these all come violently together in Roman's personality in his second crisis, where his false achievement of identity is exploded. His desires and his will, his memory and his supposed renewal, his illusions and his disillusions mingle and entangle, leaving him only with his "buried emptiness."

But precisely this becomes his new heritage: what he has is not father, friend, or wife, only the vacant, unborn self. Penn-Raven tells him what he must come to know, though he does not truly yet know it:

> *"You know as well as I*
> *That you are the inheritor to-night*
> *Of more than all the pottage or the gold*
> *Of time would ever buy. You cannot lose it*
> *By gift or sale or prodigality,*
> *Nor any more by scorn.*
>
> *.   .   .   .   .*

> You have played
> With life as if it were a golden toy,
> Till you believe that you have shattered it.
> To-morrow you will see that you have not."

Inheriting the spacious house of self, and finding it more and more filled, however tragically, by the experience to which crisis has opened his personality, Roman sells his ancestral house and goes alone (as Robert Penn Warren puts it at the end of *All the King's Men*) "out of history and into history and the awful responsibility of Time." The concluding lines, elegiac, yet trembling with anticipation, are among the best that Robinson ever wrote:

> He locked the door,
> Aware that even the key to the old house
> That had so long been his was his no longer,
> And in the twilight went away from there.
> Over the footworn flagstones and the gravel,
> Under the trees and over the long road
> Between him and the gate, he walked away,
> Knowing that he had seen for the last time
> The changeless outline of those eastern hills,
> And all those changing trees that flamed along
> A river that should flow for him no more.

V

Robinson wrote most of his late narratives during the summers at the MacDowell colony in Peterborough, New Hampshire. Each one left him exhausted. *Roman Bartholow*, he said half-way through it, "bids to finish me before it is done." After two months' work on *Matthias At the Door* his words were "all used up," and his head "so empty that it rings like a kettle when I pound it in a frenzy." After completing *Amaranth* he was stricken with a succession of violent headaches. And *King Jasper* was completed not long before his final illness and death. Yet, he said, writing these poems was as "easy as lying," and he proposed to produce one a year so long as he lived. "I had to do them," he insisted in 1932. Compulsively repeating the same poem in various narrative guises, he seems never to have been able to resolve his crisis of achievement except through them; and he never maintained it for long without them: annually he sought again his own resolution by projecting characters in whom such resolutions would take place.

"I'm glad that you are 'Knowing Yourself,' " he remarked ironically to Josephine Preston Peabody in 1914. "I've been trying to do something of the kind for forty years." He would continue to do so for twenty more, and would create, in poetry, a vehicle devoted to *knowing* far more than to *knowledge*, a heroic substitute for what he was unwilling or unable to know of himself. It was, in any event, a resolution of identity. And if in some part, his inability fully to understand what impulses drove him was a personal incapacity, one which he shared with all men, he turned it into a capacity for poetry in which, for others as well as himself, he dramatized the forms of resolution most available to twentieth-century man. He thought of poetry as a way of preserving personality and thus civilization. "The socialistic dark ages are coming," he told Edith Brower, "and the individual is going to 'wither.' " This explains why he remained cold toward poets whose subjects derived from society, groups, and classes, and spoke, for instance, of Auden and Spender as "for the youngsters."

Hermann Hagedorn, Robinson's authorized biographer, used as the epigraph to his biography Robinson's advice: "In the great shuffle of transmitted characteristics, traits, abilities, aptitudes, the man who fixes on something definite in life that he must do, at the expense of everything else, if necessary, has presumably got something that, for him, should be recognized as the Inner Fire. For him, that is the Gleam, the Vision and the Word! He'd better follow it. The greatest adventure he'll ever have on this side is following where it leads." Robinson had never himself followed his own precept. He had been obliged to shift and change. Like the heroes of his narratives he was often mistaken about himself, and he suffered over and over for his mistakes. But he made of his shifts a poetry that became for him at last the gleam, the vision and the word, and learned to follow that where it led. A character in *Amaranth* declares: "Poets, whatever the end, / Should know a little more than most of us / Of our obscurities." This was Robinson speaking. And this, during years of crisis, was what he had learned to do.

Bibliographical Note

The sources for this essay follow: for Robinson's poetry, the *Collected Poems* of 1937, and the first editions of the nine narratives with which I deal; for Robinson's prose, the introduction to his *Selections from the Letters of Thomas Sergeant Perry* (New York, 1929); *Edward*

Arlington Robinson's Letters to Edith Brower, ed. Richard Cary; and *Selected Letters of Edwin Arlington Robinson,* ed. Ridgely Torrence.

I have used the biographies of Robinson by Hermann Hagedorn and Emery Neff, the memoir by Chard Powers Smith, and the book-length critical studies by Wallace L. Anderson, Louis O. Coxe, Edwin S. Fussell, W. R. Robinson, and Mark Van Doren. In addition I have drawn upon the relevant parts of Denis Donoghue's *Connoisseurs of Chaos: Ideas of Order in American Poetry* and Hyatt Waggoner's *American Poets from the Puritans to the Present.*

Other books which have affected my treatment of Robinson are: Erik H. Erikson, *Young Man Luther: A Study in Psychoanalysis and History* (New York: Norton, 1958); Louis L. Martz, *The Poem of the Mind: Essays on Poetry / English and American* (New York: Oxford, 1966); and David W. Noble, *The Eternal Adam and the New World Garden: The Central Myth in the American Novel Since 1830* (New York: George Braziller, 1968).

Robinson's Modernity

J. C. Levenson

E. A. Robinson made an easy peace, though qualified by irony, with the poetic conventions among which he grew up, and so the Robert Frost epigram on his having taken the "old-fashioned way to be new" has usually been repeated with hardly any stress on the *new*. Though his traditionalism is no longer dismissed as out-of-date, the epigram still makes a difficulty. By *old-fashioned*, Frost meant to call attention to such timeless virtues as only the new-fashioned might miss. "Plain excellence and stubborn skill," qualities which Robinson ascribed to George Crabbe and hoped that his own work would show, have never been modish—nor can they be called modern, either. Yet the traditional and the timeless in his work do not mean that he is a poet for the ages only. Looking to tradition is his cultural habit and generalization is his characteristic mode of speech, but he is also a full-fledged citizen of the twentieth century. When he defines the present in relation to the past, he is trying to fix a particular present. And when he generalizes most broadly, he still is giving expression to a particular historical moment. Thus, in "The Man Against the Sky," he meditates on a grandly isolated man, seen looming against the sunset, who goes down a distant hill as if to death. General though the subject is, it places the poem historically. Even without explicit mention of world war, this is a poem of 1916: an ode on the very faint intimations of immortality that remained a century after Wordsworth. The man who descends to darkness contrasts with Wordsworth's child who stands in an aura of cascading light and cosmic reassurance. In the flame-lit gloom of Robinson's poem, an inward steadiness exists without evident bulwarks of spirit outside oneself—or even within. Except for one brief positive statement, faith is tentatively expressed in questions, or else it is implicitly affirmed by elaborate conditional sentences of which only the negative side is worked out. Now I do not mean to deny that Robinson in his later years had the poetic vice of liking to go the long way round, but in this case the method of tentativeness and implication is right for the poem. In the poet's meditative process as in his represented subject, darkness almost envelops the scene and the source of light is below the horizon of consciousness. There is an unfortunate touch of Dumas in his concluding dungeon image, but he could justly assert that his terrors are not of Monte Cristo but of the soul:

> *If after all that we have lived and thought,*
> *All comes to Nought,—*
> *If there be nothing after Now,*
> *And we be nothing anyhow,*
> *And we know that,—why live?*
> *'Twere sure but weaklings' vain distress*
> *To suffer dungeons where so many doors*
> *Will open on the cold eternal shores*
> *That look sheer down*
> *To the dark tideless floods of Nothingness*
> *Where all who know may drown.*

Doubt is certain, disbelief plausible, despair sympathetic, and hope obscure. These are the first principles of Robinson's imaginative world. That they have also been primary facts of twentieth-century life accounts, in my view, for the continuing modernity of his work. My argument is that he derived these principles not only from temperament and the circumstances of his private experience, but also from the cultural situation of his time. I believe that by fitting him into his milieu, we can recover something of his historicity and of our proper relation to one of the early masters of twentieth-century American literature.

The quality of Robinson's newness has almost always been a subject for argument. But by the time of his *Man Against the Sky* volume, he had fairly outlasted rejection by his elders, who genteelly deprecated his work for its prosiness and inglorious realism. Almost at once the tables were turned, and he found himself classed as obsolete by young men who denounced him as genteel and conventional. With his long look back to Wordsworth and the language and form in which he cast his latter-day Immortality Ode, he was identified with the nineteenth-century world whose passing he tried to measure. His juniors were tempted to think that Prufrock's evening "spread out against the sky / Like a patient etherized upon a table" reduced to triteness the old-fashioned sunset which, early and late, was a controlling symbol in the older poet's work. Within five years, Eliot was dismissing Robinson as "negligible," and all the disdainful young men joined in. Readers who were arrested by the highly dramatic language of Eliot's monologues felt themselves merely deterred by Robinson's slow-paced reflectiveness. His grave manner did not call attention to itself in any case, but when minds were tuning to the flashing wit of a brilliant modernism, his subtlety and strength were easy to miss. His being formal was misunderstood by those who were reacting against the politeness of polite letters. His tone of consideration and reconsideration led them rashly to conclude that he was stolid. Formality, thoughtfulness, and reticence concealed his emotional depth—though not from everyone. I would suggest that the most notable and interesting witness to the immediate usability of Robinson's art is John Crowe Ransom, who, in his development from *Poems about God* (1919) to *Chills and Fever* (1924), learned what one could make of a native bent for formality, thoughtfulness, and reticence. In his verse Mr. Ransom more than half mocked the qualities of scholar and gentleman which as a critic he could professedly admire—when the distance was right. His model *seventeenth-century* poets were, in words he might have spoken of Robinson too, "weighty yet idiomatic; polite conversationalists perhaps, who do not have to make speeches in order to offer important observations." Mr. Ransom has, of course, spoken up for Robinson directly, but the indirections are what best illustrate his acute reading and deep absorption of the older poet's art. And as different from Mr. Ransom as from each other, Yvor Winters, Winfield Scott, and Louis Coxe have also shown—by profession and by practice—how much there is to build on in this perennially unfashionable and valuable poet. But the fact remains that for about thirty years the surest way to praise a poet was to claim for him qualities that could first be attributed to a seventeenth-century poet, and idiomatic weightiness was not likeness enough. Harking back to Wordsworth rather than to Donne seemed to place Robinson, for many a young avant-gardist, as a creature of academic taste and presumptive gentility.

When gentility is a pejorative term, I suppose that it means being insensitive to experience and incurious about truth and not simply being well-mannered or well-educated. In that case, Robinson transcended the Genteel Tradition in the simplest way, by being immune to it. Notoriously not a revolutionary, he drew great benefits from the standing order of society and culture, and he discriminated accurately between benefits and liabilities. When we attempt a like discrimination, we can understand how he stood with the old America, middle-class, Republican, and confident of an unchanging domestic tranquility. His father, who first shifted the family from the artisan to the business class, no doubt helped instill in the boy an obsession for demonstrably —that is to say, economically—making something of himself; but Edward Robinson also read with his son through *Bryant's Library of Poetry and Song* and other books of his ample collection. Gardiner, Maine, reinforced the boy's small-town economic ethic and his guilty sense that poetry was not a decent calling nor art an acceptable success; yet Gardiner also provided him with a first-rate high-school education (including a little Latin and less Greek) among friends who were intellectually serious. The town, in his later view, hardly could number half a dozen people who cared for poetry. But among those few were the gifted amateurs, a homeopathic physician and a spinster schoolteacher, who welcomed the boy into their literary conversation and taught him the intricacies of verse; with their encouragement, he became the virtuoso of villanelles whose scorn for mere technicians had the authority of a master. And among the old and well-established families of the town were discerning, generous people who were quick to value him: after seeing *The Torrent and The Night Before*, which he had printed at his own expense in 1896, they sought out his company, they tactfully underwrote his next books at the publisher, and offered more direct support, they knew how to find him a job in Cambridge, they put him in touch with other writers when he went to New York. The well-known story of his rescue from demoralizing poverty by Theodore Roosevelt in 1905 recapitulates on a national scale the intelligent and practical openness of late-Victorian America at its best—just as Taft's new broom, which swept him out of his custom house in 1909, may stand for another kind of reality which was never far from Robinson.

Circumstance encouraged the poet to stay on good terms with the official culture, but temperament accounts still better for his apparent submissiveness. His youthful discovery of Whitman heartened him in his calling, but almost as soon as he understood the radically anti-traditional meaning of Whitman's work, he decided that his own way must be different. His was a nature that chose discipline, and through discipline he gained the freedom to speak in his own voice. Any other kind of self-reliance might have been disastrous, for it would have left him prey to his normal uncertainty of taste. For example, he seriously thought of ranking James Lane Allen next to Hawthorne, and he read *Stand Fast, Craig-Royston* and *Jude the Obscure* with the same reverent enthusiasm. He could easily have lapsed into mute inglorious provincialism if the prevalent culture of small-town America had not offered solid nourishment to the critical intelligence. As it was, he became an exacting reader of poetry by training his judgment on Tennyson and Arnold, Wordsworth, Milton, and Shakespeare, and beyond them on the classic writers of Greece and Rome. His literary education was simple, academic, and in some respects even meager. But it disclosed standards by which a young man could take the measure of his time.

As he proceeded to do just that, Robinson acted for the absolute inconvenience of those literary historians who like to divide the American scene between radicals and traditionalists, new men on the one hand and decadent respectables on the other. In the first place, he set himself ironically apart from the great national tendency to sing of fresh dawn and crow lustily over prospects. Even in his twenties, he was not young enough to find much to brag about. His early sonnet "Oh for a poet—for a beacon bright" announces that he can find no beacon among the flickering versifiers of his time. "To rift this changeless glimmer of dead gray," a true poet would "wrench one banner from the western skies" and take to himself the one available glory—of sunset. But while he rather undercut the chanticleer strain in American letters, he gave no comfort to timid conventionality in this sonnet in dispraise of "little sonnet-men." Having declined to cheer with American dreamers of unlimited possibility, he equally kept himself from the more temperate optimism of proper classicists. He had a little chill for either side, as he showed in his quatrain—

> Drink to the splendor of the unfulfilled,
>   Nor shudder for the revels that are done:
> The wines that flushed Lucullus are all spilled,
>   The strings that Nero fingered are all gone.

We may legitimately suspect that he enjoyed playing Banquo's ghost at the national barbecue. He had noticed of himself that the smoothest part of his face was around the mouth "where the only wrinkles of youth rightfully belong." But the quick wry grin has its own place in a nation of legendary roarers, and that place was not necessarily at the Saturday Club. As one who neither gave way easily to laughter nor ever altogether tamed his sense of humor, he managed from the beginning of his career to look before and after with equal eye. He splendidly chose as the epigraph of his first book: "Qui pourrais-je imiter pour être original?"

Given a critical acceptance of the past, Robinson proved that the supposed conflict between received tradition and direct experience need never occur. He simply assumed that one major use of culture was that it enabled a man to confront his destiny with more than his single strength. The tradition that gave him Hawthorne and Hardy scarcely led him to think that culture spared a man anything. On the other hand, he could not swallow the past indiscriminately. He gave up his early admiration for Browning's poetry because, he said, "its easy optimism is a reflection of temperament rather than of experience and observation." His own experience and observation led to a more somber view. The lifelong chronic earache which hurt so acutely and constantly that he sometimes feared it would drive him insane; the early, utter crack-up of his promising older brothers, one caught by drugs, the other by drink; his father's slow dying, accompanied by the spiritualist manifestations with which he managed to haunt his own house, and his mother's horrible death by black diphtheria, when neither doctor nor minister nor undertaker would cross the Robinson threshold for fear of infection; the alcoholism that fastened on him when artistic failure seemed as final as his poverty, and the heat and racket of his job as time-checker for a construction-gang in the New York subway—the list of ordeals could be extended, but length is not its proper measure. The quality of his experience depended on his making a discipline of suffering. As he fathomed his own powers of survival, he came to see in men's capacity to endure, the mysterious touchstone of dignity, and in their going down an equal mystery, "too far beyond the scope of our poor piddling censure to require of our ignorance anything less kind than silence." The habit of regarding human life *in extremis* conditioned his idea of reality in the literature of the past as well as the presented reality of his own poems.

Robinson's sense of the absoluteness of things has its complex origins in experience, temperament, and culture, but though such perception is old as tragedy, his mode of seeing was new. Before our own time men had been able readily enough to conceive a world in which "everything is to be endured," but they had been unwilling to reconstruct their idea of the tragic accordingly. It is very much of the twentieth century that Robert Frost should have adapted a phrase of Matthew Arnold's and declared that Robinson sang of "immedicable woes," meaning something like eternal truths. In a century of total violence, actual and threatened, poets have explored new regions of the unshakable once-and-once-only world where "nothing is to be done," and Robinson for one came to believe that endurance might stand out against the waste of life even when more practical affirmations could not. But not even survival was an unquestioned value with him. Exploring the last of doubts, at a point where he was literally engaged in the criticism of life, he found that he could not make meager joy balance out enormous pain, positing nothing beyond them. For one of his experience, he decided that for life to be worth living he must posit both idealism and immortality. He never became so much a philosopher as to argue his beliefs or so much a visionary as to elaborate their content; but the need not simply to believe, but to think through the meaning of his experience made him a meditative poet. Experience, not faith, was his subject; thought, not faith, was his way of handling it. That the resulting work should have coherent form, furthermore, was not an accident of genius merely, but the most important instance of Robinson's instinctively making the most of his academic education. And in this case, his debts were not so much to the past as to the liveliest and most advanced of contemporary thinkers. For Robinson's cast of mind was critically affected by his two years at Harvard, and by the great philosophic dialogue of William James and Josiah Royce to which he was eyewitness for a time. They, more than any others, provided him with the intellectual equipment for handling the irreducible facts of his experience.

Of course, Robinson was utterly candid when he said that he was not a philosophical poet to be read for his philosophy. He never wanted to be a philosopher, never developed the skill or talent to become one, never even fully understood how much his own thought depended on their speculative achievements. As a student he would happily have settled for the apostle of gentility, Charles Eliot Norton, whom he regarded as the greatest man on the Harvard faculty or in America for that matter. As a young man, during his Cambridge years and after, he was supercilious about the greatest collection of philosophers that has ever been gathered in America: he gave Royce's lectures second priority below Friday afternoon symphony, and he wrote of James as a "metaphysical funny man." Yet I believe that the arguments of Estelle Kaplan (in *Philosophy in the Poetry of Edwin Arlington Robinson*) and Robert Stevick (in "Robinson and William James") set us on the right track with respect to the philosophers who made Harvard resound with the clash of ideas. For James and Royce technical proficiency and even profound originality were not the only ends of their speculative careers. Their philosophies, as James once said, were like "so many religions, ways of fronting life, and worth fighting for." In their Thirty Years War of the intellect, they could not help setting the issues for young men and forcing, at some level of consciousness, a choice of sides. Young Robinson responded out of his constitutional need to compose the facts of experience for thought and to proceed only on a rational path toward supernatural belief. James's questions and Royce's answers affected him for life. The ideas with which they equipped him for his own reflections account for the largeness and the structural strength of his imaginative world.

James's energy usually set the direction of intellectual controversy in Cambridge, and his warmth kept the discussion focused on elemental human concerns. Two of his addresses of the nineties, "On a Certain Blindness in Human Beings" and "Is Life Worth Living?", specify topics to which he constantly recurred. His themes, taken up by Royce, were translated from what he gaily called "my crass pluralism" to terms out of the Hegelian idealist vocabulary. But James recognized what was different about Royce among the idealists when he spoke of his colleague's "voluntaristic-pluralistic monism." James did not hide his satisfaction that monistic Hegel should have been pluralized in the Harvard environment, but he never claimed influence. He generously granted, rather, how much Royce nourished his own mind, and he indulged himself in the notion that they might go through eternity locked "in one last death-grapple of an embrace." Something like that wish is fulfilled, I believe, in the way their ghostly presences survive in the imaginative world of E. A. Robinson.

In his essay "On a Certain Blindness," James defined our imaginative need to recognize human claims which usually escape perception in our myopic habit-crusted lives. He said what the poet was ready to hear, since Robinson had early decided that "widening the sympathies" was one effect of his personal isolation which could become in turn the moral aim of his poetry. What James did for him was clarify the theme and give it intellectual standing. The philosopher spoke of "how soaked and shot-through life is with values and meanings which we fail to realize because of our external and insensible point of view." But it is not James's rich sense of life shot through with values that comes through in the poet who worked towards the same general proposition from a base in deprivation and hardship. James's more negative formulation is closer in tone: "The subject judged knows a part of the world of reality which the judging spectator fails to see. . . ." Thus, the shallow business-like "dear friends" of the poet who kept asking him what he was going to *do* appear not only in his letters but in his poems. They become the typical witnesses to the stories he told, the chorus of townspeople who ironically miss the meaning of the tales they tell. The chorus envy Richard Cory, seeing his glitter rather than his humanity. They think they tell all when they give the outsider's view of unrequited love in "Eros Turannos" or of unmerited love in "The Gift of God." The irony is often compounded, furthermore, by the chorus being called "we" or "I," for then the reader's illusion of reality and his moral involvement in this human blindness are most immediate. Yet Robinson carries his dramatic manipulation only so far: the unreliable "I" of such poems does not entirely control what readers may learn, for the chorus with a limited point of view blends into a narrator who quietly presides over the story, not as a technical makeshift for passing information, but somehow to let us see both our common insensitivity and what it misses. But his departure from the dramatic mode reminds us that James affected the poet more by his expression of a common truth than by the metaphysical application he made of it. When we turn from the relative knowledge of the dramatized chorus to the narrator's quest for stable meaning, we see how James's influence is interlocked with that of Royce.

While James may be thought of as proposing the theme of moral blindness, it was Royce who provided the poet with a conception of what it is that the "judging spectator" fails to see. Challenged by James's reverence for individuality, and by James's charge that Hegelian idealists let everyone in particular be swallowed up in the all-inclusive Absolute, Royce devised the "pluralistic monism" which his colleague saw as complementary to his own philosophy. Royce's in-novation rested on his idealist analysis of individuality itself. His argument runs that our minds know an object only as it fits general categories that are common to other objects, and so we cannot be said to know anything that is truly unique; the unique can be known only to an all-inclusive Mind that transcends the human need for categories; so the idea of uniqueness implies both unknowability to human minds and the logical necessity of Absolute Mind. When the argument is reduced from metaphysics to plain poetry, we have the individuality of a Robinson subject coming through to us from an unknowing chorus who cannot see and an omniscient narrator who does not tell. The poet's problem is how, without saying more than he can know, he may convey an apprehension of his subject that is greater than the sum of what the spectators in the poem may see. This is one aspect of Robinson's effort to make, as he said, "a lan-guage that tells us, through a more or less emotional reaction, some-thing that cannot be said." His starting-point is a conviction about individuality. His fictional Hamilton says of the Washington he ad-mittedly cannot fathom:

> *It seems to me the mystery that is in him*
> *That makes him only more to me a man*
> *Than any other I have known.*

Assuming that he faced a challenging difficulty but not an impos-sibility, Robinson proceeded to set his subject in traditional categories and to keep us aware that our conventional ways of knowing give only partial truths. He thus presents Eben Flood as a Down East Roland, silhouetted with his jug as if he were winding a silent horn, and he requires that we discern both the mockery and the fitness of the heroic image. Such judgments on our part imply a larger context than the "time-born" categories of literary convention. So the poet has prepared us for the ending in which conventions and ironies are discarded; as Ellsworth Barnard put it, "the humor and the glamour go, and the world of unadorned fact is left." Yet when he gives us this sense of unadorned fact, he presents his subject not simply as dis-crete, isolated, and fragmentary, but as unique and somehow fulfilled by being part of a world where its existence and meaning can be apprehended justly. The loneliness of Eben Flood, though it transcends both his gross absurdity and his pathetic dignity, is less lonely in that its meaning is known. The organic wholeness of the poem, while our minds dwell in that context, stands for the wholeness of the world.

Context gives us the ideal whole, but poetic representation has to stay with the ordinary human world in which we encounter the blindness of most people and the impenetrability of the individual. "Richard Cory" is a useful example since the poem conceals its powerful particularity by appearing almost tritely conventional. But since the surprise ending of Cory's suicide does not, after a first reading, surprise anyone but the "we" of the poem, it is worth looking for deeper causes of its hold on readers. On the one hand, there is Robinson's tact in presenting the title figure. By his scheme, moral blindness is overcome, not by factitious insight into another mind, but by respectful recognition of another person. So he avoids the nineteenth-century, common-sense method of realistic characterization and gives us nothing of his subject's motives or feelings. He sketches in Cory's gentlemanliness and his wealth, but not his despondency, and he lets the suicide seal the identity of the man forever beyond our knowing or judging. On the other hand, he can characterize the chorus just because they lack individuality, and he invites us to judge their blindness on pain of missing the one sure meaning of the poem:

> So on we worked, and waited for the light,
> And went without the meat, and cursed the bread;
> And Richard Cory, one calm summer night,
> Went home and put a bullet through his head.

They do not serve who only work and wait. Those who count over what they lack and fail to bless the good before their eyes are truly desperate. The blind see only what they can covet or envy. With their mean complaining, they are right enough about their being in darkness, and their dead-gray triviality illuminates by contrast Cory's absolute commitment to despair.

"Richard Cory" is but one instance of Robinson's handling the question "Is Life Worth Living?" On that topic, he would have agreed with James that "The nightmare view of life has plenty of organic sources, but its great reflective source in these days, and at all times, has been the contradiction between the phenomena of Nature and the craving of the heart to believe that behind Nature there is a spirit whose expression Nature is." But James went on to recommend that we by-pass the tragic contradictions of natural theology; think of nature just as background like *weather*, "doing and undoing without end"; accept a pluralistic world in which spirit may express itself as a force for good among other forces, contending for mastery and calling on us to join battle on its side. Whatever the cosmic weather, then, we ought to exercise our right to believe and take sides with the power of good. Given the problem of evil in a God-ruled universe, what James prescribed for the theologically distressed was a radical change of metaphysics. To Robinson, who could no more become a pluralist than he could change his genes, James seemed to treat the human symptom but not to touch the tragic problem, and what is more, the Jamesian hypothesis seemed to him a fiction, a mere placebo. An unshakable monist, he could satisfy his own religious craving only under a system which dealt with all being as a unified whole. Royce's idealism fitted his need. Furthermore, Royce's temperament harmonized with his own, for the idealist had a tragic philosophy which made endurance rather than moral exertion the ultimate ethical value. Just as Mind was affirmed in the recognition of individuality, so Spirit was affirmed in the recognition of woe. Acceptance and courage rather than more strenuous virtues were called for by Royce's psychological approach to the problem of evil. What suited Robinson best, however, with his will to believe so nearly overmatched by his capacity for doubt, was that Royce founded his idealism on the very fact of doubting: his most famous contribution to philosophy was his proving the existence of his "Absolute" from "The Possibility of Error." This modern version of the ontological proof argued that the conception of error logically implied a standard of truth and a knowing mind to discriminate truth from error. Instead of assuming a world shot through with values waiting to be intuited, Royce began with a world in which nothing was sure but doubt and then, by the effort of logical speculation rather than the seeming-easy way of private insight, reasoned his way from doubt to faith. Assuming only the very opposite of what one wanted to believe, trusting neither perceptions nor feelings, one might still work his cautious way to affirmation encompassing all.

Royce's logic authorized Robinson to work out his own dark-side religious psychology, a kind of negativist revision of James. Where

James set up the healthy-minded once-born and the sick soul as stages towards conversion of the twice-born, Robinson developed somber parallels: he identified the once-born with the morally unborn, insensitive and egoistic; he emphasized that moral awakening might be the cause of soul-sickness, for sensitivity must principally be sensitivity to grief, of which the most likely consequence was all-consuming doubt; and having thus divided most people into the "comfortably blind or wretchedly astray," he put into his third and ultimate category "The Man Who *Died* Twice," once to complacency and once to despair. The hero of *The Man Who Died Twice* arrives at a dreadfully simple, though carefully respected, assurance that he has been born anew, but Robinson usually stops with presenting the inadequacy of un-faith. Illusion and despondency are his frequent subjects because they predominate among men; whatever else there may be he leaves to ironic implication. "The faith within the fear," Robinson declares, is what "holds us to the life we curse." What could transform his "Children of the Night" into "Children of the Light" would be the ability to cast off illusion without falling into belief that chaos rules the world: the task of declaring the tragic truth without being unmanned by it is symbolized in his injunction to "put off the cloak that hides the scar." And since truth-finding rather than conversion experience is the end he has in view, Royce's dialectic is even more important to him than James's dynamic psychology. The symbolic movement from false light through darkness to genuine light, however faintly perceived, does not occur dramatically through revelation scenes, but meditatively through taking thought.

Sometimes Robinson pursues his reflections to the point of philosophical abstraction, and then the poetry shows its intellectual workings more explicitly. Thus Merlin's special wisdom lies in a capacity for seeing the world from the vantage of Roycean idealism; he can perceive

> In each bewildered man who dots the earth
> A moment with his days a groping thought
> Of an eternal will. . . .

The malady of the race and of the time he sums up in a formulation which covers both the failure of belief and the moral blindness of human beings: though men objectively are parts of an ideal universal scheme, subjectively they seldom even reach the stage of doubts, for they are

> strangely endowed
> With merciful illusions whereby self
> Becomes the will itself and each man swells
> In fond accordance with his agency.

The illusions of self, while they mercifully keep a man from the awful qualms of theological anxiety, can wreck the world. The assertive will may keep men out of a psychological darkness, but the ensuing works of powerful men, each fondly thinking his partial cause to be the highest, brings down historical darkness over Camelot. But the philosophizing within Robinson's poems is usually turgid and ineffective; the benefit of Royce's influence is to be found, rather, in the generalizing which grows out of the represented action. The poet rightly concentrated on the world of experience; the function of philosophical ideas, as of literary culture, was to help him find order and meaning in the lives of men.

Robinson's speculative education affected the shape of reality as it is represented in his poems, and it affected the form of the poems as well. His preference for narrative over dramatizing techniques, so that immediacy is less with the event than with the thinking over; his concern for the organic unity of each poem, so that context might give poetic effect to even the plainest words; the dialectical progression that leads us past egoistic blindness and fond illusions till we confront even the most dismal truths, and confront them with acceptance and courage; the irony that affirms by indirection—these hallmarks of his poetry all testify that his thought helps account for the form as well as the substance of his work. All the technical elements converge in the poet's handling of symbols with such subtle casualness that they seem to operate almost below the level of consciousness. The emergent symbol has its cumulative effect without coming into focus in a climactic epiphany. It discloses its meaning, not in a single blazing moment, but through slow reflection; and as that meaning comes home, plain words and unpoetic subjects turn out to have been poetry after all. The basic anecdote of "Isaac and Archibald," for example, does not seem far removed from its prosy origin in the coincidence that two of Robinson's older friends each confided in him that he thought the other was slipping into dotage. The poet gave the incident a country setting and made it over as a boyhood episode, recollected in tranquility by a reflective story-teller. The boy goes with old Isaac to see whether Archibald, lamed by years, needs help in harvesting his oats; they find the oat field harvested smooth, they visit for a while, and after the old men have played cards in the shade, they eat supper and come home. Changing things thus, Robinson seemed to do little more than shape his material in accordance with century-old Wordsworthian conventions. His strength appears to lie simply in old-fashioned qualities like just representation and tactful humor. But the changes make the difference between an odd coincidence and an event in which the simplest facts may become symbolic. Walking, in the revised plot, becomes a constant underlying movement in the narration. The walking is unobtrusive "stage-business," a touch of realism; but in one local context after another the fact takes on meaning. The pace that Isaac sets is not explicitly heroic, but the boy sees the old man as striding along "like something out of Homer." In his short-legged, never-quite-surrendering struggle to keep up, there are emulation and respect that bespeak a kind of greatness. Again, when Isaac muses on the sadness of "being left behind . . . when the best friend of your life goes down," the language is so nearly trite that we may hardly notice the imagery of movement; but after the next pause on their road, the boy lets us see that the figure, far from being vague, is accurate, just, and intrinsic to the context:

> . . . *Isaac had a desert somewhere in him,*
> *And at the pump he thanked God for all things*
> *That He had put on earth for men to drink,*
> *And he drank well,—so well that I proposed*
> *That we go slowly lest I learn too soon*
> *The bitterness of being left behind,*
> *And all those other things. That was a joke*
> *To Isaac, and it pleased him very much;*
> *And that pleased me—for I was twelve years old.*

Woven in with the old man's blessing what he has to drink, even if it be only water, and the young boy's unconscious aping of his companion's solicitousness, even if it be unneeded, is the remark about being left behind which casually and lightly proves the earlier image to have been exact, though lightly handled. Life goes toward death, and the living are characterized by their relation to dying. The relation of boy to man and of both to life and death comes through forcibly on reflection, even though each separate touch that contributed to the picture has little intensity by itself.

The most vivid moment in "Isaac and Archibald" occurs when Isaac and the boy, after their long hot walk, go down to the cellar to refresh themselves with some of Archibald's fine cider. From the glare of the August sun, they enter the dark, and with that movement into the dark, a new and special sensitivity to minute details affects the narration:

> Down we went,
> Out of the fiery sunshine to the gloom,
> Grateful and half sepulchral, where we found
> The barrels, like eight potent sentinels,
> Close ranged along the wall. From one of them
> A bright pine spile stuck out alluringly,
> And on the black flat stone, just under it,
> Glimmered a late-spilled proof that Archibald
> Had spoken from unfeigned experience.
> There was a fluted antique water-glass
> Close by, and in it, prisoned, or at rest,
> There was a cricket, of the brown soft sort
> That feeds on darkness. Isaac turned him out,
> And touched him with his thumb to make him jump,
> And then composedly pulled out the plug
> With such a practised hand that scarce a drop
> Did even touch his fingers. Then he drank
> And smacked his lips with a slow patronage
> And looked along the line of barrels there
> With a pride that may have been forgetfulness
> That they were Archibald's and not his own.
> "I never twist a spigot nowadays,"
> He said, and raised the glass up to the light,
> "But I thank God for orchards." And that glass
> Was filled repeatedly for the same hand
> Before I thought it worth while to discern
> Again that I was young, and that old age,
> With all his woes, had some advantages.

Isaac is not a Down-East Ulysses making his descent to the underworld; the cider-cellar remains just that. The scene stays in memory because it is the graphic center of the story. Its significance is not to be intuited by classical analogy, but comes out through Archibald's rational discourse. When Archibald in his turn has the boy's ear, the old farmer discreetly states his worry that Isaac is losing his acuteness; but he has something else on his mind, which transcends that dismal partial truth and keeps weaving into his talk:

> Remember, boy,
> That we are old. . . .
> You look before you and we look behind,
> And we are playing life out in the shadow—
> But that's not all of it. The sunshine lights
> A good road yet before us if we look, . . .
> The shadow calls us, and it frightens us—
> We think; but there's a light behind the stars
> And we old fellows who have dared to live,
> We see it. . . .
> I'm in the shadow, but I don't forget
> The light, my boy,—the light behind the stars.

Archibald lacks the heroics, we learn, to be figured as a Greek hero out of Flaxman's Homer quite so easily as Isaac. He has, of course, harvested the oats that Isaac thought he had lost the skill and strength to do, and so in the world of supposed fact, he has proved himself a man on just as large a scale as the friend he loves. But in the context of the poem, he is lame and Isaac walks, and talking as he does of light and shadow, he seems to ramble more than the friend whose mind he thinks is aging. Yet he speaks a faith that Isaac has acted out:

> "I never twist a spigot nowadays,"
> He said, and raised the glass up to the light,
> "But I thank God for orchards."

In his casual talk he illuminates, after the fact, a casual gesture that almost escaped notice.

By the end of the poem the several images come together in a unified vision of life. The tired boy, resting in the orchard shade, has the sensation that all time is summed up at once, that the whole of existence may be comprehended as a unity. His fancy, filled with the landscape and the day's incidents, catches now and then

> A flying glimpse of a good life beyond—
> Something of ships and sunlight, streets and singing,
> Troy falling, and the ages coming back,
> And ages coming forward. . . .

And the "flying glimpse of a good life beyond" is not merely subjective in the boy's half-dreaming mind, for walking home with Isaac in the twilight, he sees the flaming sunset beyond the boundary of the forest horizon. Nature herself seems to confirm the image that Isaac acted out, that Archibald expounded, that the boy dreamed. The "flame beyond the boundary" is as much a reality as the man and boy walking altogether naturally together towards the night.

The genius by which Robinson made such simple, telling poems was his own. But if we wish not to be self-deceived in the face of his simplicity, it is worth an effort to see him in his historical context. Before we can do full justice to his particularity, we would do well to understand what he made of the literary conventions and philosophical conceptions that came to him ready for use. Like every major artist, he changed in using them the methods and ideas which were a part of his culture, and at this distance in time, we should be able to discern his originality as well as his traditionalism. Informal in tone, he could match any modern formalist in the care with which he made a poem. Realistic in manner, he developed a complex symbolic technique. He was a man of doubt who could not finally get round the absurdity of unbelief. And as one who knew what deprivations could do to a man, he hated sniveling and he honored honest praise. Apart from temperament and experience which made him responsive to the leading themes of William James, he saw life according to the conceptions of Josiah Royce. In his imitation of life so conceived, he had his originality.

Tilbury Town Today

Radcliffe Squires

Time gives us two different ways of looking at the poetry of our contemporaries. In youth we read that poetry as the truth of the present as well as of the future, as reportorial as well as prophetic knowledge. We are taken up, if we are lucky, by the modes of language which create the ruminant spirit of our history whose facts often fail to survive the moment of their birth. The facts sag away, but we are borne by the spirit into dim but paradisiacal guesses into the life of the future. In maturity we stand partly in a friendly territory of a few confirmed guesses and partly in an enemy territory, the existence of which we could never have imagined. We are no longer then among *our* contemporaries: we are among other men's contemporaries. We look back through time at the poetry of our time. And it is different to us. What had seemed a vocabulary of audacity may seem only the slang of bravado. The forms and tones that once squirmed for very life in our embrace may seem as static as poor sculpture, as finished and set as the verse of Tennyson or Dryden or Chaucer. The time is an unhappy one, yet we compensate for sorrow by claiming for it "objectivity," by supposing that at this moment criticism may really begin. Criticism comes, true enough, but not in the state of cool objectivity that we hopefully suppose; rather in a state of dual subjectivities somewhat at war with each other, somewhat neutralizing each other. The impressions of the past remain nostalgically monumental, but the chaotic present is running like a flood over everything. Somewhat at war within, somewhat demobilized by neutrality, I find that in the centennial year of the birth of Edwin Arlington Robinson and thirty-four years after his death, I see him as a quite different poet from the one I knew in my youth.

The fact is I could not but neglect Robinson's virtues at the time I first became interested in poetry. The flood running in the 1930s was not one to pay much heed to Robinson. Homage to his technical assurance, yes, to his "plots," certainly; but in one major way he seemed remote and unexciting: he seemed too much dedicated to direct statement, and his statements seemed to belong to some previous century. The poetry which particularly enthralled me and my friends was that of T. S. Eliot and of Wallace Stevens. Eliot and Stevens are dissimilar poets but in one way they are alike. They do not *assert* meaning or theme; they do not *achieve* it, not really, from the materials of their poems. They *assume* theme, and their poetry is an elaborate design embroidered on the cloth of an assumption. Their poetry is result rather than consideration of cause. Both Eliot and Stevens could move gracefully into their respective fields of surmise because those fields had already been surveyed and mapped. For Eliot the withering away of an aristocratic eminence in society and the attendant flourishing of Apeneck Sweeney (or Flem Snopes) were both incontrovertible and, in a masochistic way, exhilarating. The evolutionary myths of progress were turning back upon themselves. Retrogression, sterility, pluralistic chaos had become the new myths. For Stevens the two sources of his poetry—the scientific and philosophical subjectivism of this century along with the artistic subjectivism of the various modes of impressionism—presented him with his basic concern with a sensuous epistemology. In the 1930s these large assumptions floated like cloudy fates, pervasive determinations. In a way they seemed like one fate. For if the end result of civilization was emptiness—as Spengler taught—then perhaps all that one's life could or should be was an interior set of endless variations, endless combinations where the concrete became the abstract, the abstract became the concrete and whatever the state of being it was to be taken only as an arbitrary "state," water or ice in a glass, sensation or configuration in a mind, all of this conducting us to the delicious paradox that claimed beauty as beauty could only be immortal in the flesh. In short, the fatal and sterile subjectivity assumed by T. S. Eliot, raged at by Robinson Jeffers, became in Stevens' poetry a kingdom of the mind. The wasteland, the perishing republic which punished us extravagantly, could also reward us sumptuously. But Edwin Arlington Robinson's poems, modestly confined to lives which themselves appeared too confined, gave no such punishment or reward, seemed trivial, almost sophomoric. That, at any rate, is an approximation of my feelings when I first read poetry seriously. It is not my feeling as I look back from a present scene and view Robinson's poems through the haze of poetry today.

Poetry today is divided into a number of camps which, thanks to the natural ardor of their spirits, have not been able to avoid some miscegenation. Only two of these camps, however, seem to me important. Well, three, if one includes such poets as Allen Ginsberg and James Dickey, the shock troopers of a neo-Whitman army, accompanied by a barefoot Karl Shapiro dressed as a drummer boy. Yet both Ginsberg and Dickey are, despite the contemporaneity of their journalism, rather traditional poets; their rhetoric would not have astounded anyone in the nineteenth century. The two camps I have in mind derive from the complex of the poetry of the 1920s in the sense that they have stretched the preoccupations with decadence and epistemology farther than did Eliot and Stevens. They stretch to the breaking point. One school, sometimes called the "New York School," has, like Stevens' poetry, a relationship to graphic art. It bases itself on the latest manifestations of abstract painting. Words discover relationships less in syntactic logic, less in the structure of crises, than in the occupying of space. And since the field or space of a poem—or, is it the page?—is either infinite or infinitesimal, depending on how you view it, no question arises about the emotional largeness or smallness of the segments of the poem. Nor indeed of the poem itself. A poem does not mean, it occupies. This poetry is scrimshaw poetry. The second school, sometimes called "the poetry of protest," both accepts and rejects an assumption of doom. It accepts the assumption of historical decay, sees its manifestations everywhere. At the same time it rejects the history which has created the manifestations. It feels, in other words, that the present can save itself by dissociating itself from the past. The poet believes he has been dragged into some death bed where he doesn't belong. He never lived in the house, never walked up the stairs, step by step, into the room. It is difficult not to have sympathy for such a poet. Yet Oedipus (and surely Oedipus is relevant here) must accept the fact of his birth, of his parents, of his past, for these are his truth and his fate, the one being the other. He cannot dissociate himself, he cannot be saved by blaming badness on the past, on "society." This poetry is the poetry of "social science." My words contain doubt rather than hostility. And my only reason for mentioning my doubts is that they are a factor in my feeling about Robinson's poetry today.

Others have commented with justice and brilliance on Robinson's style, and I have no hope of adding new insights. Nevertheless, with Robinson's style my re-evaluation must begin. It must begin with the observation that the apparent conventionality, the seeming timidity of his verse have come to seem more and more original, more and more brave. Perhaps Yvor Winters always knew this, but few of us could have known this so well at any earlier time, for most of us could not have known that experimentalism as preached and practiced by Pound or Eliot or Crane would some day blur into a convention. We feel it is convention because the poetry cannot surprise, if only for the reason that we know that it is intended to surprise. All of the packrat gleanings, the allusions, the prodigality of images contract before our eyes into something as expectable as one of Pope's couplets. And the symbol, the mother of modern subtlety, becomes not subtlety but obvious device. But Robinson's poetry exists almost without symbols; it offers few images; it does not seek to make God over in the image of language. Its immense surprise lies in its humble poetic fact. It is poetry that has primarily the ambition to be poem; the ambition to convert the artesian sub-pressure of creativity into that which is created; the ambition to make the half-known truly known in the way that only the strait geometry of form can make it known. We can never say of Robinson's poetry, as we might of Eliot's, that it is becoming obvious, for in always intending to be obvious it remains mysteriously obvious. We can never say that his contemplative lyrics become small, as we might of Hart Crane's once we understand them well enough to count just how many eggs there really are in the nest, for Robinson always made his poems as mysteriously irreducible as they could be made. But that is not to postulate that it would be impossible to expunge a word here or there from the verse; it is to postulate that no one in his right mind would want to. The reason is not far to seek. The reason is the singular consistency of Robinson's language. As consistent as water. His poems do not occupy a page: they fill a vessel just to the top. To remove a few drops might not drastically alter the weight or substance. But one would know that the vessel was not quite used.

These are surface matters, but beneath the surface lies a very odd profundity: Robinson's remarkable modesty. It is as if Robinson, not wishing us to think he considered his insights superior to our own, politely refused to surround them with claims of brilliance. It is as if he suggests that his perceptions scarcely deserve anything more intense than the language of the polite essay. That one element of his poetry may in the long run turn out to be quite the most brilliant thing about it. Certainly, the calm susurrus of his "drab style," to borrow a phrase from Allen Tate, is not boring, but haunting; not tiring, but entreating. Yet the poems do not haunt to inspire terror, nor entreat to nail down our affection. They haunt and entreat because we are aware of their fine, natural courtesy, their unassuming intelligence. Even the apoetic operatives, the "albeits" and "whatevers" of the style, even the Latinate abstractions take us into their confidence. The lines do not bargain with images, nor do they parlay an image into a "chain of images." In some way, however, the whole style, language and form, creates one large image, not solely auditory, of a speech sufficiently calm to be sure of its grief, sufficiently ordinary to secure the grief from the inevitable temptation of over-dramatization. Such poetry never recedes from its climaxes. It keeps a measured but firm pressure through all its parts. Only such poetry can create simultaneous qualities of pathos and acceptance, as, for example, in the first section of "Romance":

> We were all boys, and three of us were friends;
> And we were more than friends, it seemed to me:—
> Yes, we were more than brothers then, we three. . . .
> Brothers? . . . But we were boys, and there it ends.

These four lines suggest that statement which is also understatement can obtain as much in the way of emotion and subtlety as can concrete images. The argument is not for doing away with images, of course, but for appreciating what can be obtained without them. Even beyond emotion and subtlety, one remarks that the bareness grants a grave honesty and a high confidence to the formal surface of the poems. It invests the rhythms with a quality of inevitability. It deputes a necessity to the rhymes. And those rhymes in Robinson's poetry close like hands about the ends of the lines. They hold on for dear life.

In a sense, then, the effect of this formal but drab style derives less from focusing attention on important predications than from refusing to distract from those predications. And so the substance comes forth in such a way that we call it clear rather than luminous, comprehensible rather than suggestive. I pause, smiling, to see that, still dominated by Eliot's power, I am unable to avoid describing Robinson's poetry in terms of what it does not do, rather than what it does do. My failing must now be remedied.

Let us return to the observation that Eliot works from an assumption. His soliloquies, whether Prufrock's or the committee members' of *The Waste Land,* take place, like important soliloquies in Shakespeare's plays, after the dramatic situation has been established. These soliloquies do not make the dramatic condition: they exploit it. Thus we may say that Eliot's poems depend on a dramatic situation but do not create it. And Eliot's method is unquestionably appropriate to his aim. Never arguing the truth of his assumption, he compounds examples of it. His intent being to intensify the drama, he employs richness, reiteration, and a complex linguistic mirroring. He is not interested in proving the assumption. Nor would his technique be appropriate to proof. The opposite is true of Robinson's technique.

The nearly bare, the nearly gray properties of Robinson's verse demand that something happen, that dramatic change occur. Even more important, these properties, in contrast to Eliot's, *permit* the dramatic change. Eliot's technique of rich, metaphorical demonstration thus can only properly lead to an effect of pageant. Robinson's technique can only properly lead to an effect of dramatic change. Eliot's poetry demonstrates a condition. Robinson's poetry proves a condition. At this point I think one can see why Robinson's poetry has never been influential in the way that Eliot's or Stevens' has been: because it proves a case, it has seemed to lose too much to reason. At the same time, however, one must observe that poetry which depends upon an assumption, loses a good deal of its power when the assumption fades. The poetry that proves its case, poem by poem, remains what it has always been. Its substance continues because it is created within the poem rather than by an external climate. But what is it, this substance that is both demanded and permitted by the tone and procedures of the poetry?

Robinson's poems, the best of them and those that will last, emerge from an awareness that life is continuously menaced: that innocence and experience alike are threatened by the bland modular construction of society and the soulless press of industrialism. Not that Robinson continuously harps on the menace. The contrary is true. His specific mention of materialism or industry could not be called frequent, and where we do find mention, the language, while clear, is not strident. Still, the reader recognizes the corrosive presence of a puritanic and materialistic society as an ambience about much of the poetry and most of the lives he considers in that poetry. Even the idylls, such as

"Isaac and Archibald"—seemingly remote and immune pastorals—are, like Wordsworth's "Michael," surrounded by a mundane ruthlessness only the more emphatic for being unstated. At this point, exactly here, Robinson's great theme appears. Oddly enough the theme has often been dismissed as being an "O. Henry ending," frequently as being "negative" or "bitter." Neither of these assessments is just. Neither is sensitive to the true deportment of Robinson's poetry.

Robinson is brusquely realistic about American social attitudes. He sees a life where emotion is not approved. He sees a life where imagination is suspect and where non-conformity expires early or evolves toward a painful eccentricity. Yet in the midst of these repressive proscriptions, Robinson saves life itself, for over and over again, he allows his Tilbury people to turn at bay and to fulfill themselves emotionally, imaginatively, and individually.

The word "individually" is of quintessential importance, for to accept this word is to reject the claim that Robinson was chasing after the melodramatic loot of surprise endings. The suicide of Richard Cory is not, or ought not to be, a surprise. It is an inevitability, predetermined by the subjugation of selfhood. Even more significantly, however, the subjugated self reclaims itself in the act of suicide. Not that the poem recommends suicide as a way of asserting individuality. Rather, it observes an extreme gesture in an extreme case. To see the poem in this way is to see it as neither bitter nor negative, at least not entirely so. We read ill if we cannot see that Richard Cory is granted an oblique triumph at the end, for he has refused to suppose himself made happy by what "everyone" supposes will make everyone happy. In short, Richard Cory's self emerges neurotically perhaps; still it emerges triumphant over the imposed role of "success."

"Richard Cory" is doubtless a convenient example for my purpose, but if it seems too convenient, one may turn to others. "Miniver Cheevy" is usually described as a mocking self-portrait, but such an observation tells us little about the poem itself. Indeed, such phrases as "mocking self-portrait" are usually a means of dodging a poem. I suggest that one must ask why Miniver Cheevy (*not* Edwin Arlington Robinson) prefers an earlier, more "romantic" era than his own, what it is that he loses, if anything, by being out of phase with his time, and, finally, if his anachronistic attachment is virtuous or vicious. These questions burden an admittedly middle-weight poem and I shall not burden it further with specific answers. Still, does not the sum of reasonable answers amount to an impression that Miniver's escapism is really an effort to establish an individuality which a world of "progress" denies?⌋

But possibly it will seem that I have added perversity to convenience. In that event one is directed to the poem "Reuben Bright" which is so unequivocal that no two readers are apt to differ greatly. And here we are definitely told that the world would prefer to ignore the essential capacity of a man for grief. But the poem continues on resolutely to detail not merely the delicately imaginative ritual of the butcher's grief, but most significantly to bring him to a gesture whereby he destroys the symbol of the world's idea of himself: he tears down the slaughterhouse. Reuben Bright's gesture is parallel to Richard Cory's suicide. But this gesture—which is also Robinson's primary theme, this stubbornly beautiful discovery of the self within, this ultimate insistence that individuality survives and in some devious way supersedes society—this gesture has also a parallel outside Robinson's poetry. It is the most important gesture in the American imagination, simply because it is the most necessary.

The acknowledgment that the self must create itself even as the railroad tracks unreel onto the land is the real meaning of Emily Dickinson's solitary room. The realization that the self must recreate itself—even if perversely and destructively in an inverted image of the Christian soul—is the real meaning of Poe's poem "Alone." All of Melville's "isolatos" are desperate, last-ditch preservers of self. His Bartleby has lost all will except one negative will—he "prefers" not to accommodate the vestigial soul to Wall Street. And even Whitman, the presumed celebrator of simple democracy, complicates his celebration. For even as he is touching everything, learning as an infant learns indiscriminately, he stops short to remind us from time to time that we cannot possibly learn him, that we cannot truly know *him*. He is not hiding a secret, he is saving a unique and finicky self.

But Edwin Arlington Robinson is not so hermetic as Emily Dickinson, not so upside down as Poe, not so renegade as Melville, nor so cryptic as Whitman. As soon as he had saved a soul from society he wanted to return it to society. And he did. He did this by the same means that Thomas Hardy—whom he admired—employed for a similar aim: he created a neutral, choral voice that murmurs above, below and through the lives of Tilbury Town. The knowledge of self, sacred grief, even of Faustian diabolism, is given through this choral voice to the town (New York City as much as Gardiner, Maine). It is given somewhat as a saint's life is given to be pondered by the conscience of the community of men, except that for Robinson, it was the sensibility rather than the conscience he wanted to affect. For this reason in his finest poem, "Eros Turannos," Robinson drifts away in the last two stanzas from the tortured wife and the "secured" husband to the commentary of the town, to his chorus. The chorus cannot absorb all of the pain that is pressed into the one devastating image of "the foamless weirs / Of age," but the chorus can take in much of it, can modulate the water image in another, diminished water image. In this way the chorus mediates in the classical manner between tragedy and society. One remembers that in his youth Robinson labored with his friend Harry de Forest Smith on a translation of Sophocles' *Antigone*. Like that drama, much of Robinson's poetry contemplates the problem of how the self might separate itself from a rigid society, yet remain as a tutelary spirit. In the end Robinson's decision would seem to have been that this could best be done by eschewing the dramatic catastrophes—vengeance, martyrdom—and offering instead temperate ironies, cool understatements and a language calculated, like Wordsworth's, to heal. This decision, as one looks back now from the present with its poetry of scrimshaw, its poetry of sociology, requires one to say that Robinson chose not to write for any particular time, for "any particular time" likes to have salt in its wounds. Equally it requires that one say that Robinson wrote for all time, for "all time" wants to be made healthy and to survive.

Notes on Contributors

Wallace L. Anderson is Professor of English and Dean of Undergraduate Studies at the University of Northern Iowa. He is a graduate of Trinity College (Connecticut), with a Ph.D. from Chicago, and has been a Fulbright Lecturer and a Guggenheim Fellow. Mr. Anderson is the author of *Edwin Arlington Robinson: A Critical Introduction*, and the editor (with Norman C. Stageberg) of *Introductory Readings in Language* and *Poetry as Experience*. He is currently editing, for the Harvard University Press, *The Collected Letters of Edwin Arlington Robinson*.

Ellsworth Barnard is Professor of English at the University of Massachusetts at Amherst, of which he is an alumnus. He received his M. A. and Ph.D. from the University of Minnesota, and earlier this year was honored with an L.H.D. from the University of Massachusetts. Mr. Barnard is the author of *Shelley's Religion*; *Edwin Arlington Robinson: A Critical Study*; and *Wendell Willkie: Fighter for Freedom*, as well as the chapter on Robinson in *Fifteen Modern American Authors*. He is also the editor of *Shelley: Selected Poems, Essays, and Letters*.

Christopher Brookhouse is Assistant Professor of English at the University of North Carolina at Chapel Hill. He was educated at Stanford and Harvard, receiving his Ph.D. from the latter institution. He has edited *Sir Armadace and the Avowing of Arthur: Two Romances from the Ireland MS*, and has published a volume of poetry entitled *Scattered Light*. Mr. Brookhouse is presently writing a novel which will be published by Little, Brown.

Charles T. Davis is Professor of English at the Pennsylvania State University. He is a graduate of Dartmouth College, with advanced degrees from the University of Chicago and New York University. Mr. Davis is the editor of *Edwin Arlington Robinson: Selected Early Poems and Letters*; *A New England Girlhood* by Lucy Larcom; and (with Gay Wilson Allen) *Walt Whitman's Poems: Selections with Critical Aids*. He has also published a number of articles on Whitman, Robinson, and other American poets.

William J. Free is Associate Professor of English at the University of Georgia. He is a graduate of the University of Chattanooga, and received his M.A. and Ph.D. from the University of North Carolina at Chapel Hill. Mr. Free is the author of *The Columbian Magazine and American Literary Nationalism* and of numerous periodical articles on American literature. He is also co-editor of *History into Drama: A Sourcebook on the Lost Colony*.

Scott Donaldson is Associate Professor of English and History at the College of William and Mary. His undergraduate work was done at Yale and his graduate work at Minnesota. Mr. Donaldson's background also includes some ten years as a newspaperman. He has published one book, *The Suburban Myth*, and a number of articles on American writers, in various scholarly and literary periodicals. He is currently at work on a critical biography of the American poet Winfield Townley Scott.

David H. Hirsch is Associate Professor of English at Brown University. His degrees are from New York University (B.A. and M.A.) and Ohio State University (Ph.D.). He has written articles on American literature which have appeared in various periodicals, including the *Sewanee Review*, the *Southern Review*, and *Texas Studies in Literature and Language*.

J. C. Levenson is Edgar Allan Poe Professor of English at the University of Virginia where he teaches American poetry and cultural history. Mr. Levenson's degrees are from Harvard, and he taught for some years at the University of Minnesota. He is the author of *The Mind and Art of Henry Adams* and the editor of Twain's *Life on the Mississippi* and *Discussions of Hamlet.* Professor Levenson is also well known for his work on Stephen Crane in the University of Virginia Edition and elsewhere.

Jay Martin is Director of the Undergraduate Program in American Studies at the University of California at Irvine. His undergraduate work was done at Columbia; he received his M.A. and Ph.D. from Ohio State. His published books include *Conrad Aiken: A Life of His Art* and *Harvests of Change: American Literature, 1865–1914.* A third volume, on Nathanael West, is scheduled for publication in 1969.

Radcliffe Squires is Professor of English at the University of Michigan. He was educated at the University of Utah, the University of Chicago, and Harvard University. Mr. Squires has published several volumes of poetry, including *Fingers of Hermes* and *The Light Under Islands,* as well as three critical studies: *The Loyalties of Robinson Jeffers, The Major Themes of Robert Frost,* and *Frederic Prokosch.*

Nathan C. Starr is Lecturer at the New School for Social Research and Professor Emeritus of English and Humanities at the University of Florida. His doctorate is from Harvard, where he also did his undergraduate work. In addition, he holds a B.A. and an M.A. from Oxford University and a Litt.D. from Rollins College. He is the author of *The Dynamics of Literature* and *King Arthur Today,* editor of *The Pursuit of Learning,* and co-editor of *The Humanistic Tradition.*

Robert D. Stevick is Professor of English at the University of Washington. He received his bachelor's and master's degrees from the University of Tulsa and his Ph.D. from the University of Wisconsin. He is the author of *English and Its History: The Evolution of a Language* and *Suprasegmentals, Meter, and the Manuscript of Beowulf;* co-author of *Rhetoric for Exposition* and *Composition and Research: Problems in Evolutionary Theory;* editor of *One Hundred Middle English Lyrics* and *Five Middle English Narratives;* and author of many scholarly articles on linguistics and on Middle English literature.

General Index

As a rule, published works are listed under the name of the author rather than by title.

Index to Robinson's Works

The title is given even when the poem is only quoted in the text.